ALUMNI VOICI

ALUMNI VOICES

The Winchester University Press
EDUCATION IN CONTEXT SERIES

The Winchester University Press EDUCATION IN CONTEXT SERIES, edited by Stephanie Spencer, aims to explore new theoretical and methodological directions in educational research. Education is conceptualised as an ongoing process that occurs both inside and outside the classroom within a range of historical and geographical settings. Titles will draw on interdisciplinary and transnational methodologies in order to emphasise the relationship between education and society across time and place.

ALUMNI VOICES

The Changing Experience of Higher Education

Stephanie Spencer, Andrea Jacobs
and
Camilla Leach

With a Chapter by Tom James

WINCHESTER
UNIVERSITY PRESS

Published by the Winchester University Press 2015

First Published in Great Britain in 2015 by
The Winchester University Press
University of Winchester
Winchester SO22 4NR

British Library Cataloguing-in-Publication Data
A CIP catalogue record for this book is available
from the British Library.

ISBN: 978-1-906113-15-5

Printed and Bound in Great Britain

CONTENTS

Permissions vi

Acknowledgements vii

List of Illustrations viii

1. Alumni Voices: The Changing Experience of Higher Education 1

2. From Diocesan Training School to University 27

3. The Institution as a Community: Introducing Gemeinschaft and Gesellschaft 45

4. The Community and the Church 79

5. Place and Space 117

6. Gender and 'The Culture of Care' 153

7. Management, Leadership and Change 191

8. Alumni Voices Past, Present and Looking to the Future 227

Appendices 245

Bibliography 281

Index 293

PERMISSIONS

By permission of Taylor and Francis, extracts have been reprinted from Andrea Jacobs, Camilla Leach and Stephanie Spencer, 'Learning Lives and Alumni Voices', *Oxford Review of Education* 36.2 (2010): 219-232.

By permission of Taylor and Francis, extracts have been reprinted from Andrea Jacobs and Camilla Leach, 'Teacher Training and the Public Good: The University of Winchester Alumni Project', *History of Education Journal* 40.2 (2011): 213-228.

ACKNOWLEDGEMENTS

The research on which this book is based would not have been possible without funding from the University of Winchester; in particular, the authors wish to acknowledge the generosity of a Research and Knowledge Exchange grant from the University. We would also like to thank Dr Zoe Milsom for additional research support and Professor Tom James for contributing Chapter 2.

Most of all we would like to thank all those who participated in the project by completing questionnaires and agreeing to be interviewed.

This book is therefore dedicated to the alumni of an institution whose voices are now part of the official record.

List of Illustrations

1. A Great Sense of Camaraderie	50
2. Ascension Day Picnic	56
3. A Valedictory Dinner	59
4. The Old Dining Hall	61
5. Once the College Chapel	93
6. Bargate, Southampton, January 1960	102
7. The Old Student Union	128
8. Once the Junior Common Room	132
9. The First Mini Skirt	163
10. Studying and Leisure on Campus	172
11. Miss Robina Macintyre on the Drums	182
12. Graduation in Winchester Cathedral	237

1.

ALUMNI VOICES: THE CHANGING EXPERIENCE OF HIGHER EDUCATION

> It was quite exciting, there were those challenges, and then of course we had the planning challenge. If the College was going to diversify who was going to diversify, how were we going to do it, where were we going to get all these bright new teachers from, could we afford it, what were we going to do with these cosy attitudes in which we were simply little offshoot clients of Southampton University, how in fact were we going to grow up, stand on our own feet, devise our own courses, diversify, defy the Universe?[1]

Introduction

Over a period of at least the last half century, and against a background of profound worldwide economic and social change, the landscape of higher education in the United Kingdom has become unrecognisable.[2] In answer to demands to widen access, the numbers of students, staff and institutions have increased: the cohorts of students now come from a wider social and ethnic spectrum with a more even gender balance and the institutions they attend are more varied in type, curriculum and function.[3] Inevitably the actual experience of higher education for both students and staff has changed over this period and continues to change, particularly with the potential of developments in technology and social media in delivering courses and the likely long-term effect of the introduction, from 2012, of the trebling of course fees.[4] This book, focusing on the day to day experiences of those who studied and worked in one institution, uses data from an oral history project, the Alumni Voices, to explore a way of writing the history of higher education of the recent past. It includes testimony from senior managers, academics, administrators and students, thus presenting the history of the institution from many perspectives across the power spectrum. While data from just one institution are used, the book will reflect many of the changes in higher education within the United Kingdom as a whole over the last sixty years and will highlight the relationship between alumnus and institution. It is intended that by reflecting on the history of people's experience, and in particular the way that the experience of being part of a higher education community has changed, the book might provide additional insight into the nature of higher education at the beginning of the twenty-first century: Do providers of higher education offer their students the means to individual success, measured in personal financial gain and professional advancement, or is there something more intangible in the benefits of the time spent within a community of learners, the value-added component of the higher education experience? How does the institution itself change to accommodate the increasingly small amount of time that students spend on campus, while also working outside to finance their studies? How can the ethos of an institution be defined? In particular is it shaped by staff, by students, by foundation values?

As we note above, higher education is in a state of constant change, possibly moving ever further away from John Henry (Cardinal) Newman's *Idea of a University* that embraced a Liberal model of education for its own sake.[5] Fears have been expressed that as a result of the introduction of higher fees, the field will become market and consumer driven; the relationship between student and lecturer will change;

students will choose courses on the basis of future earning capacity; the range of degrees may narrow; those who might aspire to higher education will be limited and the concept of higher education as a public good might be reconceptualised as a private good.[6] Along with the specific research questions mentioned in the opening paragraph, these possible changes for the future will be considered in the book's conclusion.

While 'alumni voices' are at its core, alongside these the book examines the methodological dilemmas facing those who write histories of higher education and more especially the exploration of the wider implications of the contribution of the individual voice. This exploration is carried out, as will be described later, utilising voice relational methodology (VRM) which derives from Carol Gilligan's work.[7] While each chapter in the book includes facets of both change in higher education and oral history methodology, those focusing on the former are written in a chronological format, while the latter are written thematically. Our methodology and its wider implications will be of interest to those interested in creating oral histories of communities. The detail of the project will be of interest to historians of higher education and alumni of higher education institutions, especially those of the University of Winchester, on whose experiences this book is based.[8]

While this book has a remit beyond being a history of the development of a single institution, it may be seen as within the same genre. Institutional histories can be written for different purposes and audiences, and it is essential to define our parameters at the outset. Gary McCulloch argues that such work has too often, in the past, been written by 'insiders' and has been commissioned for the purposes of the institution itself, either to commemorate a specific anniversary or more generally to celebrate its growth and successes. He suggests that in such histories 'the institution is viewed from the top down and as a symbol of growth and progress, finally dissolving into a mass of lists and statistics'. As a result he argues that what can be termed "house history' has a poor reputation owing to a lack of independence and its tendency to develop uncritical accounts devoid of candour'.[9] Harold Silver notes that, to counter this, over the last twenty five years or so, there has been a search 'for more comprehensive and less parochial and antiquarian approaches to the history of higher education institutions':[10] approaches that would respond to complaints that such histories had previously been pious domestic histories of only parochial interest[11] foregrounding 'the views of the people at the top' that offered little sense of 'the community of students and professors'[12] and might, instead, become 'holistic studies of individual institutions over a substantial period of time'.[13] Hilary Young, writing of the construction of an oral history of the Open University, supports the role of oral history as a different way of approaching institutional history: 'As opposed to the focus on the physical development of campuses and academic luminary accounts of university management, oral history allows other stories of universities as places of pedagogy, culture, social change and personal relationships to be told'.[14] Similarly the authors of the oral history of the University of Strathclyde, Callum Brown, Arthur McIvor and Neil Rafeek, based their history on the testimonies of alumni of the institution; the resulting book constituting 'determinedly a history of people's experience'.[15] We situate our project within these developments.

Recognising, McCulloch's criticisms of 'insider' histories and 'house' histories, we wish to highlight our positions as the authors of this book, the designers of the project as well as the interviewers of the participants.[16] The three main authors have both studied and worked at the institution over a number of years.[17] Professor Tom James, who has written the second chapter, worked at the institution for more than thirty years prior to his retirement. Although we did not directly include our own experiences in the project, in view of our positions in relation to the area of research, it was essential that we ask two questions: the first whether as authors who are also alumni, thereby both researchers and researched, we are 'outsiders' or 'insiders' in this research and therefore the extent to which our objectivity is compromised: the second, the extent to which our analysis of the data is likely to be coloured by the demands of the project funder, the institution itself.

One of the objects of VRM, which as stated above is central to our methodology, is to allow the researcher to examine how his or her own views and assumptions might affect their interpretation of the respondents' words.[18] We decided that we needed to pay more than lip-service to the problems raised when the interviewers have a close 'inside' knowledge of the subject under analysis even if 'outside' the time period being discussed. Each of us separately wrote about our own reflections on our place in the research and how we felt this impacted on our reaction to, and analysis of, the interviews.[19] We did not reach definitive conclusions either about our objectivity, other than that absolute objectivity is not possible, or the extent to which we were both insiders and outsiders, as we found ourselves regularly crossing boundaries between the two. We recognise that while the historian always has a duty to the people of the past, the present and to search for a truth,[20] oral history in particular makes demands on its practitioners that include a careful reflection of our place within the process of the research and in this case our place in the institution itself. In a presentation to a university audience, based on our written reflections mentioned above, we highlighted our possible dilemma in working within an institution and 'going public' with any negative stories that might emerge even though it was in no way our intention to 'set the record straight' with regard to changes in policy or status, to confirm angels and demons in the official record or to unlock skeletons from cupboards. While recognising that there is a bias inherent in the interviews, in that the interviewees chose to take part, in common with Brown and others, our research demonstrated that, 'The optimism, the regard for university and for the university experience [...] was a powerful feature of the testimony'.[21] Former students prepared to be involved in the project generally wished to celebrate their time in higher education rather than to criticise it. Where criticisms were made, they were usually tempered by a positive comment on the overall learning experience. Many staff recalled their period of employment with similar regard. Other staff were more vocal in their criticism particularly in relation to working against a backdrop of changes in higher education more generally (such as that highlighted in the quotation at the beginning of this chapter) and at the institution in particular. Many, but by no means all, perceived that the changes had an adverse effect on their career trajectories and the quality of their working lives. At this point, it should be noted that one of the skills required of an oral historian is to re-direct an interview if the respondent names colleagues who are not able to put their version of events into the record, and we have been careful to avoid using hearsay as evidence of events.

The Alumni Voices Project at the University of Winchester

The University of Winchester may be a comparatively new name but the institution has a long history, from its beginnings as a male teacher training college in 1840 to one achieving full university status by 2005.[22] (This transition will be described in more detail in Chapter 2.) The Alumni Voices Project was carried out in three stages between 2004 and 2009. While the book itself was not originally planned to celebrate any special occasion or anniversary, the first stage of the project was undertaken to mark King Alfred's College, as the institution was then known, being awarded University College status. This stage of the project concentrated on female students only, alumnae voices, and therefore started at 1960, the year that King Alfred's College became coeducational. The decade was a pivotal one, in relation to the gender dimension, with many other institutions taking similar measures to broaden their student base.[23] The second stage of the project included male students, (almost 60 per cent of the respondents were male), and specifically addressed the subject of the institution and the wider community. At the third stage, the project was extended to staff. These were mainly academic staff but included management and administrative staff and some who moved between different roles.[24]

Although the Alumni Voices Project is a comparatively small scale one in terms of the participants involved, it has yielded a wealth of data, only a small proportion of which can be included here. In our design of each of the three stages we utilised well-established practices of questionnaires followed by one-to-one interviews.[25] Data that we collected in this way have also been complemented by letters, emails, photographs and other memorabilia that the participants added and by our own research in student magazines, prospectuses and the official University archive held at the Hampshire Record Office. In terms of interviewing respondents, the main criterion was to obtain a historical cross section although consideration was also given to their geographical location. In the second and third stages, we also tried to obtain a gender balance. Most interviews took place in the homes of the interviewees but there were some instances where the interviewees chose, or it was more convenient for them, to be interviewed at the University or at their place of work. In two cases, where distance was a particular problem, the interviews were conducted by telephone. As the participants were all volunteers, we did not find that the place or mode of interview made a great difference to their willingness to tell their stories or their openness in responding to our questions. Except for three of the filmed interviews, where people were interviewed in pairs, the interviewees were interviewed on a one-to-one basis. The interviews lasted for between about half an hour and almost two hours: those conducted with ex-staff being among the longest. Each interview was transcribed verbatim and a copy forwarded to the interviewee for their records and for them to alter should they, on reflection, be uncomfortable with anything they had said.[26]

Oral History as Methodology

Oral history is not an exact science and professional views on its use vary widely. As a methodology it has its own extensive literature,[27] which discusses in detail its advantages and disadvantages.[28] On the one hand, oral history allows us to create a more rounded picture by documenting the lives of those whose stories might not otherwise be told and as Philip Gardner acknowledges:

> One of the great qualities of oral history as a method is that it offers our best bridging point between the two forms of narrative - between narratives of identity and narratives of history - with each always having something to say to the other. The first of these forms has an ontological foundation and is rooted in the way we live with the past as a part of ourselves; the second has a representational character and is founded in the attempt to live with the past as it was. In other words, as revealed in oral history interview, the story of a life may also become the story of the historical landscape within which that life has been lived.[29]

On the other hand a range of concerns has been traditionally raised against the practice of oral history interviews. These have been summarised by Gardner writing with Peter Cunningham:

> The charges rest principally upon three grounds: that such data draw upon the vagaries of individual memory; that they are the products of the present and not, as with the historical document, of the past;

> and that they are always critically influenced by, perhaps fundamentally shaped by, a conspiring interlocutor wearing the guise of objective historian.[30]

In order to address these concerns as far as possible, we had to decide on the best way to conduct our interviews. To take the last concern first and also to recognise the implicit power dynamics between interviewer and respondent particularly relevant in a project where those interviewed range from the powerful to the relatively powerless, our first decision was to employ feminist friendly practices and take the role of listener. Kristine Minister argues that 'feminist interviewers let their natural communication encouragement work by uttering positive minimal responses' and that 'this kind of work does not interrupt narrators; it supports them'.[31] On the other hand, in discussing the first two concerns, Penny Summerfield explores how individuals create their life narratives into stories 'composed' over the years which are rehearsed, revised and retold until the narrative satisfies the current demands.[32] The interviewer is faced with the decision whether to listen to the narrative on its own terms, or whether to 'disrupt' this process and take the narrative as a starting point from which to probe individual memory for more precise and verifiable information about the past.[33]

The process we employed was a compromise between being content to listen to the narrative without interruption and interrupting or 'disrupting' it. We felt that this compromise could best be achieved by establishing a framework for the interviews as each stage of the project had a slightly different theme and it was essential that the interviews reflected this. We therefore decided to look at the qualitative data, the individual comments, from the questionnaires, which were substantial, and see which ones appeared to be typical and which ones atypical. A draft document was then drawn up listing some of these and this was sent to the interviewees as a suggestion as to what they might like to think about in advance of the interview. For our purposes we refer to this as Participant Elicitation through Peer Comments. The intention was that the draft document would serve as an aide memoire and the interview, reflecting Minister's view above, would not be one solely of questions and answers but rather a narrative in which the interviewer would only interrupt/disrupt the narrative to ask additional 'open' questions required as explanation or to move the interview on when necessary. Our success in ceding control of the interview and remaining in the background as an active listener varied, being dependent on the confidence of the interviewee. Each interview was also personalised to include questions relating to the individual's own responses to the questionnaire and to reflect the specific period when he/she was at the institution. The interviews were, therefore, co-constructed.

Interpreting the oral history interview is a heavy responsibility if we are to take seriously our intention of analysing the way that the experience of being part of a higher education community has changed over the last half century or so, and suggesting what this might tell us about the nature of higher education at the beginning of the 21st century. As historians of the institution we have the difficult task of drawing conclusions about 'the' student experience from multiple stories from a variety of different time periods, each in their own way noting the significance of the institution in general to their own future life in particular. The discussion below considers the analytical process which retains the individual voice within what might be described as 'collective memory'. The relationship of memory to historical analysis is the subject of a long-running debate and can only be touched upon here, but its role, or even the tricks it plays on our remembering, is highly relevant to individual and collective narratives of higher education.[34]

The Changing Experience

As discussed elsewhere, and as we have already briefly mentioned above, we have, over the course of the project, developed VRM as a framework for understanding how collective and individual memories, as articulated to us in oral history interviews, can be effectively analysed.[35] VRM was originally proposed by Carol Gilligan and Lyn Mikel Brown and derived from Gilligan's work on the female voice.[36] It was taken forward by Natasha Mauthner and Andrea Doucet[37] and involves reading the interview transcript several times. Most commonly the readings can be summarised as follows:

- First for the overall plot and story to include the main events, recurrent images, narrative and contradictions.
- Second, a reflexive reading, for our response to the interviewee emotionally and intellectually and how our assumptions affect our reading. As discussed in more length above, in this case we needed to situate ourselves as alumni of the institution as well as employees. We also needed to recognize that the reading might differ depending on which member of the team was undertaking the analysis.
- Third, to identify the 'I' and how the interviewees speak about themselves, particularly looking at how they represent themselves; whether they place themselves at the periphery or the centre of the story, how they see their contribution, or whether they consider they had a contribution to make.
- Last to consider the broader context and wider relationships within the story.

Deriving from work on the female voice, this methodology was particularly appropriate for the first stage of the project which was an all-female team researching the experience of female students. The 'different' voice of the female students enabled us to highlight the significance of gender within the student experience. It also helped us to understand the importance attached to the previously homosocial nature of the institution as we moved to the next stage of the project which included interviewing male students. As men were included in the research, we considered whether this method of analysis was still appropriate. Male voices can hardly be said to have been 'marginal' in a college that was all male until 1960. On reflection we considered that the legacy of the development of feminist oral history which informs VRM provided the strongest frame for theorising the individual voice.[38] While the professional voice of those who had held positions of power in the institution undoubtedly found its way into the official record, and indeed members of staff who had held positions in senior management were among our respondents, there is no note of individual narratives which relate a history of people's experience. Although VRM is more usually associated with the voices of the oppressed, Laurence Hopkins suggests that it is excellent at producing a thorough account of the phenomenological world of the subjects without neglecting a material and cultural analysis of their environment.[39]

An advantage of VRM is that it can be adapted to the individual project and additional readings of the interviews can be added. Hawkins suggests that:

> By focusing on a single institution the project becomes a study not only of individuals and the science they practise, but of the institution itself. As a result, an additional 'voice' is added to the mix, even if it is a proxy voice – the voice of the institution, given expression through the words of its employees. The influences the institution brings to bear, consciously or subconsciously, on the responses of the individual have to be taken into account when both planning and interpreting the results of such a project.[40]

Taking account of this, and the way that the interviewees talked about the significance of the institution itself and its location in the city of Winchester to their learning experience, suggested that a fifth reading for the 'spoken visual' would further enhance our understanding of the centrality of the whole university experience to the composing of self.[41] This fifth reading will be developed further in Chapter 5.

To conclude this chapter we offer an example of how one interview from the project has been analysed using VRM.[42] It will be seen that the readings are not carried out in any particular order: often they overlap and in most interviews one reading takes precedence over the others. The interview highlights the wider significance of the data we collected in understanding change in the history of higher education.

Interview Analysis

Robert (not his real name) joined King Alfred's College in 1956 for a two year teacher training course. Unlike many of his contemporaries he joined as a school leaver, rather than as someone who had recently completed two years of national service. He was required to study two main subjects and selected Music and Horticulture. His narrative painted a vivid picture of student life and of the city of Winchester more than half a century ago. Evoking the spirit of the 1950s, students were proud to wear their blazers with their 'gold braided badges' and 'wonderful black and gold and red scarves' which 'could be seen everywhere'; life centred around College with a variety of sporting and social societies, all of which were well supported; students avoided the more lively pubs in the town, preferring somewhere more 'respectable' such as the Black Swan or the Cadena Cafe where dances were held; modern music that the students enjoyed was no more 'wild' than 'Rock around the Clock'. In an all-male college, female companionship was provided by the local nurses' home which was mentioned several times in the narrative.

Describing the transition from home into the wider world, Robert anticipated with relish the prospect of belonging to the community at the College. Although it was not directly stated, the tenor of the interview implied that although his family lived in the city, he felt he had physically to leave home and live as a college student, in order to gain access to and become part of the College community. Like many others he had a possibly idealised, almost school boyish, concept of how a college community should be. At one point he expressed disappointment that there were no 'rags' during his time although he had heard stories of 'rag' events that had happened in the past. This notwithstanding, the sense of community that he found and the sense of common purpose among the students were both strong themes in the interview. He spoke of 'a little oasis, all with a common purpose, at the top of the hill', opined that 'at all times I felt very much part of the College' and that 'other students seemed to help each other'; and recalled the Principal saying that, 'You're all part of the same community'. Highlighting the relevance of family background to the higher education experience, Robert revealed his as that of a clergyman's son. The importance of the College's Church foundation to him was therefore unsurprising as was his use of concepts associated with the idea of a Christian family to describe the community and the behaviours and attitudes of the students and staff.

For Robert, the most important aspects of college life were those connected with music and particularly music associated with the Church and Chapel (where he felt very 'at home') whether it was playing in concerts, singing in the choir or playing the organ in the Cathedral. Music was therefore a recurring theme particularly as a way of bringing people together. Another recurring theme in the narrative related to how he benefitted from his time at King Alfred's. He stated that he had attended an independent school and therefore although not born with a 'silver spoon', had had some privileges. He admitted to arriving at college a 'bit full of myself', thinking 'I knew everything and the way they dealt with that was excellent. I came out a much wiser person'. He recalled:

> When I came here I was full of very immature ideas and the staff always had a wonderful way, whatever their age, of being fatherly and saying, 'That's a jolly good point but have you thought about this?' So you were never put in a corner and told you were stupid, as you were at school.

He emphasised that, almost more than anything else, what he learnt was to have dignity and respect for other people especially for the children whom one is teaching. Quite poignantly during the interview he mentioned a well-known picture of the institution as it was in the 1860s, a copy of which he had on his study wall, saying: 'I look at that building every day and am reminded of what it did for me which was really to finish off the job, or take the job on to another stage'.

Wider relationships were important to Robert. He defined himself and described himself by his relationship to others. The concept of family was important to him. However, family became a discourse. He moved from discussions of his biological family to the family of the College. He made reference to losing his biological father at a young age and seemed to appreciate and take comfort from the paternalistic care and concern from the staff most especially the Principal for whom he obviously had had enormous respect. He repeatedly talked of the support he garnered from all around during his time at the institution and it was taken as axiomatic that that level of support would be returned by him. He emphasised the importance of the relationships that were made through sport which again indicated his concern for the dignity and respect of all he encountered:

> Life is a playing field and it levels everybody out. People I've played cricket with for example in the Second XI at King Alfred's, who I'd never really met, but just because we all went to play cricket together we had a wonderful time and a great sense of fun and relying on other people for cadging lifts or whatever.

Beyond King Alfred's he mentioned two particular instances where he encountered other 'King Alfred's' men. In his first job in a state school, the headteacher was also an alumnus of the College which led to a common bond, an expectation of shared ideals with regard to education. Robert said, 'It was wonderful to work for him because we had something in common from the word go and he was a very wise person and always spoke very highly of the College'. In later years he met up with another alumnus, with whom he had played piano duets, who was by now the conductor of the Hampshire County Youth Orchestra touring Australia and giving a concert near to Robert's home:

> I actually met him at that concert and it was a great moment in my life to find an old King Alfred's student out here beating about the bush with his orchestra and impressing everyone to death. It was just wonderful.

There was one jarring note in terms of his relationship with others. Members of the Christian Union caused him to question and consider how Church and religion was presented although it did not apparently cloud his attitude to Christianity:

> They used to go and knock on students' doors in the evening and pretend they'd come for a cup of tea and then try to get you to kneel down and take Jesus into your heart...I found that very disturbing.

Robert used 'I' throughout the narrative but not in a self-centred way. There was a sense of understatement, of not wanting to highlight the achievements of the self. 'I' was used but he swiftly moved on to include others. For example he talked about his own musical accomplishments but moved to the more impressive musical contacts of the Head of Music who 'really had contacts all over Hampshire...she had a madrigal group I was part of, so we were always out and about'. He used 'we' to emphasise the sense of community particularly in reference to the societies and organisations of which he was part. There was a clear sense of moving from the 'I', the somewhat opinionated youth that he was when he commenced his teacher training course, to becoming one of the 'we', one of the larger community of King Alfred's men, by the time he left two years later. Speaking of the time after he had left College, the 'we' takes on an intergenerational and wider geographical concept in terms of the discussion of his first headteacher and the meeting with his old friend in Australia.

As we have described above, because of our own associations with both the institution and the city, there are particular difficulties in analysing our response to the interviewee emotionally and intellectually which could affect how we write about the subject. We recognise that the response to the interviewee can differ between individuals and especially between the interviewer and another member of the team. The member of the research team who carried out the interview recalls it as an extremely pleasant and relaxed one to conduct, even though it was carried out somewhat impersonally by telephone. Robert responded generously and enthusiastically to the questions. There was little need for the interviewer to say anything other than prompt or move on to another subject. As his memories of his college life were so positive, it would be difficult to write about him in any way that was not similarly positive. His experiences of the institution were completely different from our own but not so different from experiences of other alumni to whom we had spoken and who were also at the College during the 1950s. He mentioned places in Winchester with which we were familiar which helped link the passage of years. Another member of the research team who also analysed the interview felt an immediate affinity with the interviewee because, although from a different generation, gender and social class, she also came from a clergy family: the issues that are of importance to the interviewee resonate with values that were considered important in her own upbringing. The references to Christianity and the nuances of the different types of Christianity are something that she could instantly understand and did not make her feel uncomfortable in any way.

The analysis of Robert's interview reveals one reading of many of the themes we are seeking to pursue in this study. In the following chapters we will explore the data from other interviews and questionnaires under the specific headings of The Institution as a Community, The Community and the Church, Place and Space, Gender and 'The Culture of Care' and Management, Leadership and Change. While some of the chapters have a direct relevance to the questions we originally set out to attempt to answer, others have been driven by the results of the project, in the manner of grounded theory methodology.[43] As conversation often comes in the form of a long sentence, on which we then impose a researcher's punctuation, we have deliberately chosen to often use long extracts from the interviews. This also highlights the dilemma of the oral historian in selecting beginnings and endings to quotes. Before turning to the alumni voices, we take the opportunity in Chapter 2 to set out the context of the history of the institution and bring the previously published record up to date.

Notes to Chapter 1.

[1] Interview 19 (Stage 3), 1969-1985.

[2] Harold Silver, 'Higher Education and Social Change: Purpose in Pursuit', *History of Education Journal* 36.4-5 (2007): 535.

[3] See Roy Lowe, 'The changing role of the academic journal: the coverage of higher education in *History of Education* as a case study, 1972-2011', *History of Education Journal* 41.1 (2012): 103-115.

[4] From 2012, universities were permitted to charge up to £9,000.00 per year following the recommendations of the Browne Report, *Securing a Sustainable Future for Higher Education: An Independent Review of Higher Education Funding and Student Finance* (12 October 2010): www.gov.uk/government/uploads (accessed 7 March 2013).

[5] Sophia Deboik highlighted John Henry Newman's 1852 avowal of the purpose of a university education as one which eschewed narrow vocational education in favour of a 'university as a community of thinkers, engaging in intellectual pursuits not for any external purpose but as an end in itself'. She noted: 'He offers us little help on how the balance can be struck between pursuing knowledge for its own sake and giving students the saleable skills they surely deserve. He has even less to offer on the pressing matter of how the whole enterprise may be paid for.' Deboik indicates that the end of a university education is still a matter of debate. See Sophia Deboik, 'Newman Suggests a University's "Soul" Lies In The Mark It Leaves On Students', *The Guardian* (20 October 2010): www.guardian.co.uk (accessed 28 March 2013).

[6] See especially Stefan Collini, 'From Robbins to McKinsey', *London Review of Books* 33. 16 (August 2011): 9-14.

[7] Carol Gilligan, *In a Different Voice: Psychological Theory and Women's Development* (Cambridge: Harvard University Press, 1982).

[8] Data from the Alumni Voices Project has been disseminated in papers at the History of Education Conferences in Dublin, 2004, Cambridge, 2008 and London, 2010 as well as at the Australia and New Zealand History of Education Conference, 2008. It has formed part of other discussions on institutional and organisational history notably at a colloquium 'University History and Histories: Official? Celebratory? Critical?', University of Sheffield, 2006; at a conference 'Persistence and Disappearance: Educational Organizations in their Historical Context', University of Erlangen, Germany, 2007 and at the Oral History Society's Annual Conference 'Corporate Voices: Institutional and Organisation Oral Histories', University of Sussex, 2013.

[9] Gary McCulloch, 'Historical Insider Research in Education' in *Researching Education from the Inside: Investigations from Within*, ed. Pat Sikes and Anthony Potts (London: Routledge, 2008), 51-63.

[10] Harold Silver, '"Things Change but Names Remain the Same": Higher Education Historiography 1975-2000', *History of Education Journal*, 35.1 (2006): 121.

[11] Harold Silver, "Things Change"', 122, citing Eric Ives, Introduction in Eric Ives, Diane Drummond and Leonard Schwartz, *The First Civic University: Birmingham 1880-1980. An Introductory History*, (University of Birmingham, 2000) xiii.

[12] Harold Silver, "Things Change"', 122, citing Paul H. Mattingly, 'Structures over Time: Institutional History', *Historical Inquiry in Education: A Research Agenda*, ed. John H. Best (Washington: American Educational Research Association, 1983) 43-44.

[13] Harold Silver, "Things Change'", 122, Eric Ives, Diane Drummond and Leonard Schwartz, *The First Civic University*. Examples of histories to which Silver might be referring (although some were written to celebrate particular anniversaries) include Richard Aldrich, *The Institute of Education 1902-2002: A Centenary History* (London: London University, 2002); Helen Mathers, *Steel City Scholars: The Centenary History of the University of Sheffield* (London: James and James, 2005); *Jennifer Bone, Our Calling to Fulfil: Westminster College and the Changing Face of Teacher Education 1951-2001* (Bristol: Tockington Press, 2003).

[14] Hilary Brown, 'Whose Story Counts?: Constructing an Oral History of the Open University at 40', *Oral History* (Autumn 2011): 94-106. Similarly many of the universities founded in the 1960s have undertaken oral history projects to celebrate their fiftieth anniversaries. See, for example, 'Fifty Voices, Fifty Faces', University of Sussex, www.sussex.ac.uk (accessed 5 January 2013); 'Oral History: 50th Anniversary,' University of York, www.york.ac.uk (accessed 5 January 2013). Girton College Cambridge pioneered an oral history project (ULE Project) which began in 1995 and which set out to examine the life histories of university-educated women over the twentieth century using Girton records and input from successive alumnae who entered the institution between 1918 and 1985. S Frances Gandy, 'The University and Life Experience Project: Phase Two' *The Year: The Annual Review of Girton College* (2011-2012) 33.

[15] Callum G. Brown, Arthur J. McIvor and Neil Rafeek, *The University of Strathclyde 1945-1975: An Oral History of the University of Strathclyde* (Edinburgh: Edinburgh University Press, 2004).

[16] Sue Hawkins has recently acknowledged that much has been written about the interrelationship between the two and how this can affect the tone quality and content of the resulting interview. See Sue Hawkins, "'Whose Story

is it Anyway?": The Challenges of Conducting Institutional Histories', *Journal of Conservation and Museum Studies*, 10.1 (2012): www.jcms-journal.com (accessed 5 January 2013).

[17] At the time of writing, they have, between them, a combined experience of six years as undergraduates, fifteen years as post graduates and more than twenty years as staff or research fellows within the institution.

[18] See Natasha Mauthner and Andrea Doucet, 'Reflections on a Voice Centred Relational Method', in *Feminist Dilemmas in Qualitative Research: Public Knowledge and Private Lives*, ed. Jane Ribbens and Rosalind Edwards (London: Sage, 1998), 119-146, especially 130.

[19] These reflections formed the basis of a paper, Stephanie Spencer's 'Alumni Voices: Claiming a Place in the Institutional Archive', presented at the 'Work, Work, Work' Conference of the Australia and New Zealand History of Education Society (ANZHES) at Sydney, Australia 8-11 December 2008. In 2008 the annual ANZHES conference was held jointly with the History of Education Society (UK).

[20] Richard Aldrich, 'The Three Duties of the Historian of Education', *History of Education Journal* 32.2 (2003): 133-43.

[21] Brown and others, 258.

[22] This book is intended to complement the existing histories of the institution: Martial Rose, *A History of King Alfred's College, Winchester 1840-1980* (London: Phillimore, 1981); Martial Rose, *King Alfred's College, Winchester, 1980-1990: A Decade of Change* (Salisbury: Salisbury Printing: 1990); Tom James and Martin Doughty, *King Alfred's College Winchester: A Pictorial Record* (Stroud: Alan Sutton Publishing, 1991).

[23] As Girton have noted in their ULE Project, the 1960s was a pivotal decade connected as it was with 'going mixed'. See Gandy 'The University and Life Experience Project'. The decision to become a coeducational college

followed the steps that the then government took to initiate the recommendations of *The McNair Report* 1944. The recommendations were to double teacher training capacity by the end of the decade, to reduce class sizes, and to increase the Teacher Training course from two to three years.

[24] The scope of the project did not encompass interviewing governors of the institution.

[25] See the appendices for a fuller description of the questionnaire process.

[26] All questionnaires and copies of interviews (as amended by the interviewee where appropriate) have been lodged with the Hampshire Record Office as part of the University archive.

[27] For example, see Joanna Bornat and Hanna Diamond, 'Women's History and Oral History Developments and Debates', *Women's History Review* 16.1 (2007): 19-39, which discusses developments and debates over a forty year period; Philip Gardner, 'Oral History in Education: Teacher's Memory and Teachers' History', *History of Education Journal*, 32.2 (2003): 175-188; Andrea Jacobs and Camilla Leach, '"No Women, Please": Co-education and Expansion, Crisis and Change at King Alfred's College Winchester in the Mid-Twentieth Century', in *Persistence and Disappearance: Educational Organizations in their historical Context*, ed. Michael Göhlich, Caroline Hopf and Daniel Tröhler (Wiesbaden: VS Press, 2008), 41-53.

[28] Cunningham and Gardner term this the 'optimistic' and the 'pessimistic' camp. See Peter Cunningham and Philip Gardner, *Becoming Teachers: Texts and Testimonies 1907-1950* (London and Portland Oregon: Woburn Press, 2004) 4-5.

[29] Gardner, 'Oral History in Education', 184. See also Paul Thompson, Introduction in *Oral History, Health and Welfare*, ed. Joanna Bornat, Robert Perks, Paul Thompson and Jan Walmsley (London: Routledge, 2002) 3-4.

[30] Cunningham and Gardner, *Becoming Teachers*, 5.

[31] Kristina Minister, 'A Feminist Frame for the Oral History Interview' in *Women's Words: The Feminist Practice of Oral History*, ed. Sherna Gluick and Daphne Patai (London: Routledge, 1991) 38.

[32] Penny Summerfield, *Reconstructing Women's Wartime Lives: Discourse and Subjectivity in Oral Histories of the Second World War* (Manchester: Manchester University Press, 1998).

[33] See Gardner, 'Oral History in Education', 179.

[34] Ewa Domanska, 'Frank Ankersmit: From Narrative to Experience', *Rethinking History* 13.2 (2009): 175-195.

[35] See especially, Andrea Jacobs, Camilla Leach and Stephanie Spencer, 'Learning Lives and Alumni Voices', *Oxford Review of Education* 36.2 (2010): 219-232; also see, Jacobs and Leach, '"No Women, Please"'.

[36] Gilligan, *In a Different Voice.*

[37] Mauthner and Doucet, 'Reflections on a Voice Centred Relational Method'.

[38] See for examples: Helen Roberts, *Doing Feminist Research* (London: Routledge and Kegan Paul, 1982); Sherna Gluck and Daphen Patai, *The Feminist Practice of Oral History* (London: Routledge, 1991) and Shulamit Rheinharz, *Feminist Methods in Social Research* (New York: Oxford University Press, 1992).

[39] Laurence Hopkins, 'The Path of Least Resistance: A Voice-Relational Analysis of Disabled Students' Experiences of Discrimination in English Universities', *International Journal of Inclusive Education* 15.7 (2011): 711-727.

[40] Hawkins, 'Whose Story'.

[41] Stephanie Spencer, 'A Uniform Identity: Schoolgirl Snapshots and the Spoken Visual', *History of Education*, 36.2 (2007): 227-246.

[42] Interview 8 (Stage 2), 1956-1958.

---

[43] Grounded theory is the discovery of theory through the analysis of the data as developed by Barney Glaser and Anselm Strauss in *The Discovery of Grounded Theory: Strategies for Qualitative Research* (Chicago: Aldine Publishing, 1967).

2.

FROM DIOCESAN TRAINING SCHOOL TO UNIVERSITY

Origins

The Diocesan Training School, later College, Winchester (DTC), was founded by the Diocese of Winchester in 1840, one of the oldest institutions of higher education in the country beyond a handful of universities.[1] Only St John's, (1838), the first training college, and Chester, (1839) are older, while Bishop Otter, Chichester was also founded in 1840. The establishment of these colleges was intended to remedy the existing inconsistencies in teacher training. A further ten Anglican Colleges were established between 1841 and 1963. These institutions included the women's Salisbury Diocesan Training School, later the College of Sarum St Michael, which was in fact part of a joint diocesan project between the Winchester and Salisbury dioceses: a training college for male teachers for the dioceses in Winchester, and for female teachers in Salisbury. These early training institutions embodied the post-Reformation Anglican ethos of Oxford and Cambridge – an ethos under challenge by 1850 as the ancient universities struggled to change from their historic focus as training grounds for clergy.[2] The DTC became King Alfred's College in 1928, became University College, Winchester in 2004, and the University of Winchester in 2005 by order of the Privy Council.

This chapter charts the development of the college to a university and focuses on the period covered by this oral history: the final years of the college as a monotechnic institution and its approach to, and successful acquisition of, university status as the curriculum and staff-base broadened and the training of teachers ceased to be the main activity of the College. This necessarily addresses the period since the Second World War when exile to Carmarthen and Culham College, Abingdon, ended and a new start was made. In 1945-46, negotiations to persuade the War Department, who had requisitioned the college in 1939, to hand back the buildings were protracted. Meanwhile the governors decided new management was required and the contract of the Principal, R C White, was not renewed.

From Triumph to Tragedy 1946-1958

The new Principal was W P Dickinson, formerly headmaster of Ormskirk Grammar School. Dickinson was not, as his predecessors, an Anglican clergyman. He was a scholar of Corpus Christi College, Oxford and a lay preacher, who did much to sustain the fundamental Christian ethos of the College, and to encourage collegiate life among the men. He surrounded himself with Oxbridge staff and met the challenge of military personnel returning as staff and students to academic life, and subsequently dealt with successive generations of national servicemen and those who had served, for example, in Korea, who came into the College. Student testimony among our interviewees, for example 'Robert' in Chapter 1, bore witness to the strong spiritual and educational values of the institution. Students from this era were significantly more numerous in their response to requests for interviewees for the project than more recent collegers. This could be partly because they are now largely retired and therefore have more leisure. However, as will be suggested in subsequent chapters, other reasons may have underpinned this statistic – the binding male ethos renewed in those early post-war years, the residential nature of the institution, the more overtly

Christian foundation characterised by Chapel attendance and the experience of these men in wars or as national servicemen.

However, behind this convivial male facade there was a range of problems. The new Principal was unable to start work because his predecessor was in place. Fortunately the Reverend Spencer Leeson, Headmaster of Winchester College, helped.[3] He advised on property availability, for example West Hayes, a former prep school west of the College on Sarum Road. A recurring issue was the size of the College which had still not attained the 200 set as a target in the mid-1920s, languishing at some 130. To add to these problems some 55 new colleges, largely Local Authority-based, were founded by the government. These new foundations, while ensuring a special place for the religious-based voluntary colleges, also constituted a threat. However, the purchase of West Hayes together with refurbishment of the Main Building allowed a recruitment of 180, more than The Dining Hall and teaching space could adequately accommodate.

In contrast to the situation in 1919, in 1946 military adaptation of the buildings had left them forlorn. Principal and staff, on occasion on their knees scrubbing, prepared for the return of students. The Chapel, used as a store of College papers during the War, was cleared and re-commissioned and appropriately on King Alfred's Day, 26 October 1946, staff and students met together at 9.45 am, Principal Dickinson recording 'I want this College to be a Christian family where each works for the good of all'.[4]

In the following decade the tide flowed strongly for teacher training at King Alfred's: the raising of the school leaving age to 15 (1947), a rising birth rate, and the realisation in government of the implications of this latter development fuelled a decision announced in June 1957 to expand teacher training courses from two to three years from 1960, thus taking steps that had been long recommended by the *McNair Report* of 1944.[5] This decision was to have major implications for the College which was already, apparently, struggling for space even with 180 students in the late 1940s. Nonetheless it continued to expand by a further 50 students in total by 1957. As the new academic year approached in the autumn of 1958 further pressures were rapidly becoming felt, as it became known to the Principal that Hampshire County Council was contemplating making a bid for an additional teacher training college to contribute to the predicted national shortfall of 12,000 teachers by 1962, and that such a College should be located in Winchester. This confronted Principal Dickinson with an insurmountable dilemma. On the one hand he could preserve the community on the scale and of the type for which he had prayed on that King Alfred's Day 1946, but this option might be blighted by a Local Education Training College on his doorstep in Winchester. Alternatively he could go for massive expansion at King Alfred's and, it seemed to him, by so doing bring about the end of much for which he had worked since 1946. In reply to the Governors' enquiry about maximum size he presented his proposal which was that in moving from a two- to a three-year training programme the size of the College could expand to 250, the maximum he could envisage on the site.

On 9 October 1958 the executive committee of the governors had conducted a site tour of the College to explore possibilities for expansion in view of ongoing debates about the future. On the eve of King Alfred's Day, 25 October, the full governing body met to receive their report and took the decision to forward a proposal much more bold than the small increase in numbers favoured by the Principal: to increase to 400-500 male students. That day also the plan for the second training college in Winchester and the wider plans for expansion of teacher education were printed in the

Hampshire Chronicle. But Principal Dickinson was no longer alive to hear the outcome of the deliberations for suddenly, on 14 October, he had taken his own life. Worries about the future, the changing world, the size of the site, the threat of a competitor built anew with modern accommodation elsewhere in Winchester were too much for him.

Gender and Growth

As outlined above, before the momentous events of October 1958, change was already inevitable for the College in the late 1950s. One aspect of the change was the matter of admitting women students. Events moved quickly: on 22 December following the decision to expand to 400 students, a statement from the governors was issued to staff by the Secretary to the Governors. It began by stating the known: that the College would expand over the next four years taking account of the lengthening of the course to three years from 1960. The second paragraph, however, no doubt caused significant discussion namely that 'King Alfred's College will become a mixed College for approximately 250 men and 150 women students' a change that will conform 'with national policy' and further that 'the life will become more similar to that of a university student'.[6] This bold decision, it should be noted, was taken by the governors. It was not what Principal Dickinson would have hoped for and indeed, at the time this was agreed, there was no Principal as the incoming John Stripe was not formally appointed until a week later on 29 December. 'The two training colleges in Winchester' proposal had already been abandoned by 8 December, and the Governors' Executive Committee, led by Sir Desmond Lee (Headmaster of Winchester College) seized the moment to grasp the opportunity of admitting women, following 'the Ministry's view' on the matter, which was key to the growth of the institution and, ultimately, led to university status. Already in 1960 the Ministry was pressing for equal numbers of 200 men and 200 women. In 1959-60, the first women academic staff were appointed, Robina Macintyre as Vice-Principal, Jennifer Nias and Pat Pemberton and female governors were also engaged.[7]

The gender balance reversed over the succeeding half century. Expansion occurred at a faster pace than initially planned. It was a period of great optimism: during the election campaign of 1959 the Prime Minister, Harold Macmillan, chaffed the nation that they 'had never had it so good'. Already at Winchester in 1959 numbers exceeded the proposed 250 by over 10 per cent: the planned 400 for 1962 was exceeded by 22 already in 1961, although the number of women grew slowly at first and fell short of the 250:150 split envisaged in 1958 for 1962.[8] However, by 1967 women were already some 40 per cent of the total and were outnumbering the men by 3:1 by 1990: in 2005 the percentages were 71:29 per cent.[9]

One of the key changes in the early years was that it was clearly impossible to accommodate all the students as boarders on site, and equally impossible to sustain the high percentage of resident students as opposed to day-students. The long tradition of daily attendance now contributed significantly to numbers so that, for example, in 1965 when there were 688 students, 296 were resident, 195 were in approved lodgings and 197 were day students.[10]

During these rapid and unprecedented changes principals and staff continued to promote fundamentals of the Christian foundation. Principal Stripe, appointed to oversee the introduction of women students, provided both 'spiritual and academic leadership'. In addition Stripe made it his business to be familiar with staff and students and to know their names, to welcome them to Holm Lodge, the Principal's residence on nearby St James's Lane – no mean feat in a period of expansion amounting to a threefold expansion of the College in the eight years he was Principal.[11] All this took its toll on him; he died in May 1967.

Stripe's successor, Martial Rose, previously Vice-Principal and latterly Acting Principal, stepped up. A graduate of King's College, Cambridge, Rose had experience both in schools and far from Winchester at Bretton Hall College in Yorkshire, where he had put on a production of the medieval Wakefield Mystery Cycle of plays on which he was expert. In 1967 he was only the ninth Principal since 1840. He had entered a new world, captured in the photographic record of the 1960s: changing social *mores* and mini-skirted women and long-haired men unfamiliar with the church parades which had been a part of the lives of their servicemen predecessors. Rose provided a strong spiritual example, attending morning Chapel on a daily basis, always wearing his gown. He worked hard to draw the various constituencies of the College together. An early achievement was to fill in the details and see through to completion the already planned theatre which was opened in 1969 as the John Stripe Theatre.[12]

Meanwhile the *Robbins Report* (1963)[13] and its successor by Weaver (1966)[14] had given the College more autonomy because close relationships with universities and outside controls of curricula were restrictive. However, the road ahead was impeded by the minister, Tony Crosland, in 1965 when he effectively prevented the development of a 'unitary' higher education system (promoted by Robbins) and instead espoused the 'binary' system in his speech at Woolwich Polytechnic. This bifurcation left polytechnics on the other side of the tracks from universities, tracks which were to prove difficult to cross in the next generation: colleges were not in Crosland's sights and were potentially in limbo.[15]

Rose, however, realised that there was danger in sole reliance on a teacher-training income stream and planned to widen the institution towards being a College of Higher Education. The building programme of the Herbert Jarman and Tom Atkinson buildings also included science and television facilities and did much to ease pressure on the site as did the establishment of an 'outpost' for seventy-five students in Basingstoke, and from 1969 a system of 'hot-desking' was introduced on the main site where cohorts of students were recruited to attend while their seniors were out on school teaching practice. New courses emerged initially in a consensual way arising from a day conference 'involving the whole of the college's academic staff'.[16]

In 1971, a memorandum to Southampton University proposed that Winchester would double in size to 2,000 students 'half of whom would enter the teaching profession'. This suggested departure from the monotechnic model was prescient. In 1972 it became apparent that oversupply of teachers and a falling birth rate challenged the very existence of colleges of education. Rumours that colleges would close abounded: a significant number of colleges did close in the following years. The women's college of Sarum St Michael closed after negotiations with Winchester for merger failed and was one of many colleges which disappeared. Others engaged in wary and fractious mergers and, at Cheltenham and Gloucester, merger was followed rapidly by 'defederation'.[17] In these years, 1970-80, when 'most polytechnics and all the former colleges of education were engaged in a virtually continuous process of institutional change', these institutions, including Winchester, secured impressive educational achievements despite successive cuts and 'increasing pessimism'.[18]

A mission: 'To educate, to advance knowledge and to serve the public good'. From College of Higher Education to University.

One reason for pessimism in Winchester was that links with the local university at Southampton became problematic in the mid-1970s. The Southampton Vice-Chancellor's suggestion that Winchester and other affiliated Colleges should become Southampton's Education Faculty, met with alarm from educationists on the Southampton campus, and opposition from the chairman of the University Grants Committee. Winchester's desire to validate new, non-education courses was neither welcome in Southampton University, which despite being largely scientific in focus, had an arts faculty and also a theatre, nor to the Regional Advisory Council (RAC) which had overview of higher education provision.

These hurdles were addressed in two ways by the autumn of 1976: first the College approached the Council for National Academic Awards (CNAA).[19] This organisation's 'insistence on qualitative parity with best practice higher education' was a highly formative influence on all subsequent developments, not only at Winchester but elsewhere in institutions which experienced the undoubtedly 'arduous and stressful' process which led to CNAA validation.[20] Second it handled objections from the RAC which, for example, opposed the teaching of single honours courses already offered by universities in the region at Reading and Southampton, by offering joint degrees in History, first with Drama or English, later with Archaeology, and in English, with Drama, History and later with American Studies alongside the BEd awards. However, developments also took place in Education with the introduction of the College's first Masters' degree in Special Education, in preparation in 1980.[21] A DipHE began in 1977 in Social and Economic Studies.[22] These changes were as fundamental as the admission of women. For the first time there were many students in the College who were not being trained for the teaching profession and these students had a different weekly organisation of their time and different aspirations.

If the experience of the students contrasted on the different courses, the Senior Common Room was no less affected. The traditional timetable of stopping for coffee, for lunch and to take tea was a ritual.[23] This and other traditions, such as not sitting with your subject colleagues, but migrating round the SCR to learn from other staff, are recalled by interviewees, but the new subject area staff sat together. Nonetheless, however new, and for some painful, these experiences were, the College survived because it diversified and under Rose's leadership held on where many others failed. One of the ways in which the College attracted new funding and opened its doors was by the establishment of overseas links. [24]

When Martial Rose retired in 1984, the College was not free from problems. By contrast to the student unrest of the late 1960s the decade or so following the early 1980s was characterised by staff unrest. This was over various matters: pay was one, declining staff-student ratios another, both because successive governments followed the 1970s cuts with an unwillingness to fund Colleges of Higher Education with the same pay-scales and ratios as in the 'traditional' universities. These problems continued through the decade and the Education Reform Bill of 1988 once more raised the question of mergers and closures.[25] Indeed Principal Cranmer, who replaced Rose in 1984 and was the first Wintonian (i.e. alumnus) Principal, came to Winchester with experience of closing down his previous College, and no doubt realised he might have to repeat the experience.[26]

Between 1985 and 1995 significant advances were achieved in key areas, led by the Vice-Principal C N C 'Tim' Drey, latterly with Principal John Dickinson. First a formula was found to increase numbers which rose from under 1,000 to some 4,500 in that decade. Second, and equally important, a model for widening the curriculum was introduced through a 'modular' degree. This enabled departments beyond Education, English and History to grow autonomously giving the spread of subjects in Arts and Social Sciences including Psychology and provide a viable basis for a university.[27] Meanwhile in 1990 the College celebrated 150 years of its foundation. Despite the anxieties of the previous 25 years there was much to celebrate. Changing external constraints meant that, for example, by 1990 single honours Drama was permitted and had recruited highly successfully. Winchester had been tested in the national field of higher education by its interaction with the CNAA, which required among much else a focus on research and scholarship aspects of the specialist staff appointed to teach the diversified courses. [28] There was an ever-growing stream of publications from its academics, an ever-increasing attendance at international conferences and an ever-rising list of appointments as visiting scholars. Staff contributed to the development of national curricula abroad. There was development of postgraduate courses at masters' level and, from a start in the late 1980s, in MPhil and doctoral study which contributed signally to the attainment of university title in 2005. From teacher training origins a distinctive aspect of the Church Colleges has been the development of humanities courses and subsequently the caring professions such as nursing. This contrasts with the polytechnics which developed a broader curriculum with more scientific and vocational work starting from a larger student base.[29]

Educational change is always linked to politics and never more so than in the last two decades. The CNAA was abolished and, in 1992, the College returned to accreditation by Southampton University. This was uncomfortable for Winchester and encouraged its leaders to seek independence. Principal Dickinson boldly declared in 1995 that the College would seek university title by 2005.[30] This seemed wholly unrealistic, but circumstances conspired to enable this to be achieved. In this the institution was helped by the government. Anxious over the titling of institutions, the Conservative government became concerned that European Union students might not be attracted to institutions not entitled 'university'. The results were that while the polytechnics were all quickly dubbed universities in the mid-1990s, by contrast some 150 institutions, including King Alfred's, were omitted from the list and ways were sought in succeeding years to remedy this. [31] Another hasty decision was local government reorganisation (1994). This resulted in wealthy local authorities, like Hampshire, being broken up by the bestowing of unitary authority status on cities in Hampshire exemplified by Portsmouth and Southampton. This removed both these universities from Hampshire and, in a welcome development, encouraged the County Council to focus on Winchester as the county's sole institution of higher education. Former members of the College had gone elsewhere and had moved their institutions forward rapidly. Most notably Dame Janet Trotter, inspired by Martial Rose, had moved on to Gloucestershire where she cut through the restraints and led the former colleges of St Paul and St Mary, together with other partners, to become the University of Gloucestershire. It was apparent that the proposed university title was not, therefore, impossible.

In 2003 The Quality Assurance Agency (QAA) established that the College's 'standards and quality were fully commensurate with the university sector as a whole'. The following year undergraduate and masters' degree awarding powers were conferred on the institution which became known as University College, Winchester. This was a double benefit: first it began to break the link with Southampton University which was proving restrictive. Second it released significant sums of money paid to the University of

Southampton. In 2005, following a further QAA audit[32], the Privy Council conferred the title of The University of Winchester. The only remaining hurdle was to gain Research Degree Awarding Powers (RDAP), the autonomous awarding of degrees of Master and Doctor of Philosophy, awards which had remained vested in Southampton University. Winchester met the criteria for RDAP in terms of numbers of students graduating 'past the post' at Master and Doctor of Philosophy level and there was a sufficient body of staff with the experience to carry this forward. Notwithstanding delays, RDAP was finally granted in August 2008, and this too was ratified by the Privy Council. The transformation from School to College to University was complete.

Notes to Chapter 2.

---

[1] Teacher training colleges were distinct from universities and until the mid-twentieth century existed on the margins of, or totally beyond, what was understood as higher education. See Harold Silver, 'Higher Education and Social Change: Purpose in Pursuit?', *History of Education Journal* 36.4-5 (2007): 527.

[2] For fuller accounts of the institution's history, see Martial Rose, *A History of King Alfred's College, Winchester 1840-1980* (London: Phillimore, 1981), Martial Rose, *King Alfred's College, Winchester, 1980-1990: A Decade of Change* (Salisbury: Salisbury Printing: 1990), and Tom James, *Winchester University: From School to College to University* (forthcoming).

[3] Winchester College (College of St Mary's, Winchester) is the famous public school. In 1928 the headmaster urged the governors of the Winchester Training College to find a means of avoiding confusion between the two. It was then that the latter became King Alfred's College. See Rose, *A History*, 83.

[4] W. P. Dickinson, Notebook, quoted in Rose, *A History*, 96-97.

[5] Arnold McNair, *Teachers and Youth Leaders,* known as *The McNair Report*, (London: His Majesty's Stationery Office 1944), paragraph 208. See McNair Report (www.educationengland.org.uk, accessed 29 February 2012).

[6] Statement by the Governors, 22 December 1958; Tom James and Martin Doughty, *King Alfred's College*

Winchester: A Pictorial Record (Stroud: Alan Sutton Publishing, 1991), 56, no. 91.

[7] Principal's Report to the Governing Body (PRGB), October 1960; Rose, *A History*, 105.

[8] The 1962 Education Act required Local Authorities to provide grants, inter alia, for teacher training. See Education Act, 1962 (www.educationengland.org.uk, accessed 29 February 2012).

[9] Quality Assurance Agency (QAA), *Institutional Report on the University of Winchester* (www.qaa.ac.uk, accessed 29 February 2012).

[10] QAA, *University of Winchester*, 104.

[11] Joyce Tuffill, for example, recalls arriving to work in the Library and being surprised and delighted to be sought out by Principal Stripe with the words 'You must be Mrs Tuffill, welcome'.

[12] James and Doughty, *King Alfred's College,* 137, no. 228.

[13] *The Robbins Report* (1963) refers to the foundation of the Council for National Academic Awards (CNAA), the award of degrees in Colleges of Education, and the intention to ensure parity between different institutions of higher education. See *The Robbins Report (1963) on Higher Education*, paragraph 832 (www.educationengland.org.uk, accessed 29 February 2012).

[14] The Weaver Report focused on the government of Colleges of Education. See T. R. Weaver; *Study Group on the Government of Colleges of Education* (London HMSO, 1966).

[15] Harold Silver, *Tradition and Higher Education* (Winchester: Winchester University Press 2007), 64.

[16] Rose, *A History*, 110-111. See also Brian Tippett, 'Diversifying the Colleges' in *150 Years: The Church Colleges in Higher Education Chichester: West Sussex Institute of Higher Education*, ed. Trevor Brighton Tippett, (Bognor Regis: West Sussex Institute of Higher Education,

1989), 50, 53. This report caused much discussion in the College with its recommendations for part-time BEd degrees and regional organisation of training. In October 1972, Rose could report that 22 in-service teachers had enrolled in the BEd degree. (PRGB October 1972) This was part of the shift to making teaching a wholly degree-based profession rather than a certificated one.

[17] See for example Geoffrey D. C. Doherty, *A Case Study of the amalgamation of Crewe and Alsager Colleges of Education* (Crewe: Crewe and Alsager College of Higher Education, 1981), its text illustrated with some telling cartoons demonstrating mutual suspicions of staff from the two institutions and general suspicion of new managers. See also Alan Matterson, *Polytechnics and Colleges* (London and New York: Longman 1981), 10 and 253.

[18] Matterson, *Polytechnics*, 10.

[19] The CNAA had been awarded its charter to be a degree-awarding body in 1964 following the Robbins Report and is discussed in more detail in Chapter 7.

[20] Tippett, 'Diversifying the Colleges', 51-2; Silver *Tradition*, 63.

[21] This report and Lady Warnock's place among the College governors were acknowledgements of the College's national status in this area of Special Needs. (PRGB, October 1980). See Mary Warnock, *Meeting Special Educational Needs* (London: HMOS, 1978), paragraph 12/55.

[22] Rose *A History*, 125.

[23] James and Doughty, *King Alfred's College*, 8, 10, 11 nos. 12, 15 and 18.

[24] Rose had visited Shoei College in Tokyo in 1982, and soon thereafter had established a link which has sent groups of young Japanese women to Winchester each year to be accommodated and taught in their own, Shoei-funded, buildings. Links with American liberal arts colleges and universities were established, such as with Bowdoin

College, Maine, Chapman College, California, the University of Southern Maine, the University of Wisconsin and elsewhere. Links with Canada and Poland were also initiated and sustained. See James and Doughty, *King Alfred's College*, 27, 29, 156, nos. 45, 46, 49, 262.

[25] P. J. Black, *National Curriculum Task Group on Assessment and Testing*, known as the Black Report, (London: Dept. of Education and Science and Welsh Office, 1988), 2: 129, 132.

[26] Rose, *1980-1990,* 9, 11; James and Doughty, *King Alfred's College*, 30, no. 50.

[27] Underpinning this establishment of critical mass and the broader curriculum were a mission statement and a strategic plan, both prepared by Tim Drey, supported in the development of modularisation by Martin Doughty together with Brian Bull and Brian Tippett. Drey's College Academic Committee Structure of November 1994 which set out the committees with their terms of reference showed that the administration had come of age.

[28] Tippett, 'Diversifying the Colleges', 55; readerships and professorships were introduced c. 1990.

[29] Tippett, 'Diversifying the Colleges', 56-57.

[30] In Chapter 2 of 'The Making of the University of Winchester', an unpublished typescript account of developments at this time, John Dickinson described the relationship with Southampton University in the years following this announcement in 1995 as 'a protracted and, for the most part good-natured, game of cat and mouse'.

[31] By the time of the Education Act 1996 and the Education (Student Loans) Act 1996, the word 'polytechnic' had disappeared from government vocabulary.

[32]QAA, *University of Winchester*, (accessed 29 February 2012.)

3.

THE INSTITUTION AS A COMMUNITY: INTRODUCING GEMEINSCHAFT AND GESELLSCHAFT

> The College provided everything for you academically, spiritually and socially...We all lived so closely together. We ate together. We carried out all kinds of sporting activities together and all the social clubs...you were constantly interacting with other people in your year group and the year above. There were never occasions when you were on your own. You were surrounded by people and you were mixing with people all the time.[1]

Introduction

This was the response of one of our interviewees to a question relating to the nature of the community at King Alfred's College in the 1950s, at a time when the majority of students were accommodated on site, or in the nearby West Hayes building which, as described in Chapter 2, had been purchased by the College and first occupied in the summer term of 1948.[2] From this and similar responses it was clear that the principle adopted by the pioneers, who in the 1840s created the English training college, that, like the universities, teacher training colleges should be conducted as close knit communities of learners and should be residential,[3] was firmly in place. Harold Silver suggests that: 'Providing or offering students somewhere to live has, for some eight centuries in Britain and mainland Europe, been part of the need and the mission – even the definition – of a university and other kinds of higher education'. [4] Although the nature of 'somewhere to live' has changed in the recent past, the idea of residence, whether it be in on-site accommodation, halls of residence, hostels, or lodgings at least for some part of the academic course, is still considered important in encouraging shared values and a sense of community.

In this chapter we question to what extent this same esprit de corps, evidenced by our interviews with alumni of the immediate post-war generation, as exemplified above and in the analysis of Robert's interview in Chapter 1, survived during the period covered by our research. As already acknowledged the period was one of enormous change in the nature of higher education institutions as a result of social, political and economic influences. The period also encompasses trends away from the residential towards the growing numbers of students living at home, studying part time, studying as mature students with a home life elsewhere or working outside the institution during term time to offset the ever spiralling costs of the higher education experience. We also analyse the contribution of the staff to the feeling of community within the institution and their own experiences of a community spirit within a generally non-resident staff group.[5]

As a way of analysing the changes within the community that took place over time as the institution adapted and changed, this chapter also introduces Ferdinand Tönnies's sociological concepts of 'Gemeinschaft' and 'Gesellschaft'.[6] Tönnies elaborated these concepts in the late nineteenth century in his quest 'to study the sentiments and motives which draw people to each other, keep them together, and induce them to joint action'.[7] In brief, Gemeinschaft can be interpreted as natural will and pertains to relationships where individuals associate themselves together 'as friends do, because they think the relation valuable as an end in and of itself'.[8] It is therefore appropriate to ideas of friendship based on common work or calling and thus on common beliefs in a community where the welfare of the whole has precedence over the individual. It is best exemplified by family or neighbourhood community. In contrast, 'Gesellschaft' can be interpreted as rational will and pertains to relationships willed 'because those involved wish to attain through it a definite end and are willing to join hands for this purpose'.[9] Unlike the fellowship of Gemeinschaft, Gesellschaft relationships are governed by rationality and self-interest. Gesellschaft is best exemplified in business or nation; individual loyalty is of less importance. Tönnies is careful to observe that Gemeinschaft or Gesellschaft are types of communities and not ideals: they do not exist in pure form and no society could exist if one form or type existed to the exclusion of the other.[10] They are rather 'found interwoven in all kinds of associations'.[11] In relation to the work of Tönnies, we are grateful for the suggestion of one of the interviewees, from Stage 3 of the project, who used the concepts on both his questionnaire and in his subsequent interview as a way of describing the changes in the nature of community at the institution as he perceived them.

While the three stages of the Alumni Voices Project had different foci, at each we posed questions regarding the community, particularly whether the respondents felt there was a sense of community at the institution and whether they felt part of it. Our raw statistical data show that in the first stage of the project 91 per cent of the respondents felt there was a sense of community at the institution and 80.5 per cent felt part of that community. The figure rose for the second stage when almost 98 per cent agreed there was a sense of community and 85 per cent felt part of it. At the third stage, the staff stage, we phrased our questions differently and asked whether the respondents felt there was a sense of shared beliefs, whether they felt part of the community and whether they felt part of their particular faculty. In response 26 per cent felt that the community shared beliefs; 44 per cent felt that the community shared beliefs to some extent; the remaining 30 per cent thought there was little or no evidence of shared belief, or chose not to respond. To the question regarding feeling part of the community 60 per cent did feel part of the community, a further 26 per cent felt part of the community to some extent while the remaining 14 per cent either didn't feel part of the community or didn't answer. In respect of feeling part of the community within their own faculty, 72 per cent answered in the affirmative, 26 per cent felt some affiliation and the remaining 14 per cent either replied negatively or again did not answer. (The percentages total more than 100 per cent because some interviewees ticked more than one box.)

We appreciate that our use of the potent term 'community' was very general, as we made the decision to leave it to our respondents to define it in their terms. The very nature of the project seeks to reflect the change between a community of fewer than 200 men all studying to be teachers and almost all resident on the campus to one with some 6,000 students of both sexes, far more mixed in age and social class, subject and mode of study and residential affiliation. It was also a given that the staff community would respond differently from the former students since, in all but a few cases,[12] they were not resident at the institution; their purpose at being at the institution was different and most of them spent much longer and saw more changes over what was often a long working life. Whereas we could identify change in community by comparing earlier cohorts of students with later ones, in the case of the staff, changes could be identified from within their own experiences. Sociologists argue that the term 'community' might have almost one hundred definitions and this has led to significant debate on which, sociologically, there is not yet complete agreement.[13] We are historians rather than sociologists and our discussion below highlights how we have chosen to interpret the term.

To recognise the differences we observed, we will initially analyse the data chronologically in three distinct periods, the earliest covering the period when it was a men only teacher training college, the second covering the period from 1960 until the mid-1970s while the institution was still monotechnic, and the third covering the later period when courses diversified to include other degree options. Although the interviewee whose quotation opens the chapter identifies three types of community - the social, the academic and the spiritual - we will discuss only the first two in this chapter, with the third being discussed in a subsequent chapter. In both cases our interpretation goes beyond a recent, broad definition of community as 'a cooperative or interactive group sharing a virtual or physical environment and aspects of identity (such as location, race, ethnicity, age, history, occupation), culture, belief or other common bonds and/or share interest in particular issues or outcomes'.[14] Most often respondents interpreted 'community' in a less sterile way and more in the warmer, reciprocal sense of 'social capital' which Robert Putnam suggests refers to 'connections among individuals – social networks and the norms of reciprocity and trustworthiness that arise from them'.[15] Perhaps goodwill, fellowship, sympathy and social intercourse among those making up the community, avoiding any over sentimentality of harking back to the 'more harmonious type of bonds between people vaguely attributed to past ages'.[16] might be a reasonable description. The student narratives, in particular, resonate with references to 'looking out for each other', 'community spirit' and 'friends for life'. We consider this the 'social community'. This should not suggest any absence of the 'commonly held assumption that academic organisations are academic communities'.[17] Our respondents also commented on the intellectual stimulus of being involved in a learning community particularly in connection with their being drawn together with a common purpose. While this was not always distinct from the 'social community', we will refer to this as the 'academic community'. Within these analyses we will refer to the whole community of staff and students as well as the separate communities but again these are not distinct groups and there is considerable overlap.

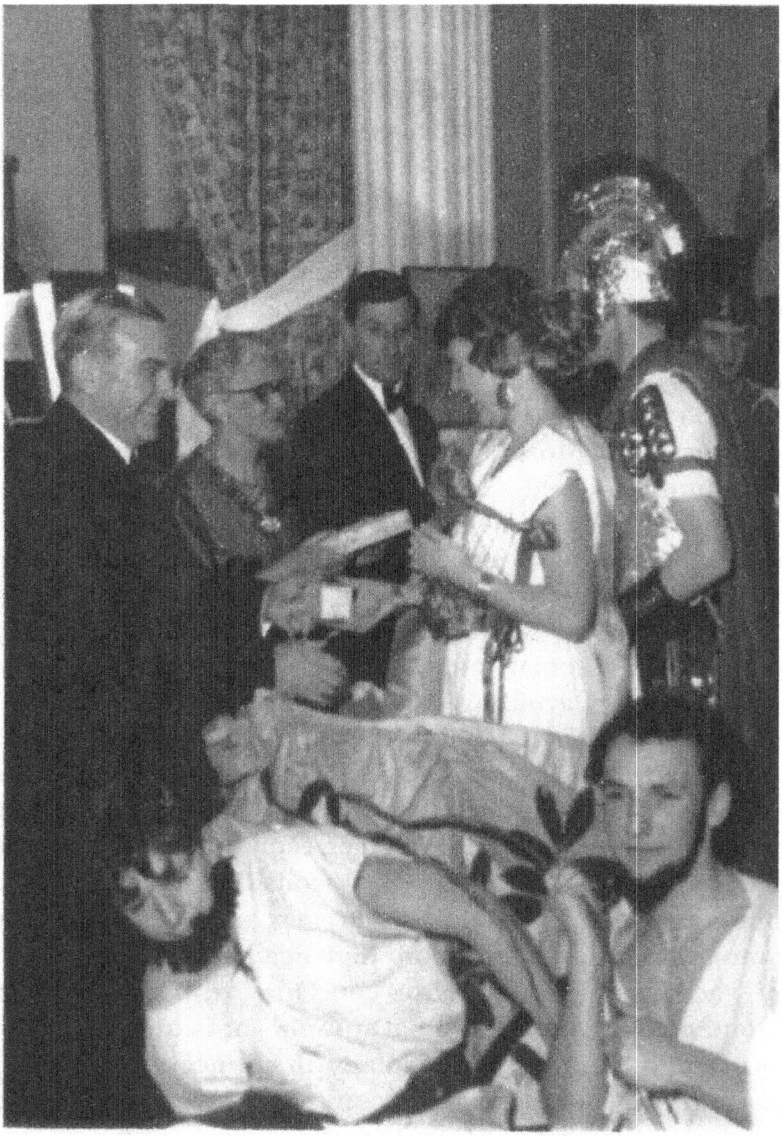

A Great Sense of Camaraderie
'There was a great sense of camaraderie among the students and staff. I found fellow students to be friendly and supportive. The college had a strong social life.'

The Male Community – pre 1960

As we have already suggested, there was a strong sense of family and community prevalent in the College in the immediate post-war period with descriptive phrases such as a 'great sense of belonging', 'almost instant camaraderie' and 'a very tight knit group' being typically used in narratives in which the 'we' was very prevalent. The College was very small at the time with fewer than 200 students. All were working in a community of learners to the common end of becoming teachers, which contributed to their sense of joint enterprise, identity and shared commitment. As mentioned above, the purchase of West Hayes in 1948 enabled almost all students to be resident on site or very close by. Only one respondent lived in private accommodation at any time during his student days.[18] Opportunities were also provided for them to spend their recreational time together, with extensive sporting activities and societies to suit most interests including Chess Club, Christian Union, Debating Society, a Drama Club known as the Irving Club, Film Society, Geographic Society, History Society and Music and Choir groups. These opportunities were taken up enthusiastically, with all but two questionnaire respondents having taken part in extracurricular sports activities and all of them joining one of the special interest societies.

Due to the distance in terms of years and highlighting the importance of the oral history interview in recording memories before they are lost, the interviews with staff are limited for this period. Those we do have make it clear that much of the credit for the feeling of family and community must go to the Principal at that time, who, as Chapter 2 indicates, strove to create a 'Christian family'. We know from a professional source close to him that he was 'very, very kind, very caring, and he was really a father figure to a lot of those students because some of them came back … one or two of them came back from war service rather nervous and in a poor state, and he was very careful to look after them'.[19] Similarly his deputy advised that, 'he was a father figure in the place and I suppose his attitude influenced staff in their relations with students'.[20]

The 'family' at King Alfred's College in the immediate post-war period, with the Principal in the patriarchal role, was comprised entirely from men other than household staff and the matron. The majority of the 'men' who were students at this time had either just finished two years compulsory National Service or may have previously been serving officers in one of the armed forces. Only a few would have come to the College straight from school which in most cases would have been single sex independent or grammar schools. Their previous experiences would therefore be of environments where male camaraderie was the norm. Two responses, one from the end of the 1940s and the second from a decade later, give a flavour of the community life that was experienced by the students:

> Of course the vast majority of our intake were ex-servicemen, so we were used to communal living ... Looking at your notes one word has kept coming into my mind and that is 'comfortable'. I felt really comfortable there – physical comforts, there again we were used to hardship. When I came to the College we were in a dormitory, which we called the 13 club. There must have been 13 of us in it, which seems odd doesn't it? Then during the time we were there they built little cubicles in what had been a dormitory and we each had a little cubicle which was painted in grey walls and features brought out in red. We called it the Woolworth building because that was the Woolworth colours. ...... The camaraderie sounds very military, but I wish there was another word to collegiality for what people all bent on the same purpose with similar experiences feel towards each other. Fraternity I suppose is the word. [21]

> I went to a boarding school when younger and then I was a day boy at what's now a public school, so it was interesting that there was a community immediately from the beginning of my course there. As soon as you arrived you were part of that community. It's very difficult to put your finger on exactly what it was. I was just looking at a photo here and I recognised the person in it. He was the senior student in the hostel I was in and he actually introduced himself to everybody who came to the hostel. He was in his second or third year I think and he introduced himself to all the first years immediately and made sure that everybody had everything and knew where they were going. Even though I'd been to boarding school, so had been through it several time before, it was very, very smooth as an entry into the place. ... I suppose everything was small and central enough in the same sense I imagine it would be in an Oxbridge college, and all the meals being taken together definitely and high tables...But really it was again that intangible feeling of being part of a community. There were no bits that you didn't know about.[22]

At the Winton Club reunion weekend in 2006, when we filmed eleven interviews, one particular event was re-lived and re-told by those involved again and again. It serves to highlight the strength of the community at King Alfred's College in the immediate post-war period that is still closely recalled. Details of the event were re-ordered but the significance lay in the constructed narrative of a student prank which demonstrated a shared sense of student identity and social capital. For the general election in 1955, a group of students proposed a Communist candidate in the name of Alfred King. They covered the city centre in placards and banners including one outside Winchester prison which read, 'Vote for Alfred King and get your freedom'. They also painted the statue of King Alfred which stands in the High Street, as a potent symbol of Winchester as the ancient capital of Wessex, a vibrant shade of red. The following day the College received a visit from a Detective Sergeant and a Detective Constable and the perpetrators of the 'crime' were asked to own up. Instead of the group who were involved taking full responsibility, '143 men stepped forward', almost the entire student population. The policemen took no further action but the Student Union did have to pay for the cleaning of the statue.[23]

We have limited information about the staff community from personal reflections of this time but like the students they would have been drawn together by coming from a background as teachers in grammar or independent schools. The pictures painted by those who joined the staff later hint that it had very much the atmosphere of an Oxbridge college or a gentlemen's club.[24] There have been suggestions that although superficially all may have seemed well, there may have been 'cliques' or factions and a particular instance where there was conflict between the Principal and the Chaplain. We will return to this in the next section. Overall, from the limited data we have, there was generally a spirit of cooperation which found people getting on with each other, 'with a philosophy of helping out, leaning on other people to get answers to the queries we may put either professionally, academically or more likely socially'.[25] In particular there was a bond between those who, like the students, had experience of life in one of the services:

> That's right … well even when I first joined I was made welcome by members of staff...we were quite close knit. It's difficult to suggest that many of us, and I think this has something to do with it at that point in time, were ex-servicemen, I was … towards the end of the war, but some of the others would have been more into it than I was. And that would also have included some of the students who were coming in who were fairly experienced if only having

> done national service or something like that you see. So there was an air of, as you would get in the services, believe it or not, of getting on together willy nilly, good or bad and so on and so forth.[26]

1960-1976

We would suggest that the community we have described above in the immediate post-war period is one demonstrating primarily Gemeinschaft characteristics, resonating as it does with ideas of family, fraternity and common purpose with a patriarch or 'tribal leader' at its head. This was to continue into the next phase when the College became coeducational. In many ways most of the period might be described as a 'golden age' for teacher training. Les Bell terms the years between 1960 and 1973 as the 'Social democratic phase', characterised by a rapidly increasing school pupil population, expansion and a broad consensus about the nature of the educative process.[27] It was the period, as Chapter 2 has described, when many of the recommendations of the *McNair Report* 1944 were implemented and the number of teachers in training grew substantially. One of our staff interviewees suggested that: 'You've also got to remember that it was the '60s, it was an exciting time to be in education. We all believed passionately in what we were doing, we all believed in the importance of education and I think we all innocently felt we could actually make a difference'.[28] This enthusiasm was prevalent in a very high proportion of the responses during this period and contributed to the sense of unity within a close community of learners and teachers, although the size of the College grew from around 200 students in 1960 to around 1,000 by 1976.

The institution's policy of holistic care, which continues today, was particularly prevalent during this period with the 'social capital' of goodwill, fellowship, sympathy and social intercourse ever present. Following Principal Dickinson's death in 1958 he was replaced by Principal Stripe who continued the ethos of the College as a family community and who, like his predecessor, 'probably liked to think of himself as a father figure'.[29] He encouraged the personal tutor system and for staff to invite students into their homes which reinforced the strength of both of the social and academic community. Speaking of one of the departmental heads and his wife, one former member of staff advised:

> Mrs S, who always used to have all the History Department up at various times for a meal, was a superb cook which really helped a lot, and she always came to everything and if we were going somewhere that involved a picnic she would always make sure there was an excellent picnic and you know I mean she was kind of a great asset in that sense, but he knew his students as people very well indeed and encouraged us to. We had a personal tutor system, and it ... I don't know whether it was made explicit or whether it was just in the air but it was clear to us that we should know our personal students better than the others, and so most of us had them round once a term or twice a term.

Ascension Day Picnic

In this period steps were being taken to lower the ratio of students to lecturers: 'I think it was eleven to eleven point five and coming down to ten point five and this was the real battle, you see, to get your staff, to get small units of students, to get small tutorial groups and that's the way to teach'.[30] This enhanced the closeness of the community, as did, emphasised repeatedly, the fact that everyone was working to the same end to either train, or be trained as, a teacher. Staff and students were obviously brought together on a day to day basis academically but beyond this some of the students especially remembered those whose tutorials they experienced and valued. One recalled in what she agreed was a 'golden age':

> Obviously I didn't have the academic qualification to have gone to Oxford and Cambridge's 'dreaming spires' and all that but many of my tutors were in fact 'Oxbridge'. I had my eyes opened to a wide array of English literature and in HB had tutorials with an expert in his field. Looking back I don't think my work was that good, but he gave me the confidence to explore ideas. [31]

The influence of good lecturers might be felt long after college days had ended. One respondent suggested: 'I think that empathy was something certain lecturers had that rubbed off on us and affected the way our relationship progressed with our students or children when we became teachers and I've got that to this day. I think it came from some of those people'.[32] Members of the staff who taught Art, Music and Drama spoke especially of the special bond that existed between them and their students academically because of the nature of the subjects:

> Art is a strange subject in that you're trying to delve into, you know, student's personalities, you're trying to get them to express some sort of inner quality or inner message that they're trying to get out, you're

> probing all the time, and you're exposing you know their feelings and their thoughts and intellect all the time really, and it's that sort of thing which makes a very close relationship.[33]

Similarly a member of the Music staff suggested that: 'If you're making music with somebody the rapport and the general understanding is uplifting'.[34] While the Drama tutor stated:

> Well I think Drama has a peculiarity in that essentially there is an informal relationship between teacher and taught, so in a sense there wasn't something called pastoral care, there was a relationship that permeated the entire treatment and the course, so it was all pastoral, it was also all academic was also all practical … but they would willingly come and talk over, and I could be absolutely frank with them and tell them my thoughts, they would tell me theirs … you can't have secrets from each other in Drama you know you have to be prepared to be vulnerable.[35]

Socially students and staff got together particularly for special occasions such as the Christmas celebrations and the Valedictory Balls:

> So the big one would be my first one would have been the Christmas carol service probably, so the Christmas carol service is a big event, and because there would be too many people to fit in the Chapel, it would carry on afterwards in the dining hall. Everybody would gather in the dining hall for a form of carol singing and mince pies and what have you, and most tutors would be there, and similarly at the end of the year the Valedictory Dinner again most tutors attended and that was a sort of black tie do, and everybody dressed up in their glad rags on the last night of the student year.[36]

The majority of the students during this period were resident in the city, if not always on campus. The nature of the residence changed as numbers increased and the College, during the late 1960s and 1970s, acquired different sorts of accommodation throughout the city to cope with the growing student body.[37] Until the late 1960s meals continued to be taken together formally. The ethos of the community was often described as 'caring for one another', 'looking out for everybody' and 'helping one another' without any 'feeling of rivalry or outdoing one another or any feeling of people rushing to get better marks or anything like that. It just didn't happen'.[38]

The Valedictory Dinner
'I have very fond memories of Winchester - dressing up for Valedictory dinners.'

For most alumni who took part in the project, extra-curricular activities still centred on College. The students seldom worked outside of the College in term time and it was possible to 'live without going out into the wider world during our three years if you wanted to. Everything was there for you. Your academic needs and social needs were all there'. [39]As in the immediate post-war period, these college centred activities continued to be an important means of bringing people together to forge friendships that in many cases were very long standing. Sporting activities continued to be important to the spirit of community. While such activities involved both male and female students, team sports seemingly continued to provide a space for the male students to enjoy the spirit of male camaraderie. Such was the feeling of camaraderie that:

> We would, for instance, travel away to matches wearing, voluntarily, grey trousers, black blazers, college tie, college badge and white shirt and the majority of the teams of choice would go dressed like that, except if we were going to London because we'd go out in the evening. That's a symbol of the idea – having a team identity.[40]

Those joining the staff in this period similarly recall that the community spirit was strong both academically and socially, with the Senior Common Room (SCR) being described as 'a very vibrant place where all the staff met'.[41] It became a focal point for discussion and intellectual argument: 'I would have said that the SCR was the key element in the sort of community feel of the place ... you could go into it at any time of the day, sit by anybody and be sure of a friendly conversation. It was also very much a kind of joint professional and social place'.[42] One interviewee recalled the many things that she learnt in her conversations in the SCR:

> I learnt about bees from the Physicist, the Head of the Art department taught me a great deal about modern Art. There was a Mathematician who persuaded me that Maths could be interesting, by talking about it as a ... talking about Geometry as a game that ... an intellectual game that the Greeks played, and various other things. I learnt all about

> you know Brecht from the chap that did Drama; it just was ... the context was right in the sense that there was a place and comfortable chairs, and the time was right.[43]

The Old Dining Hall
'We were served by the catering staff who allocated the food to the head of the table who dished out to everybody else.'

It was quite common for staff and their families to mix together socially and invite each other to their houses. In addition there were various social activities which the staff enjoyed together:

> There were staffroom walks you know. We used to organise walks with all members of different departments and tennis at weekends, but again all mixing in; and badminton. I mean for many years twice a week in the evening I'd play badminton with

> someone called MH from the English Department, TS from the RE Department and EG from the Art Department, and I was Education and it was a regular thing and it was lovely you know having that sort of friendship.[44]

The story of the community at King Alfred's College in this period as related by the staff who took part in the project was almost without exception a favourable one of a community displaying particularly Gemeinschaft characteristics. One interview, however, demonstrates how sometimes the past is looked at through rose-tinted spectacles and memory can be a slippery thing. We have noted above in our discussion of the post-war period that there may have been 'cliques' or factions within the staff body and a particular instance where there was conflict between the Principal and the Chaplain. One of the later Principals strongly suggested to us that 'ghosts' from this period pervaded the following years. To bring the staff together and exorcise the 'ghosts', a play was performed in which many of the staff took part either on the stage itself or in various background roles. Those staff who took part recalled the play in terms of it being fun and rather risqué, 'We had the Christian Union praying for us ... because it was thought to be not the sort of thing we should be doing at a Church of England College'.[45] In contrast the producer remembered:

> ...and one of the things that I thought we would do was to produce a staff play in this theatre And I chose a play by Aristophanes called, 'Ladies' Day'... and it brought everybody together and it brought not just, it didn't bring the students so much, they had something to do with the popular music but it brought the technicians, it brought Design and Technology staff in the stage stuff and it brought in all these new ladies...women's chorus. And they were just terrific. [46]

Post 1976

Towards the end of the period we have just described, changes in the nature of the community began to be felt because of the increase in student numbers. As the size of the student population increased and the institution itself became a more complex one, with the diversification into avenues other than teacher training, the feeling of being one cohesive community and one family began to decrease. Instead there were 'several different communities'...but also a sense of 'being one institution'.[47] In particular those doing the BA degrees, which were introduced from 1976, felt generally separate from those who were doing the BEd degree. In the early days this manifested itself as follows:

> I would say that at that stage the BA courses had only been running for two years and we were very much the minority. When people heard you'd gone to KAC they automatically assumed you were doing teacher training until you told them you weren't. So I didn't really get to know any BEd students very well at all. So I tended only to get to know people who were on the BA courses and mostly those doing the same subsidiary subject, which was Drama.[48]

Those coming later, as the balance changed towards more people doing BA degrees, suggested:

> We tended not necessarily to mix with people on the teaching courses, simply because of the fact that we didn't really see them and if they were away on placements, especially during the latter part of their courses, you tend to not see them for a term because they spend a whole term teaching down in Southampton.[49]

However, this separateness should not imply that the students lost their feelings of belonging, of loyalty, or of caring for one another or that they no longer had shared values. The goodwill, fellowship, sympathy and social intercourse that characterised the social capital of the earlier periods was still prevalent and the same phrases relating to caring for and helping one another were repeated, as was the use of the word 'family', albeit there were now many separate 'families': 'I was in Macintyre and in that hall you had a ready group of people that I suppose were your family in a way and I think that really helped'.[50] 'I saw my friends very much as part of my family and we had really, really good links for a long time afterwards'.[51] 'Our course was like a little community within a community... the whole College had a sense of community as it was so small and had a sense of family'.[52] To the regret of the Principal, who was in post both pre and post the College expansion and diversification, he was no longer able to be a father figure and know the students in the way his two predecessors had. In his interview he recalled a recent occasion when he had met an alumna at a local coffee morning:

> And when we met, Helen said, 'I was at King Alfred's, I was a student there,' and she said, 'I recognised you from a photograph'. ..and I felt awful that I hadn't spoken to her. It was at a time, you see, when you get this expansion of all sorts of new things that you stop knowing the students. At one time I knew all the students. But my feeling was she didn't know me, she knew of me and I was ashamed of that...[53]

Relationships with staff continued to be mostly very good with the staff being described variously as 'a great friendly bunch, who were approachable and willing to help out when needed';[54] 'very nice people...warm and friendly and intelligent',[55] suggesting that the institution continued to operate as a close community of teachers and learners although as the number of students increased so did the ratio of students to staff.

While the closeness of the community remained, responses to the questions raised at different stages of the project demonstrate that in other ways it had changed, particularly in terms of the manner of its cohesion. After the 1980s in particular, the interest in societies and sports as a means of building a sense of community declined. While we would reiterate at this point that our sample is small, the data indicate that as late as the 1970s more than 80 per cent joined one of the College societies. During the 1980s the figures had reduced to half, in the 1990s it had further decreased to around a third and in the later period to around a fifth. The figures for those joining sports teams show a similar decline with only a third of respondents joining a sports team in the 1980s, by which time any fixtures were friendly rather than competitive, a similar number during the 1990s, and none of the respondents from the more recent period. It should be mentioned that the gender ratio is also a factor here. Our figures from the 1960s, when the gender balance was more equal, indicate that sporting activities were always more popular with male students and it therefore follows that the statistics will be affected as the gender balance grew in terms of female students.

There were of course exceptions to the above including one particularly enthusiastic response relating to the importance of sports echoing those of earlier cohorts:

> I played mixed hockey, netball, anything I could, and that's how I got into my union activities and that's really where I made all my friendships, my main friendship group I suspect. It was a big, big group. The male and female hockey club – we turned every game into a huge adventure really. We used to have pre- and post-match get togethers and so it went on. It was any excuse for a party! It just went on. You came back from a match and you just all had to meet somewhere in the evening and if you didn't

> you'd get fined for not being there. We had all those sorts of things that if people didn't join in activities they were fined. So it was really great, great fun. Pressure, but fun with it. Really that dominated my life at college.[56]

More generally though the attitude was one of uninterestedness:

> I don't ever remember knowing anybody in a society. I think one of my friends was in the Free Tibet Society and a couple of the guys played football, but other than that I've no idea. I wouldn't have known which societies...In Freshers' Week they had people sat on stalls saying 'Do you want to play a sport?' but other than that I was never aware, so they must have suffered quite a bit.[57]

Writing in 2000, Putnam similarly found that during the previous twenty-five years, attendance at club meetings had fallen 58 per cent, family dinners were down 33 per cent, and having friends visit had fallen by 45 per cent.[58] He suggests that as similar patterns are also evident in many other western countries, western cultures may be losing the spirit of community that was once found in a variety of institutions. As we have mentioned above this did not seem to be the case at the College and there was not necessarily any lack of social capital. In a changing society, the students 're-grouped' and seemed more inclined to seek their entertainment elsewhere, most often in Winchester itself or for livelier nights out to nearby Southampton: 'I didn't really get involved with any of the societies in college. I tended to do a lot of my socialising outside really...'[59]

There were financial pressures on many students at this time, particularly following the decline of student grants and the introduction, from 1990, of student loans: more students were therefore working in paid employment in term time as well as in the holidays. Within our sample the figures do show some fluctuation but before 1980 it was comparatively rare for the students to work other than in the holidays. Many specifically mentioned how grateful they were to have studied during a period when full student grants were the norm. During the 1980s almost 90 per cent had jobs; the figure decreased to about 66 per cent during the 1990s but in the later period all our respondents worked in term time. While this no doubt had some effect on their interest in extra-curricular activities provided by the institution it did not necessarily have any effect on their feelings of being part of the community:

> When I was working at the hospital it didn't really affect it because I only had to work maybe three evenings a week and I was cleaning there. So it was a matter of starting at 5.00pm and finishing by 9.00pm and then I'd go and meet everyone, wherever they were. So I don't really think it affected anything.[60]

and

> I wouldn't have joined any clubs and societies and part of that was due to having a job. Obviously a lot of my friends went out a lot more than I did because I had to go to work, but I don't think it really affected the feeling of being part of the community.[61]

From our research the essence of community spirit manifested itself in the sharing of a life-changing situation, described by respondents variously as having 'moved away from home and clinging on to life without your mum to do your washing for you',[62] or building up camaraderie, 'because it was all quite new to everyone, queuing for your grant, having to go and do shopping for the first time and cooking for yourself for the first time'.[63] Often those who did not feel part of the social community were those living further away from the institution, travelling in and then travelling home without involving themselves in any way with the life of the student population and therefore not sharing the same experiences:

> A couple of my friends had commuted in from a distance and they really didn't feel there was a sense of community and I think they missed out. We would socialise and go for a meal and socialise more in the evening and it was definitely with people you lived with rather than those on your course. During the second year I got really friendly with people on my course, but it was more to do with the halls.[64]

To our respondents, it did not therefore matter that the size of the institution had increased and they only knew small groups of people: the importance of residence whether it was in on site accommodation, halls of residence, hostels, or lodgings elsewhere in Winchester was critical to their sense of being part of the community and having a shared experience. A member of staff suggested that:

> And I think for the students you know to be part of a group of fifteen friends makes no difference whether they're fifteen among 5,000 or fifteen among 50,000 really, they'll still have that you know … they'll make their own little networks and clusters of friends... I think that's what you do as a student, you coalesce with a bunch of people that are convivial and that's who you see, and it doesn't matter to you how many people are on the campus, as it were.[65]

We would suggest that the student community, or perhaps more correctly the multiple student communities, continued generally to exhibit the Gemeinschaft characteristics of friendship based on common experiences. Before we turn to discussion of the staff community during this period, it will be recalled that the data from both the student projects did not show complete agreement either that there was a sense of community or that the participants felt part of it. For some it was because they were not resident in Winchester, as we have described above, or as mature students had lives elsewhere. For others this might be attributed to their own personalities particularly if they were shy and lacking in confidence: 'I possibly kept myself to myself. I spent time in the common room and things like that but I didn't feel part – I don't know, it's just me';[66] or perhaps they felt themselves somehow 'different':

> And also little things like I was never into pop music, going to discos and things. That wasn't quite my style. Also I think I tended to be a bit shy, so it was a bit more difficult to be outgoing. The idea of going down and spending the evening in the pub drinking wasn't really my idea of entertainment, so perhaps I was a bit stodgy compared to some of the others.... I tended more to keep myself to myself a bit I think within the hostel.[67]

In one case a student described herself as feeling so alienated that she was about to 'quit' until a particular act of kindness:

> A morning I walked into the Chapel, lost and alone, and would have walked out again if not for a much older blind student called B. He always sat just inside the door with his Braille books. He heard the hesitation and invited me to sit on the chair next to him for the service, then insisted I see him down to breakfast and sit with him to cut up his food. He could manage perfectly well, I found out later, but he heard what no one else did and realised I was about to quit. Sometimes all it takes is one act of kindness to change a life.[68]

With others the reasons can be attributed to their own attitudes at the time:

> The difficulty I have here is that I didn't have a sense of community. I think I isolated myself to a certain extent. I brought down the barriers due to certain

> factors. I felt that although I was only three years older I felt a lot older than the eighteen-year olds that I was put in a room with and was sharing accommodation with. [69]

As we acknowledge in the introduction to this chapter there is an inevitable difference between attitudes of students who are resident and spend between two to four years at an institution and staff who are non-resident and spend many years of their professional life there. This was particularly apparent with those staff who joined while the institution operated as a teacher training college and remained to work in what they found as a very changed institution following the diversification into other degrees. Bell describes the period 1973-1987 as the Resource Constrained Period:

> In which there was a growing emphasis on management, especially the management of resources including teachers, a debate about the nature and purpose of education, a growing concern about the quality and relevance of teaching and of teacher training, a decline in the morale of teachers as career opportunities became more limited, increasing state intervention in the curriculum, the targeting of funding, the limiting of equality of opportunity and experiments with alternative funding strategies.[70]

It was, as described in Chapter 2, the period when King Alfred's College had to fight for its survival when so many teacher-training colleges were closing and when it was also required to approach the CNAA to validate its degrees. As will be described in more detail in Chapter 7, the staff who experienced this recalled enormous pressure: 'It was for survival very necessary but also very horrendous'.[71] 'There was a great deal of anxiety amongst people just for their lives, their jobs and so on...you were always looking out in the *Times Higher Education Supplement* to see whether your institution was on the list for the chop'. [72] Recollections of applying to the CNAA in the validation process were almost all negative and signalled the change from a staff community that had previously displayed predominantly Gemeinschaft characteristics moving to a much more complex Gesellschaft one.

The decision for the institution to diversify also caused the staff to lose their earlier professional cohesion. Initially the two subjects to be considered for BA degrees were History and English with Drama being added shortly afterwards. While some staff admitted that this was because these had the reputation of being the strongest academically, for those from other departments, 'there was jealousy on the part of some of the staff'.[73] In the case of Drama, it also caused some 'schism' between those who 'did' Drama professionally and therefore 'knew about it' and those for whom it had been a hobby.[74] The employment of new staff to supplement the existing staff working in these areas of History, English and Drama added to the loss of the earlier cohesion for various reasons: initially because of the difference of their academic backgrounds but also because of a more widespread 'clash of attitudes':

> People came into the place that had no background of teaching and teaching was the common element when I went there, teaching in school I mean, but I mean we had archaeologists coming in. Well I mean nobody taught, nobody could have taught archaeology in a primary school, they might have been interested in it and shown children, you know, things that had been dug up, but I mean it's not quite the same.[75]
>
> As you know too at around this period in the '70s there was an increasingly polemical almost politically driven attitude among many academics, and I think that for a while, although I don't think it persisted, but it was for a while it did create a sort of clash of

> attitudes to what one was there to do, and that announced itself in staff meetings, so the first time in many years that I knew we began to get that sort of polemicism that we hadn't had before and that was interesting to watch but sometimes uncomfortable to experience.[76]

As the College expanded and the faculties separated, 'people spent much more time within their faculties and particularly within their subject areas'. The Senior Common Room 'didn't have anything like the sense of a community coming together'.[77] This separation is illustrated very clearly in one particular story we were told:

> I was sitting in the Common Room and a very nice young and strong new member of the History Department called M was there, and we were all you know sitting mixed up together but the History Department staff were at one end of the Senior Common Room, which you perhaps know is a very long room, and M picked up an enormous armchair and walked with it the length of the Common Room to come and sit next to the History Department and there was this very large man with a huge armchair striding across the Common Room... [78]

The closeness that had existed earlier among the whole staff as one cohesive group could never return as the College expanded. A staff member who joined the staff in 1987 recalled that:

> There was clearly a sort of an apartheid in the institution between the teacher training group who felt themselves to be the Admiralty, the Senior Service who represented the true 'bottom' of the institution and the people that I was appointed to work with, the History department, the English department, the Drama department, who saw

> themselves as proper academics. There really was a divide between the two camps.[79]

This should not imply of course that there was no sense of either a social or academic community among the staff: it existed (and exists) as the statistics earlier in the chapter demonstrated but it was definitely more fragmented and was and is likely to exist within individual faculties or departments, communities within a community, rather than in the institution as a whole. Inevitably it also fluctuated depending on the pressures on the staff as the institution has grappled with successive changes in policy relating to higher education which have required it to adapt and change particularly since the early 1990s.[80] This is particularly the case as this book is being written and universities are being required to secure funding by way of tuition fees to secure their own futures.

Conclusion

In this chapter we have introduced Tönnies's concept of Gemeinschaft and Gesellschaft which was used by one of our correspondents in his analysis of change in the College. As the institution expanded so the nature of the community inevitably changed. The addition of alumni voices which include the reflections of staff enables us to explore in more detail the day-to-day experience of living and working at Winchester. In the following chapters we return to Tönnies's discussion of community in order to highlight how gender, religion and policy changes affected the narratives of higher education at the institution.

Notes to Chapter 3.

---

[1] Filmed Interview 5, Stage 2 (1956-1958).

[2] Rose, *A History of King Alfred's College, Winchester 1840-1980*, (London: Phillimore, 1981) 96.

[3] H.C. Dent, *The Training of Teachers in England and Wales 1800-1975* (London: Hodder and Stoughton, 1977), 8. See also Harold Silver, *Tradition and Higher Education* (University of Winchester Press, 2007), 35.

[4] Silver, *Tradition and Higher Education,* 83.

[5] Many staff were resident on site until the 1960s and the Principal and Vice Principal continued to be provided with on-site accommodation until the 1980s.

[6] We recognise the difficulties of using these terms given the link of Gemeinschaft with Hitler's 'Volksgemeinschaft' which was used to justify Nazi action against other groups. However, Ferdinand Tönnies disavowed totalitarianism including Nazism in his own country. He joined the Social Democratic Party of Germany in 1932 to oppose fascism. See *Encyclopaedia Britannica*, 'Ferdinand Tönnies,' *Encyclopaedia Britannica* www.britannica.com (accessed 12 August 12 2013).

[7] Ferdinand Tönnies, *Community and Association*, first published as *Gemeinshcaft und Gesellschaft,* 1887, (London: Routledge and Kegan Paul, 1955 fp 1887), 3.

[8] Charles P Loumis, Introduction in Tönnies, *Community*, xv.

[9] Loomis, Introduction, xv.

[10] Loomis, Introduction, xix.

[11] Tönnies, *Community*, 18.

[12] Many staff were resident on site until the 1960s and the Principal and Vice Principal continued to be provided with on-site accommodation until the 1980s.

[13] Bearing in mind all the caveats regarding the use of *Wikipaedia* as a reliable source of information, it is still interesting to note the following explanation to the search term 'community': 'In sociology, the concept of community has led to significant debate, and sociologists are yet to reach agreement on a definition of the term. There were ninety-four discrete definitions of the term by the mid-1950s.Traditionally a "community" has been defined as a group of interacting people living in a common location. The word is often used to refer to a group that is organised around common values and is attributed with social cohesion within a shared geographical location, generally in social units larger than a household." (*Wikipedia*, 'Community', *Wikipedia* (en.wikipedia.org, accessed 12 April 2011).

[14] See Leslie Hicks, Diane Simpson, Ian Mathews, Karen Crawford, Harriet Koorts with Kevin Cooper, 'Connected Communities', AHRC (www.ahrc.ac.uk, accessed 29 April 2013).

[15] Robert D. Putnam, *Bowling Alone: The Collapse and Revival of American Community* (New York: Touchstone, 2000), 19. Putnam acknowledges that the term 'social capital' itself turns out to have been independently invented at least six times over the twentieth century, each time to call attention to the ways in which our lives are made more productive by social ties. The first known use of the concept was by L. J. Hanifan, state supervisor of rural schools in West Virginia in 1916. Subsequently it was also used in the 1960s by Jane Jacobs, in the 1970s by the economist Glenn Loury, in the 1980s by the social theorist Pierre Bourdieu, by the German economist Ekkehart Schlicht and by the sociologist James S Coleman. Putnam recognises that a society of many virtuous isolated individuals is not necessarily rich in social capital.

[16] Norbert Elias, Forward, *The Sociology of Community: A Selection of Readings,* ed. Colin Bell and Howard Newby (Abingdon: Frank Cass and Company Ltd., 1974) xiii.

[17] Silver, *Tradition and Higher Education* , 185.

[18] We recognise that our sample may not be proportionate in this respect.

[19] Interview 23, Stage 3 (1953-1965).

[20] Interview 21, Stage 3 (1951-1965).

[21] Interview 18, Stage 2 (1947-1949).

[22] Interview 11, Stage 2 (1959-1961).

[23] Filmed interviews, Winton Weekend 2006, especially interviews 6, 7 and 11.

[24] A member of staff joining in 1960 suggested that the whole College had the aura of Oxbridge with 'toasted crumpets around the gas fire at tea time'. See Interview 18, Stage 3 (1960-1967).

[25] Interview 2, Stage 3 (1956-1991).

[26] Interview 2, Stage 3 (1956-1991).

[27] See Les Bell, 'Chronicles of Wasted Time? Initial Teacher Education in England: 1960-1999,' *Australian Journal of Education,* 43.2 (1999):186-204.

[28] Interview 18, Stage 3 (1960-1967).

[29] Interview 13, Stage 2 (1963-1966).

[30] Interview 22, Stage 3 (1965-1984).

[31] Questionnaire 140, Stage 1 (1961-1964).

[32] Interview 13, Stage 2 (1963-1966).

[33] Interview 8, Stage 3 (1969-1998).

[34] Interview 5, Stage 3 (1960-1991).

[35] Interview 6, Stage 3 (1967-1988).

[36] Interview 17, Stage 3 (1973-2006).

[37] See Rose, *A History*, 109-110.

[38] Interviews 3 and 4 (husband and wife), Stage 2 (1962-1965).

[39] Interview 4, Stage 2 (1962-1965).

[40] Interview 6, Stage 2 (1963-1966).

[41] Interview 13, Stage 3 (1970-2008).

[42] Interview 11, Stage 3 (1971-1992).

[43] Interview 18, Stage 3 (1960-1967).
[44] Interview 13, Stage 3 (1970-2008).
[45] Interview 7, Stage 3 (1968- 1995).
[46] Interview 22, Stage 3 (1965-1984).
[47] Questionnaire 46, Stage 1 (1985-1989).
[48] Interview 16, Stage 2 (1979-1982).
[49] Interview 14, Stage 2 (1993-1996).
[50] Interview 19, Stage 2 (1977-1981).
[51] Interview 20, Stage 2 (1985-1989).
[52] Questionnaire 92, Stage 1 (1998-2001).
[53] Interview 22, Stage3 (1965-1984).
[54] Questionnaire 102, Stage 1 (1986-1989).
[55] Questionnaire 137, Stage 1 (1991-1995).
[56] Interview 19, Stage 2 (1977-1981).
[57] Interview 17, Stage2 (1999-2003).
[58] Robert D. Putnam, 'Bowling Alone: The Collapse and Revival of the American Community', *Bowling Alone*: bowlingalone.com (accessed 16 July 2011).
[59] Interview 20, Stage 2 (1985-1989).
[60] Interview 20, Stage 2 (1985-1989).
[61] Interview 17, Stage 2 (1999-2003).
[62] Questionnaire 121, Stage 1 (1998-2002).
[63] Interview 14, Stage 2 (1993-1996).
[64] Interview 17, Stage 2 (1999-2003).
[65] Interview 14, Stage 3 (1987-present day).
[66] Interview 6, Stage 2 (1963-1966).
[67] Interview 16, Stage 2 (1979-1982).
[68] Questionnaire 68, Stage 1 (1982-1986).
[69] Interview 1, Stage 2 (1974-1978).
[70] Bell, *Chronicles of Wasted Time,* 2.
[71] Interview 3, Stage 3, (1968-1991).
[72] Interview 10, Stage 3,(1975-2003).
[73] Interview 3, Stage 3 (1968-1991).
[74] Interview 7, Stage 3 (1968-1995).
[75] Interview 4, Stage 3 (1964-1987).
[76] Interview 6, Stage 3 (1967-1988).
[77] Interview 8, Stage 3 (1969-1998).

[78] Interview 13,Stage 3 (1970-2008).

[79] Interview 20, Stage 3 (1987-present day).

[80] While Bell's descriptions of different periods, which we have used earlier in the chapter, relate specifically to teacher education, they can also be applied to higher education more generally. He terms the years 1988-1996 as the Market Phase and defines this as the period in which opportunities were available for growth as those areas defined as successful were encouraged to expand while schools and colleges branded as failures contracted or closed. Following from this Mark Lofthouse suggests that the period from 1997 under the Blair/Brown Labour government might be termed the Excellence Phase with education being placed at the centre of New Labour's economic and social agenda. See Mark Lofthouse, *Faith, Class and Politics: The Role of the Churches in Teacher Training, 1914-1945* (Oxford: University of Oxford Department of Education, 2009), 99.

4.

THE COMMUNITY AND THE CHURCH

> The Church is at present busily engaged on spending vast sums of money on the expansion of its colleges. There are not a few churchmen who doubt the wisdom of spending so much money on a project that the State could well undertake. It is, therefore, our duty as part of the products of this policy to endeavour to justify it by taking with us into our schools something that will distinguish us from the people trained by the Local Education Authority Colleges. The early apostles were first called Christians at Antioch because they had a sense of value and a set of standards which were alien to the society in which they lived. These same Christian standards should mark us out from the world at large.[1]

Introduction

Our introductory chapter indicated that in using data from just one institution, this book would situate itself within wider changes in higher education. However, while this chapter, in its analysis of general trends in religiosity and the spiritual life of the academic community, can be widely applied, it does have a greater resonance for institutions such as the University of Winchester and its fourteen sister institutions sharing a Church foundation. These universities and colleges, many of which like the University of Winchester have their origins in teacher education, are linked together in The Council of Church Colleges and

Universities (CCUC) and are now known as 'The Cathedrals Group'. This association supports the Churches' (the Roman Catholic Church, the Church of England and the Methodist Church) 'continuing role in Higher Education through the Church Universities and Colleges as a means of developing the historic partnership between the Churches and the State and of contributing to the public good and the well-being of society'. It also 'maintains oversight of the statutory duty to protect denominational education in Christian schools through the provision of teachers trained in Church Universities and Colleges'.[2]

The opening quotation is taken from a message, in 1960, from the retiring President of the Student Union at King Alfred's College. Its context was the promised expansion of teacher training colleges in order that the long-standing recommendations of the *McNair Report* might be implemented: the Church of England had supported these recommendations enthusiastically. It suggests that at that time many students who had undertaken their teacher training at a Church college were clear in the ways in which they might have been distinguished from those trained at secular institutions, and that although much had changed since the foundation of the College in 1840, there was still a trace of the distinctive belief of the early training colleges that, first and foremost, the elementary school teachers they trained should be Christian missionaries and that teaching was their vocational duty. Harold Silver acknowledges:

> The universities have at different times in their histories had to reconcile diverse and changing loyalties, both to changing circumstances and to changing perceptions of the reality and validity of their own perceived traditions. They have faced dilemmas relating to their distinctiveness and to their underlying attachment to church or state.[3]

This is particularly relevant in respect of the Churches' changing role in relation to teacher education in which, as has been touched upon in Chapter 2, they became closely involved in the early nineteenth century at a time when religious conviction dominated public life and society was imbued with a moral earnestness which encouraged philanthropy and missionary zeal. Mark Lofthouse suggests that religion and education were inextricably linked.[4] Before the nineteenth century, there was no systematic training of teachers in Britain.[5] Those who did receive the limited training available were trained in 'Model' schools or in 'Centres' attached to schools.[6] This inconsistency remained until the mid-1830s by which time the Board of Education hoped that the creation of new residential training establishments would improve the situation. By 1837 three establishments had been founded but ten years later, there were more than twenty with the prospect of more to come.[7] Almost all of these, like the Diocesan Training School in Winchester, founded in 1840, were associated with the Church of England.[8] By 1850, the Congregationalists had opened two colleges and later in the same decade the Wesleyan Methodists and the Roman Catholics opened their first colleges.[9] From 1840-1890, the denominational colleges enjoyed a monopoly of teacher training,[10] having sprung to life 'on a wave of religious enthusiasm'.[11] Sir James Kay-Shuttleworth, whom it might be reasonable to describe as the founding father of teacher training, believed that 'no skill can compensate adequately for the absence of a pervading religious influence on the character and conduct of schoolmasters'.[12]

From the standpoint of the twenty first century this 'inextricable link between religion and education' sits uneasily. Today, in contrast to the nineteenth century, Britain, following many years of immigration, is a multi-faith society and it has been argued is a country in which Christianity has, over the last forty years, died or is at least in its death throes:[13] others, notably Garnett and others, disagree with this argument and put forward an alternative one suggesting that Christianity has transformed rather than died and 'Christian Britain' still has some meaning.[14] However both sides of the argument agree that, whatever the future holds for Christianity in this country, outward signs of religiosity, such as church attendance, baptism and confirmation have decreased and immigration has increased the number of different religions practised here.

It is hardly surprising against a background of profound religious and cultural change that Church colleges and universities have faced challenges in the last sixty years in surviving as distinctly Christian bodies[15] and especially in defining their roles as such.[16] The 2001 *Dearing Report* on Church schools devoted a chapter to the Church colleges, recognising both the problem of maintaining their Christian distinctiveness and of ensuring their long-term stability.[17] In 2007, an article by Melanie Newman in the Times Higher Education Supplement highlighted tensions between Christian universities over the role that their religious mission should play.[18] While the confident tones of the website of the Cathedrals Group suggests that things have moved forward since 2007, reference to the home pages of the websites of the individual members does not overtly highlight their Christian affiliation as part of a distinctive identity. While such affiliation can be assumed from the names of the three Catholic institutions, Leeds Trinity, Newman and St Mary's University, Twickenham and five of the Anglican ones, Bishop Grosseteste, Canterbury Christ Church, St Mark and St John, Trinity St David and York St John University, only Bishop Grosseteste and the University of Winchester reference any religiosity in their logo: in the former case a bishop's mitre and in the latter a stylised silhouette of Winchester Cathedral. In contrast, some American universities choose to use their Christian foundation as an important feature of their identity.[19] Baylor University in Texas advertises itself as 'A Private Christian University' and its seal bears the motto 'Pro Ecclesia, Pro Texana'. [20] Similarly, the University of Notre Dame, Indiana celebrates being 'An independent National Catholic Research University' and refers to 'The Basilica of the

Sacred Heart and the 14 story (sic) Hesburgh Library with its 132 feet high mural depicting Christ the Teacher'.[21]

The tensions noted in Newman's article above have also been apparent in our research. While our project has covered a wide aspect of life in a higher education institution, the question, 'How was/is a Church college/university different from those with a secular foundation and what difference did/does it make?'[22] has been one of the most difficult to answer. In this chapter we will investigate the spiritual life of the community and discuss the changes that our research has noted. We will analyse the perceptions of change in the importance and relevance of the Christian ethos at Church colleges, recognising the value of the oral history interview in revealing the historical context both to the current wider debate regarding the continuing role of the Church and Christianity in higher education and to the decline in religiosity in university communities more generally. As in the previous chapter we will analyse our data, by date, in three separate sections.

At the outset it is relevant that we refer again to our description of our methodology in the opening chapter, wherein we stated that the second reading of the interview transcripts was a reflexive one in order that we might consider how our own assumptions and beliefs might affect our analysis. We feel it is appropriate at this point to state that all the authors of the book are, or have been, communicant members of the Anglican Church and have, or have had, a particular interest in religious education.

The Male Community – pre 1960

While always having a different role to the theological college or seminary,[23] this change in emphasis on Christianity and the difficulty in defining exactly what it means to be a Church college or university, has not been sudden. Lofthouse suggests that it pre-dates the Second World War:

> Gradually, the historical echoes became more distant and during the 1930s the Christian distinctiveness of the denominational colleges was finally swallowed up in the drab conformities of unimaginative rule from Whitehall.[24]

Our data to support or refute this view are limited in comparison with the later periods. It is based on only four questionnaires from former student respondents plus one audio and one filmed interview but it suggests generally that the Christian foundation of the College was important to them. In replying to the question as to why they chose to study at King Alfred's College, three of the four questionnaire respondents cited the fact that it was a Church college as one of the reasons for their choice. Discipline at this time was strict with a prefect system in operation. The Principal of the College was a member of the clergy, as had been the tradition from its foundation, and attendance at Chapel was compulsory. One interviewee confirmed that the ethos of the College was very much Church of England orientated and that attendance at Chapel formed an important part of the framework of daily life: 'You had to go to Chapel in the morning. It didn't worry me because I'd been very connected with the local church. I was a server at the local church'.[25] Another respondent, who was a prefect and held the office of 'Chapel Warden', remembered that he could fine students up to 2/6d (12.5p) for absence or persistent lateness for Chapel.[26] The senior prefect was designated 'The Bishop' and, clad in appropriate robes, was able to deal out punishments. Against such a background, it was unsurprising that all of our respondents claim to have attended Chapel on a regular basis. In spite of the apparent strictness of the regime, our respondents have fond memories of their student days. One suggests: 'Winchester was my cornerstone: A church foundation in beautiful surroundings, friendly and not too many students'.[27]

The post-Second World War period was one of reconstruction, in which Christianity was important. Rob Freathy and Stephen Parker suggest that:

> The Second World War was frequently portrayed by British clerics and politicians as a spiritual and moral crisis threatening the Christian foundations of civilisation, freedom and democracy. Such rhetoric was repeatedly coupled with an assertion that Britain's social and political traditions and values could only endure the threat of idolatrous totalitarianism abroad and pre-war trends towards faithlessness at home if the nation's Christian identity was reinforced and reinvigorated. [28]

In 1949, Sir Walter Moberly, the philosopher and university administrator, had published his book, *The Crisis in the University*. His ideas had been developed through his work with the Student Christian Movement and the University Teachers' Group.[29] The crisis he diagnosed was spiritual: he argued that academic neutrality was undermining the moral character of universities, and that the growth of academic specialisation was robbing students of a broad cultural education. The solution was a return to Christian values (though not to narrowly confessional universities), and a broader curriculum.[30] Freathy, writing of education for citizenship, notes that in the immediate post-war period, such education was 'influenced by the common belief that English national identity and political traditions have Christian foundations'.[31] Grace Davie, a sociologist of religion, in her analysis of the period from 1945 to the mid-1990s, wherein she sought 'to put some sort of time-scale on the subtle but important developments in the relationship between the sacred and the secular in post-war British society',[32]suggests that during the 1950s, the country experienced a sense of well-being and revival in Church circles.[33]

It was also a period of great change for King Alfred's College. Not only were considerable repairs required to the fabric of the institution but new challenges had to be met in preparing teachers for the changes occasioned by the 1944 Education Act.[34] A new principal was appointed at this time and for the first time a member of the laity filled the post. He was charged by the governors to provide for the students a college which was 'a real centre of spiritual and intellectual life'.[35] He has been described to us as a pious and learned man.[36] A lay preacher, his own educational philosophy was to turn out Christian teachers as opposed to just good teachers and it was the College's designation as a Church training college that particularly attracted him to the post.[37] His influence was considered significant during the period 1945-1958.[38]

In these somewhat 'traditional' and 'conservative' times, both with a small 'c' and, from 1951, with a large 'C', 60 per cent of our respondents selected King Alfred's College because it was a Church college. Although, as noted earlier, some of the students came after war, or national, service, many came straight from school which would in most cases have been independent or boys' grammar schools. They were therefore used to a 'traditional' and 'conservative' background and would not have found it difficult to fit into an establishment where all meals were taken together as a community and were both preceded and concluded by Latin grace:

Before the meal

> Benedictus, benedicat, per Jesum Christum, Dominum Nostrum, Amen
> (May the Blessed One give blessing, through Jesus Christ our Lord)

After the meal:

Benedicto benidicatur, Amen
(Let praise be given to the Blessed One)

Where college blazers were worn bearing the badge with the admonitory Latin motto:

Qualis vita finis ita
(As is our life so is our end)

And where attendance at Chapel was the norm.

From his arrival in 1945, Principal Dickinson instigated change in that attendance was no longer compulsory, although he did ensure that there was a space for everyone in the Chapel.[39] However, according to our quantitative data 90 per cent from these cohorts attended Chapel on a regular basis and almost 40 per cent also claimed to attend another local church or Winchester Cathedral regularly. In line with these figures it is not surprising that we received mainly positive responses when we asked how important it was to their student experience that the College had a Church foundation. There is a very strong emphasis on the 'I' in the narratives and in both the questionnaires and the interviews there are recurrent references to the place of the Chapel and the personage of the Chaplain. In this respect our respondents would agree with the views of Clive Jones Davies and Gordon McGregor. The former suggests that the quality of relationships within a Church college is dependent on 'formal and obvious manifestations of the Christian life... the Chapel and the Chaplaincy, regular services and the celebration of Christian festivals'.[40] The latter, writing in particular of Ripon and York St John College, now York St John University, suggests that the presence of the Chapel and the Chaplaincy in most cases appears to be a marker of a Christian presence.[41] To take just two examples of our responses:

> During the time I was at college I was prepared for confirmation by the Chaplain. I felt he was more

> than a Chaplain, he was a friend. So I was very regular at churchgoing in those day. [. . .] I used to attend very regularly the morning service and I found that a great comfort and a good start to the day.[42]

and similarly:

> For me personally, very important, because I'm very much involved with the Church. I wasn't so involved then. I was a committed Christian, but it was whilst I was there that I was actually baptised in the Chapel in 1956. .... I felt it was important. I think it (Chapel) started the day off in the correct way. It made one feel 'OK, now we're prepared for work,' and that set you up. You didn't just drift in to lectures. You felt geared up ready to go.[43]

There were exceptions to these views. One of the interviewees whom we filmed had joined the College as a mature student, declared himself an agnostic and said that, for him, an important reason for choosing the College was to have the opportunity to engage in philosophical and theological discussions.[44] Generally, however, there was a considerable degree of consistency in the responses from this cohort of students leading us to conclude that in the 1950s, the Chapel, the Chaplain and other manifestations of Christian life were central to the experience of being a student at a Church college.

As the previous chapter noted, we have very little data for staff for this period, although one interviewee did confirm that: 'We would all attend church on Sundays very often with our families ... my two children, and they're very adult now, were both christened there for example'.[45] Those interviewees who joined the staff slightly later recall that they 'were aware quite soon that some senior members of staff particularly were deeply attached to the Church of England beliefs'[46]and that a lot of their older colleagues 'were very devout'.[47] This suggests that the older members of staff they encountered were staunch members of the Church of England and it would seem reasonable to assume that not only the Principal but a good proportion of the staff would have been practising Christians committed to the nature of the College's foundation and the expectation that they should play a part in the creation of a community based on Christian principles and communicating Christian values.

We have previously suggested that this period was one where the community at King Alfred's College demonstrated primarily Gemeinschaft characteristics, being regulated by common mores or beliefs about the appropriate behaviour and responsibility of members of the community to each other and to the community at large. In some 'Gemeinschaft' communities a vital locus or common belief might be in the Church as a 'mediating institution'. Our data suggests that in this period this applied at King Alfred's College and would have applied at other Church colleges.

Our opening quotation for this chapter suggests that the cohorts leaving King Alfred's in the post-war period would have been expected to take certain values and standards with them which might mark them out from those trained at secular institutions. When asked about the most important thing that they took with them on leaving the institution, a typical response was:

> The motto of the first school I taught in, in Portsmouth, was Integrity and I really think that's the most important thing. You have a job to do and you do it honestly and I suppose that devolved from the general college atmosphere. We would have had standards we adhered to. I think it just rubbed off on you.[48]

Jones Davies acknowledges that:

> It would be arrogant and untrue for Church colleges to claim to have a monopoly of those experiences which create the best professionals or to be the only communities which are capable of producing responsible, committed or compassionate practitioners.[49]

It is impossible to say that our alumni might not have acquired the same values and standards at a secular institution and it is important to note that those who were willing to contribute to our study are likely to be people keen to 'put something back', as suggested below. However, our data reveal that in their lives outside work, some 80 per cent have been, or continue to be, actively involved in voluntary work in the community reflecting the comment: 'Whatever we've done we've wanted to put something back into the community and this is something I got from my time at King Alfred's'.[50] The same interviewee echoing the comments above about standards 'rubbing off' or in this case 'caught', also suggested:

> I think FE (Further Education), like measles, is caught and not taught. So the atmosphere in the College – I just caught it. [. . .] This is something I carried forward all the way through [. . .] and the sort of ethos instilled in me during my time there: this Christian thread running through my life.[51]

In addition to their involvement in voluntary work in their community, 72 per cent have had involvement in their local church. These activities include being an organist, a member of the choir, a Sunday school teacher, a lay reader, a member of the Parochial Church Council, a church secretary and a bell ringer.

1960-1976

Changes that took place in these years were striking. Brown suggests that in 1963, 'something very profound ruptured the (Christian) character of the nation'.[52] 'The cultural climate was less conducive to State-sponsored Christianisation envisaged by those who were responsible for piloting the 1944 Education Bill through both Houses of Parliament'.[53] Davie describes the 1960s as confident, exciting, enthusiastic and optimistic and suggests that:[54]

> The Churches were, inevitably, in for a bumpy ride in the 1960s. The world into which they appeared to fit so well was being challenged on every front. Not everything happened at once, but by the end of the decade a profound and probably irreversible revolution in social attitudes had taken place.[55]

Parker and Freathy note the significance of the decade for British secularisation, or more precisely dechristianisation, which, following Hugh McCleod, they describe as a more nuanced term which 'describes the decline in cultural affinity with Christianity rather than a decline in interest in, or attachment to religion generally'.[56] They suggest that, with regard to religious education in schools, the decade saw the calling into question of the appropriateness of 'a predominantly Christian and Bible focused RE curriculum, the relevance of the Bible to young people and the ability of children to understand religious concepts at all'.[57] The influence of Professor Ninian Smart, who began to challenge what he saw as the intellectual hegemony of much contemporary Christian theology and whose philosophy was one of critical openness in relation to religious education in schools, was substantial towards the end of the decade.[58]

In contrast to the confidence of the previous decade, and highlighted in the opening quotation, the 1960s saw a working party set up, at the behest of the Church of England and the Board of Education, with its terms of reference being not only 'the communication of the Christian Faith to all members of the colleges, staff and students, but also to their preparation for communicating the Faith, when they leave college to the children they will teach'.[59] The working party recognised that:

> Expansion has meant that the students in the Church colleges are now being drawn from a far wider spectrum of backgrounds than in the past. It has been assumed that the majority of students go to Church colleges because they are Church members or Christians of some other denomination. If ever this was true in the past, it is clearly no longer true today [. . .] on average about three quarters of the students are members of the Church of England and of those an appreciable minority are unconfirmed. Not all those who are confirmed can be assumed to be active members of the Church. We have the impression that among Third year students, who have nothing to lose by frankness the picture would be very different, perhaps seldom more than one quarter would call themselves active Christians.

Our respondents suggest that, in tune with the zeitgeist of the 1960s, it was indeed a confident, exciting, enthusiastic and optimistic place to study. It was also described as a place where the Christian caring attitude was pervasive,[60] and where 'the atmosphere was nice and a certain morality and high standards of behaviour were expected'.[61] The growing student community could no longer be accommodated in the old Victorian chapel and a new one was built on modern lines. However, Church membership figures, together with other indicators of religiosity in the 1960s, reveal the Churches' 'continued inability to stem the growth of religious indifference in Britain'.[62] Unsurprisingly our data suggest that there was correspondingly more indifference in student attitudes to the College's Church foundation in this period when compared with the very recent past.

When asked why they chose the College, around 45 per cent of both male and female alumni included that it was a Church college as one of the reasons. While a majority claimed to be Christians, a legacy from their home and school life, fewer than previously continued to practise their faith in terms of outward religiosity. Around half of the students did attend Chapel on a regular basis with almost no difference between the male and female students. About 40 per cent also attended a local church or the Cathedral. In the first stage of the project, which included only alumnae, they were asked whether they joined the Christian Union (Student Christian Movement): 30 per cent confirmed that they did so. Contrasting to the positive tone of the 1950s, about 30 per cent of those questioned did not think it particularly important that the College had a Church foundation, and almost another 20 per cent answered that, for them, it was not relevant at all. For those who did feel that it was relevant, the following are representative of interview responses:

Alumni Voices

Once the College Chapel

'I'm very sad that the modern Chapel in which I worshipped is now an ICT centre.'

> I didn't attend Chapel as often as I should have done, although I did go and it was meaningful. But I think it gave it a better foundation somehow. Faith is a strange thing because you can't give people faith. You either have it or you don't, but I think it was fairly important.[63]

> It was important to me from before I applied because it influenced my choice. I applied to Church colleges and that was due to my personal background because my father was a clergyman and he influenced me. Quite a lot of people used to go to Chapel morning and evening but I didn't go that regularly. I certainly attended though and in that sense I was continuing what I did at home.[64]

> I wouldn't have come here if it hadn't. I enjoyed developing my Christian life here and I think a lot of people did. A lot of people didn't because it wasn't a place for Holy Joes but it was here, in no small measure, and the Church was represented and everyone knew it was a Church college. We used to have very, very good preachers every Sunday morning and they were often Bishops, Archdeacons, and people of quite some substance.[65]

Although all three interviewees were clearly supportive of the College's Church foundation, the responses of two of them were less enthusiastic than those of the previous decade, with the first two admitting that they did not attend Chapel regularly. Taking these together with the ambivalent responses in the questionnaires, a trend emerged during the 1960s at the institution, which was not dechristianisation but corresponded more closely with what Davie describes as

'Believing without Belonging'. This echoes the findings of the working party referred to above.

During the 1970s, Davie suggests of religion in Britain that: 'Certain characteristics of the 1960s persist, particularly those which had acquired a momentum of their own. Widespread indifference, however, remains the norm'.[66] Of those coming to the College, as previously, 45 per cent stated that the Church college aspect was a factor in their choice. When analysed by gender, the percentage was higher for the female students, although it would be unfair to draw too many conclusions from this as there is some imbalance of data by gender for this period due to the change in the overall gender balance in the institution.[67] Chapel attendance on a regular basis, as an outward sign of religious observance, remained at around 50 per cent but it seems likely that 'regular' attendance was at the most weekly rather than daily as in the 1950s. Around 25 per cent claimed never to attend Chapel. The Principal at the time recollects a considerable falling off in numbers.[68] As in the 1960s, some 30 per cent did not consider it very important that the College had a Church foundation while 25 per cent considered it of no importance at all. Around 27 per cent of the female students joined the Christian Union. The 'manifestations of Christian life' remained important for several of our respondents. Two met at college where they were both members of the Chapel Council and eventually married in the College Chapel.[69] Other questionnaire respondents mentioned the benefit of having a chaplain in college, either citing incidences where he had helped them or more generally commenting on the reassurance of knowing that he was there if needed.

Although it is not evident from the quantitative data above, the interviews for this period demonstrate less support for the College's Church foundation than in the immediate past. Two of the respondents, who joined the College in the 1970s and with whom we carried out a detailed interview, selected the College because of its specialism in special needs education. They were both Christians but for different reasons did not find their spiritual needs completely met by the College and therefore found themselves on the periphery of any Christian community within college itself. The first, although finding the Chapel a nice place to sit, advised that: 'I think at that age too you have very, very strong views and I joined the Christian Union and was bitterly disappointed. I felt it was very enclosed'.[70] The second, who was a Roman Catholic, felt that: 'I couldn't be involved because I had a different religion and it was Church of England; definitely Church of England and not any other religion'.[71]

A third interviewee is probably representative of a growing number of the students of this period who epitomised Davie's 'norm' of 'widespread indifference' to any Church influence within the College. She stated:

> I think I ought to mention that the religious, spiritual, Christian institution had absolutely no effect on me whatsoever. In fact the Christian Union were perceived as a kind of smug, nauseating clique by the sorts of people I associated with. I don't know what that says about that or me.

Her reasons for feeling this way are particularly resonant of the 1970s:

> It's awful to say bad things about it but I am quite firmly not a Christian, partly because especially then I was quite opinionated and I felt organised religion had nothing to offer for women and I just associated the whole deal with patriarchal, patronising stuff.[72]

It is interesting to note that two of the respondents above mentioned the Christian Union in a negative way. While it was not an aspect of college life that we discussed in great detail, these comments are not unrepresentative. Although those who were not particularly interested in Christianity generally expressed a 'live and let live' attitude, criticism was sometimes reserved for members of the Christian Union as above and in Robert's interview in the opening chapter for those members who might have been perceived as overzealous in their Evangelism.

The cohorts of freshly qualified teachers who left King Alfred's College in the 1960s and 1970s exhibited similar trends to their predecessors in respect of their commitment to voluntary work and involvement in church activities. It would only be conjecture, as we said previously, to suggest this owes anything to the influence of attending a Church college. However, perhaps we can do no better than quote one respondent who opined that it was 'difficult to say how a Church college affected life [. . .] my feeling is it did affect the College but I'm not sure how'.[73] Some 70 per cent have been involved in voluntary work and 60 per cent have been involved in church activities. When asked about the most important thing they took with them when they left, they most commonly mentioned the professional qualification and standards that they had acquired. However the standards would have included, as one alumnus told us, trying to be 'a decent person in life, to have a very humanistic outlook on life, to encourage people, to reach out to every individual you come into contact with'.[74]

Until well into the 1960s, all prospective students to King Alfred's College would have required a letter of recommendation from their parish priest.[75] This did not apply to the staff who taught them. 'The appointment of staff was made on the strength of their academic abilities',[76] other than the Principal and the Vice Principal who would have been required to be communicant members of the Anglican Church. While staff members in the immediate post-war period were apparently fairly devout Christians, we were surprised at the considerable variation in the extent to which the members of staff who followed them shared this strong adherence to Christianity. While one stated:

> And then on Sundays, we turned up to Chapel with our children and it created the atmosphere that there was this influence of Christianity over the College. We belonged to the Diocese. I mean the Bishop was Chair of Governors at that time, so we were very much influenced by what the Church was doing and what the Church was saying and so on.[77]

Others were indifferent to the Christian foundation:

> Chapel existed, it was never compulsory, many staff went occasionally, I went occasionally but rather than the sense of the Conservative party of prayer as it were, I went because I rather liked the atmosphere.[78]

Few recalled being asked about their religious affiliations when they applied for their positions. One recalled:

> I don't remember being asked anything at all, and I have to say that it wasn't important to me. I was a slightly unquestioning Anglican at the time I think. I couldn't see that the Chapel [. . .] I couldn't see that it was doing any harm, and it may have done some good, and it certainly produced some lovely music.[79]

Another specifically asked about the relevance of the Church foundation at her interview and complained that 'no-one ever gave me a straight answer, even the RE department'.[80] However, they also remembered something that was distinctive about a Church college in that:

> A vast number of the governing board were members of the Church and the Bishop's diocese through various Canons and Deans, and so there was a sense of religious context or C of E context within which the institution still survived'.[81]

The Community and the Church

The influence of the Church in the overall management of the institution was still strong, if declining, in this period. Members of staff who were not believers do not seem to have challenged the religious context of the College. The following comment is typical:

> Occasionally I went in, in the morning, I used to think it was [. . .] it didn't do any harm to turn up occasionally, to show unity. I'm an institutional man, if I belong to an institution, I support it. I do what the institution requires of me, and so it was [. . .] I like singing hymns as well actually. You know I don't object to that, I think like a lot of other people I was brought up to go to Church, and I've never forgotten it but when I was in the position of making a decision for myself, I realised that I could do without it.[82]

We have suggested that the institution at this time was still demonstrating many 'Gemeinschaft' characteristics. While belief in the Church might have been one of the important common beliefs in an earlier period, it is clear that it was becoming less influential. We would suggest that instead the cohesion and consensus to be found at King Alfred's College from the 1960s until the mid-1970s, when courses began to diversify, had moved away from the Church and centred instead on the commitment to teacher education and to the care of the students themselves.[83] As one interviewee told us:

> There was a real commitment to the idea of making the students more educated in the broadest sense, educated, and nicer, happier people [. . .] and there was a very good emphasis on pastoral care, a very strong emphasis on pastoral care, and also a kind of hidden curriculum which suggested that there was something beyond the material.[84]

Post 1976[85]

The years following the diversification of courses exhibit the same trends that we have noted above, as the 1960s gave way to the 1970s, in terms of Chapel attendance by students and their overall interest in the College as a Church college. Of our questionnaire respondents who joined the institution after 1980 and into the new millennium, some 27 per cent claimed that the Church college aspect had been a factor. However this was not borne out in their responses to further questions relating to the way they displayed this outwardly. Only 4 per cent claimed to have attended Chapel on a regular basis although 8 per cent attended another church or the Cathedral. There may have been various reasons for this but one interviewee whose Christian background was not Anglican, attended Chapel on occasions but preferred worship at one of the local churches feeling that:

> Chapel was a bit ancient in many ways [. . .] It was a different approach to Christianity so I found it intriguing to discuss with people what their priorities of faith were and how they found that sort of service enriching to their Christian faith, when it seemed to me they were talking to a very remote God, who wasn't like the person or God I felt I'd built up a relationship with over the years.[86]

Such was the decrease in regular attendance at Chapel, in an increasingly secular society, both inside and outside the institution, that the new Chapel that had been built to provide a place of worship for the growing number of students in the 1960s, was deconsecrated and became an IT centre during this time. The old Victorian Chapel reverted to its original purpose. This is not to say that the enthusiasm for the College's Church foundation disappeared completely. We did have many positive responses from respondents who joined the College after courses diversified. For some this directly related to their spiritual development:

> Chapel was very important to me both as a significant part of my spiritual development and as being the first point at which I 'belonged' in the College and made friends outside my course/hostel. These are the ones I have kept. The Chapel also arranged my confirmation.[87]

Others felt that there was a gentler and more caring atmosphere,[88] that it contributed to the general atmosphere that some students were obviously attendees at Chapel which gave a feeling of 'calm and commitment',[89] that attending a Church college gave them a sense of security and a 'vague but unexpressed' idea 'that moral issues might have been more important' than at another University.[90] In contrast to some of the negativity we have noted earlier, there were several positive comments relating to the benefits of belonging to the Christian Union to which some attributed their Christian development, suggesting that it was their membership of this group that was responsible 'and the friends I made there rather than being a Church college'.[91] For others the negativity still existed with members of the Christian Union sometimes being regarded with suspicion by non-members who generally thought them to be dull and staid. One of the interviewees who had been an active member told us that people were surprised that she was a member because she did not fit the stereotype:

> They were quite surprised. I was [. . .] very active [. . .] I was on the Rag Committee. I was very active in several sports clubs. I was [. . .] Fridays and Saturdays, I'd always be involved in something at the Union either sort out a band or just going down and meeting groups of people. And because, I think, a lot of people had an image of the Christian Fellowship anywhere, wherever it would have been, as being very [. . .] very staid or very dull and people who would go there were assumed to be like that and a lot

of people were surprised that I went to it because they didn't think that I fitted with what their stereotypical opinion of a member would be [. . .] and unfortunately some members were [. . .] they did almost fit a stereotype and could be seen as very judgmental whereas I think that's what people did expect and it's what I never, always tried not to do, be judgmental.[92]

Bargate, Southampton, January 1960
'It was too snowy to do sport.'

There were many during this period who, echoing the alumna quoted above from the 1970s, had no interest in the religious aspect of college life, and gradually positive responses to the nature of the College's foundation became fewer: some were completely unaware of it. As we have indicated in our introduction to this chapter, to answer the question as to how the Church foundation affects the nature of the educational experience and how it might distinguish those who come under its auspices has been one of the most intangible in our research.

It will be recalled from the earlier chapter that the period immediately before and after diversification was a particularly difficult one for the staff of the institution when the very survival of all Church colleges was threatened. Between 1974 and 1980, the number of such colleges almost halved.[93] New staff who had been employed to teach on the new degree courses were not involved in teacher training, where the link with Christianity had once been strong. The cohesion and consensus of the earlier period was weakened as the College struggled to find a new identity for itself: the comments of our interviewees point to a jagged and less stable experience and highlight different ways in which the Christian identity changed or was challenged. The extent to which this affected the experience of the students is difficult to measure. In the first instance there was a decrease in attendance by staff members at Chapel:

> I can't quite place when that began to happen, certainly the early morning Chapel seemed to fade away and certainly we, I, other members of staff didn't begin to attend Sunday Church service as we had done for many, many years, a date I can't put anything on that at all but it was slow fading, and I can't think to put any obvious reason on that except the College was enlarging, different courses maybe were coming in and that caused people/students to look more outwards.[94]

While it had not been a requirement that the staff should be Christians, we have suggested above that those who were not, did not normally challenge the Christian nature of the institution. Following diversification this changed:

> Well, I think it was much weaker but of course because you were taking in this much wider spectrum of students, the same applied to the staff, and some of the staff that were recruited were non-believers, even the opposite you know, and they

> made their witness and they made their witness in the Senior Common Room. They were completely out of contact with the Church influence. It didn't seem to matter to them [. . .] I used to sometimes wonder why they applied to us [. . .] they wanted the job I suppose.[95]

Influenced by developments elsewhere and particularly by Professor Ninian Smart and his colleagues at Lancaster University who defended religious studies as a secular discipline and distanced religious studies from traditional theology, Religious Education, at the College, began to be taught as an academic discipline rather than as a profession of faith. Following this, the Chaplain at King Alfred's role changed. They ceased to be the Head of Religious Education, making them more available to both staff and students in both a liturgical and a pastoral role.[96] On a particular occasion we were advised that these changes caused tensions between the Principal and the Head of Religious Education:

> I remember T who was Head of Religious Education and he was a very acute philosopher who wanted to present to the RE students, he wanted to teach them about religions [. . .] so they had an understanding of the arguments for and against different religious points of view, or indeed the arguments against religion per se [. . .] and I think M brought him in and queried him on this and T, according to what he said to me, said [. . .] 'Do you want me to educate people or do you want me to indoctrinate them? [. . .] I can't present them with a single point of view.' [. . .] You know either you're encouraging people to be rational and follow the arguments wherever they lead, or you're trying to lead them in a particular direction and you might say, well that's not, as I understand it, education. Education is to promote rationality and to let people reason you know develop

> their minds and be able to work it out for themselves.[97]

Another interviewee referred to later courses in Religious Education, reflecting a pluralistic society, which covered Wicca, Paganism and Buddhism, as well as core Christianity. He mentioned that, at one time, 'we did Religious Studies with a whole bunch of people who didn't believe in God'.[98] While a third suggested that:

> I think there probably was a feeling in the late '70s and the early '80s that being a Church college was all a bit of an embarrassment [. . .] yes unfashionable, you know people were generally sort of liberating themselves from the Church.[99]

According to some of our interviewees, the changes at the College did not sit easily with members of the Christian Union who had presumably joined the College because of its Church foundation, expecting a traditional approach to Christianity. They did not always find what they wanted and, as we have commented above, many preferred to worship at local churches where, 'They would get the sort of diet of sermons and worship that they wanted rather than the sort of slightly more esoteric worship that you get in a college Chapel'.[100] A former Chaplain, whom we interviewed, found that some of them had a very rigid approach to Christianity. He claimed that, 'I always saw my job as Chaplain was to give permission to people to see things in shades of grey rather than just in black and white'.[101]

Similarly a member of staff employed to teach Moral Philosophy had difficulties with the more evangelical students in this freer approach to Christianity:

> If you're employed as I was to teach Philosophy, let's say moral Philosophy, as I was [. . .] how it applied to education, occasionally as it did [. . .] there were

> particularly some evangelical students I can think of didn't really like it at all. They wanted me to promote what they would consider Christian values, which I mean, I personally, well you know [. . .] what are Christian values on homosexuality, abortion you know [. . .] what actually is a Christian value, you know something that's discussable but which they didn't want to discuss, they wanted [. . .] they had a very fixed idea about what was [. . .] what should be taught to children, and if I attempted to open up a discussion about actually what sort of moral values should we be teaching children, and how should we be teaching them, it got them rather upset.[102]

During this later period, the relevance of Church colleges seemed to be unclear, as though they were not sure of their identities or positions. One respondent advised that:

> On one hand I've been in meetings where they've been talking about recruitment where it's been mooted that perhaps we shouldn't make too much of our Church status because we were trying to attract as many students as we could and the fact that we were Church based might put people off, either the student or the parents.[103]

But also advised that on another occasion they were asked, at the instigation of the Bishop of Winchester, to consider:

> The transfer of the excellent selling point that Church schools have [. . .] Church schools are generally more oversubscribed than non-Church schools, and generally have a better reputation than non-Church schools and why shouldn't that carry on with the colleges.[104]

This debate is a continuing one and emphasises the tensions we highlighted at the beginning of the chapter about the religious mission of Christian universities.

Conclusion

This chapter has analysed the change in the spiritual life of the community at a Church college, and our broad conclusion can hardly be anything other than the expected one that there has been a substantial decline in the importance of this aspect of college life over the period of our research. However while it has declined, it has not disappeared, and many of our interviewees have suggested reasons for this, particularly relating to the emphasis on the importance of the Christian history and surviving traditions of the university, the context in which it has continued to operate:

> I think people [. . .] I don't know, you sort of imbibe a tradition don't you? If you [. . .] it's well people like us (historians) respond to history to the appeal of tradition, however much we may dislike some of its manifestations, so I'm talking about something mystical here, osmosis really, you absorb it in the air.[105]

And:

> Well it had grown out of that (Church foundation) of course, and therefore you couldn't [. . .] that was its roots, and therefore something of that growth was still in its growth and its greens [. . .] but it was never, there was never any sense of imposition but quite clearly the whole ethos and nature had been partly shaped by its starting in that way [. . .] . So it affected everybody, whether they were practising Christians or not, really, because it became a kind of touchstone whereby we judged ourselves, if you see what I mean.[106]

In analysing all the interviews and the questionnaire data, we would argue that, whatever their religious beliefs, there was considerable agreement that, in their experience, the institution operated within a context of care for the students, in pastoral terms. As we have explained previously Gemeinschaft and Gesellschaft do not exist in pure forms and no society could exist if one form or type existed to the exclusion of the other.[107] They are rather 'found interwoven in all kinds of associations'[108] and an essence of the softer Gemeinschaft continued to exist in the otherwise more modern, harder, Gesellschaft context.

While the tradition might be rooted in the Christian foundation of the College, it continued because people, whether they had any religious beliefs or not, cared about each other. If being a caring community is the 'touchstone' by which the University is judged, perhaps we are some way to promoting one of Mark Lofthouse's ideals for a Church college, that of promoting 'a theology of kindness' as the basis for good human behaviour. [109] The *Dearing Report* of 2001 suggested that, in addition to providing courses in teacher education including specialist religious education and courses relating to the needs of other caring professions, a Church college should be a community:

- which is welcoming, caring and supportive;
- which displays values of honesty, openness, friendliness, trust and respect;
- in which all students and staff are valued as individuals and helped to reach their full potential;
- which recognises and tries to meet responsibilities to serve those in need in the wider community and to act as stewards of creation.

This is in accord with the objectives of The Cathedrals Group as stated on their website suggesting that after a long period of uncertainty and tension while the debate continues, the members are clear on the way forward.

Notes to Chapter 4.

[1] A departing President of the Union (1959-1960), quoted in *Wintonian* 14 (1960). The *Wintonian* was the King Alfred's College magazine.

[2] The Cathedrals Group, 'Welcome', *The Cathedrals Group*: cathedralsgroup.org.uk (accessed 20 February 2013).

[3] Silver, *Tradition and Higher Education,* 37-38.

[4] Mark Lofthouse, *Faith, Class and Politics: The Role of the Churches in Teacher Training 1914-1945* (Oxford: University of Oxford Department of Education, 2009), xiii.

[5] Harold C. Dent, *The Training of Teachers in England and Wales 1800-1975 (London: Hodder and Stoughton, 1977)*, 1.

[6] Dent, *The Training of Teachers*, 8.

[7] Dent, *The Training of Teachers*, 10.

[8] Dent, *The Training of Teachers.*

[9] Dent, *The Training of Teachers*, 14.

[10] Lofthouse, *Faith* , xiv.

[11] Lofthouse, *Faith*, xiii.

[12] From Sir James Kay-Shuttleworth's second report on Battersea, reprinted in his *Four Periods of Public Education* (London: Longman Green, 1862), 359, quoted in Dent, *The Training of Teachers*, 15.

[13] Callum Brown, *The Death of Christian Britain: Understanding Secularisation 1800-2000* (London and New York: Routledge, 2001).

[14] Jane Garnett, Matthew Grimley, Alana Harris, William Whyte and Sarah Williams, *Redefining Christian Britain: Post 1945 Perspectives* (London: SCM Press, 2006), 6.

[15] James Arthur, 'Changing Patterns of Church College Identity and Mission', *International Journal of Research and Method in Education,* 24.2 (2001): 137.

[16] As well as James Arthur's article mentioned in the previous note, there is a body of literature that has dealt with these difficulties over a period of years. It includes: William R. Niblett, *The Church's Colleges of Higher Education* (London: Church Information Office, 1976); John Gay, Brian Kay, George Perry, and Diana Lazenby, *The Future of the Anglican Colleges, Final Report of the Church Colleges Research Project* (Abingdon: Culham Educational Foundation, 1986); Church of England, *An Excellent Enterprise: The Church of England and its Colleges of Higher Education* (London: Board of Education of the General Synod of the Church of England, 1994); James Arthur, *Faith and Secularisation in Religious Colleges and Universities* (London: Routledge, 2006).

[17] Ronald Dearing, *The Way Ahead: Church Schools in the New Millennium* (London: Church House Publishing, 2001), 65-74.

[18] Melanie Newman, 'Christian Colleges: Our Higher Purpose'. *Times Higher Education Supplement* (30 November 2007): www.timeshighereducation.co.uk (accessed 3 August 2010).

[19] This is not to imply that American universities have not similarly faced challenges to their Christian heritage. See especially George Marsden, *The Soul of the American University: From Protestant Establishment to Established Non-Belief* (New York: Oxford University Press, 1994); James T. Burchall, *The Dying of the Light* (Grand Rapids: Erdmans, 1998); Robert Benne, *Quality with Soul* (Grand Rapids: Erdmans, 2001). Douglas and Rhonda Jacobsen, writing in 2012, claim that religion is essential for the work of American higher education in the twenty-first century. See Douglas G. and Rhonda H. Jacobsen, *No Longer Invisible: Religion in University Education* (Ebook: www.oxfordscholarship.com, accessed 26 April 2013).

[20] Baylor University, 'About Baylor', *Baylor*: www.baylor.edu (accessed 25 February 2013).

[21] University of Notre Dame, 'University News', *University of Notre Dame*: www.nd.edu (accessed 25 February 2013).

[22] Arthur, 'Changing Patterns', 138.

[23] Arthur, 'Changing Patterns', 39.

[24] Lofthouse, *Faith, Class and Politics,* 85.

[25] Interview 5, Stage 2 (1939-1945).

[26] An alumnus (1934-36) in *Venta* 10 (2004): 10 (The University of Winchester Alumni Magazine).

[27] Questionnaire 24, Stage Two (1934-1936).

[28] 28. Rob Freathy and Stephen G Parker, 'Secularists, Humanists and Religious Education: Religious Crisis and Curriculum Change in England, 1963-1975,' *History of Education* 42.2 (2013): 223.

[29] The autobiography of the first overseas student (from Jamaica) to King Alfred's College suggests that support for the Student Christian Movement was strong in the immediate post war period. He states: 'I was instrumental in staging a medieval religious play in the College Chapel, the proceeds of which were used to pay the expenses of 14 students to attend a SCM meeting in Derbyshire'. See Edmund H Dale, *Relentless Struggle* (Victoria: Trafford, 1999), 81.

[30] Matthew Grimley, 'Moberly, Sir Walter Hamilton (1881-1974)', *Oxford Dictionary of National Biography*: www.oxforddnb.com (accessed 6 January 2011).

[31] Rob Freathy, 'The Triumph of Religious Education for Citizenship in English Schools, 1935-1949', *History of Education* 37.2 (2008): 295-316.

[32] Grace, Davie, *Religion in Britain since 1945: Believing without Belonging* (Oxford: Blackwell, 1994), 29.

[33] Davie, *Religion*, 31.

[34] The 1944 Act introduced the primary/secondary divide for all pupils, effectively abolishing the old all-through elementary school.

[35] Rose, *A History*, 93.

[36] Interview 22, Stage 3 (1965-1984).

[37] *Wintonian* 12.1 (1958): 2.

[38] The Principal, W. P. Dickinson, died in 1958.

[39] Interview 21, Stage 3, (1951-1965).

[40] Clive Jones Davies, 'The Anglican Colleges of Higher Education', in *Faith for the Future*, ed. Graham Leonard, (London: Church House Publishing, 1986), 94.

[41] Gordon P. McGregor, *A Church College for the 21st Century?: 150 years of Ripon and York St John, 1841-1991. A Study of Policy and Its Absence* (York: William Sessions, 1991) 154. This college history is particularly useful as it seeks to address the question of the differences between Church colleges and those established by LEAs.

[42] Interview 18, Stage 2 (1947-1949).

[43] Interview 12, Stage 2 (1954-1956).

[44] Filmed Interview 11 (1954-1956).

[45] Interview 2, Stage 3 (1956-1991).

[46] Interview 6, Stage 3 (1967-1988).

[47] Interview 18, Stage 3 (1960-1967).

[48] Interview 18, Stage 2 (1947-1949).

[49] Jones Davies, 'The Anglican Colleges', 92.

[50] Interview 12, stage 2 (1954-1956).

[51] Interview 12, Stage 2 (1954-1956).

[52] Hilary Brown, 'Whose Story', 1.

[53] Freathy and Parker, 'Secularists,' 224.

[54] Davie, *Religion*, 36.

[55] Davie, *Religion*, 33.

[56] Stephen G. Parker and Rob J. K. Freathy, 'Ethnic Diversity, Christian Hegemony and the Emergence of Multi-Faith Religious Education in the 1970s', *History of Education* 41.3 (2012): 381-382, citing Hugh McCleod, *The Religious Crisis of the 1960s* (Oxford: Oxford University Press, 2007).

[57] Parker and Freathy, 'Ethnic Diversity', 382.

[58] See Brian Gates, 'Obituary Ninian Smart', *The Guardian* (2 February 2001): www.theguardian.com (accessed 9 April 2014). The introduction into schools of the

Birmingham Agreed Syllabus for Religious Instruction as an attempt to introduce children from the earliest ages to other world religious and non-religious 'stances for living', followed from Smart's philosophy. See Parker and Freathy, 'Ethnic Diversity', especially 382 and 389.

[59] See Church Colleges of Education, *Report of the Working Party on the Communication of the Christian Faith* (London : Church of England Board of Education, 1966).

[60] Questionnaire 96, Stage 1 (1961-1964).

[61] Questionnaire 28, Stage 1 (1968-1971).

[62] Davie, *Religion*, 34.

[63] Interview 10, Stage 2 (1962-1965).

[64] Interview 13, Stage 2 (1963-1966).

[65] Interview 9, Stage 2 (1964-1967).

[66] Davie, *Religion*, 38. Other suggestions by Davie relating to the 1970s which she terms 're-emergence of the Sacred' are not discussed in this chapter.

[67] The ratio between male and female changed during this period due to the College's gradual move to teacher training in primary education which is more traditionally associated with female teachers.

[68] Interview 21, Stage 3 (1951-1965).

[69] Questionnaire 66, Stage 1 (1972-1975).

[70] Interview 1, Stage 2 (1974-1978).

[71] Interview 10 Stage 1 (1974-1977).

[72] Interview 2, Stage 2 (1974-1978).

[73] Questionnaire 95, Stage 1 (1969-1972).

[74] Interview 4, Stage 2 (1962-1965).

[75] One interviewee said that it was 'useful' that he dug the garden of the local vicar, who gave him a reference even though he made no claims to be a Christian. Filmed Interview 10, 1964-1967.

[76] Interview 22, Stage 3 (1965-1984).

[77] Interview 1. Stage 3 (1962-1984). Although the Bishop is no longer the Chair of Governors there is still a requirement for diocesan representation on the governing body.

[78] Interview 6, Stage 3 (1967-1988).

[79] Interview 18, Stage 3 (1960-1967).
[80] Interview 3, Stage 3 (1968-1991).
[81] Interview 6, Stage 3 (1967-1988).
[82] Interview 4, Stage 3 (1964-1987).
[83] The concept of care is explored in more detail in Chapter 6.
[84] Interview 18, Stage 3 (1960-1967).
[85] Although during this period the country was becoming more multi-cultural, our sample, while perhaps representative of the institution itself, was not representative of the country as a whole. None of our interviewees was from an ethnic minority or suggested that they followed any religion other than Christianity.
[86] Interview 19, Stage 2 (1977-1981).
[87] Questionnaire 68, Stage 1. (1982-1986).
[88] Questionnaire 120, Stage 1(1993-1997).
[89] Questionnaire 42, Stage 1 (1981-1985).
[90] Questionnaire 46, Stage 1, (1981-1985).
[91] Questionnaire 117, Stage 1, (1981-1985).
[92] Interview 7, Stage 1, (1989-1992).
[93] *The Church Colleges of Higher Education* (reprinted from *The Church Times*) 15.8 (1980): 1.
[94] Interview 2, Stage 3 (1956-1991).
[95] Interview 1, Stage 3, (1962-1984).
[96] See also John Hull, *Studies in Religious Education* (Lewes: Falmer Press, 1984).
[97] Interview 13, Stage 3 (1970-2008).
[98] Interview 16, Stage 3 (1993-2004).
[99] Interview 9, Stage 3 (1982-1987).
[100] Interview 9, Stage 3 (1982-1987).
[101] Interview 9, Stage3 (1982-1987).
[102] Interview 13, Stage 3 (1970-2008).
[103] Interview 15, Stage3 (1993-2004).
[104] Interview 15, Stage 3 (1993-2004).
[105] Interview 19, Stage 3 (1969-1985).
[106] Interview 12, Stage 3 (1973-1996).
[107] Loomis, Introduction, xix.

[108] Tönnies, *Community*, 18.
[109] Lofthouse, 115.

5.

PLACE AND SPACE

> Winchester is a beautiful city and I always enjoyed walking through its streets. I remember walking along by the railway past the Green Jackets Barracks and being thrilled to receive wolf whistles from the soldiers! The walk along by the river at the far end of town was one of my favourites. Ken's café at the bottom of St Giles Hill was a favourite venue as was The Rising Sun pub and The Green Man (for birthday celebrations) I also remember having some lectures in the Carfax Hotel. My future husband also took me for a very romantic meal at the then newish Wessex Hotel during my final year, 1968. We went by taxi and I felt very grand![1]

Introduction

In this chapter we reflect upon how alumni recall their memories of the physical environment of the institution in their interviews and questionnaire responses in order to explain their experience of higher education at Winchester. In doing this we can identify how histories of higher education and its institutions can be enriched through memories attached to events. We argue that these events and, more importantly, the significance of such events, can be explained in more detail as a result of the visual recollection of space both within and outside physical campus boundaries. At a distance of over forty years the alumna in this opening quote articulates a sense of continuity of place against which to recall her student experience, she notes that Winchester *is* a beautiful city, as well as the distance of time, remembering the pubs that *were* favourite venues. As Hawkins notes in her study of institutional history, any analysis of the stories people tell of their learning and working lives cannot be detached from the environment in which the events they describe actually took place.[2] Pierre Nora suggests that 'memory attaches itself to sites whereas history attaches itself to events'.[3]

While the institution's buildings changed substantially during this period, its geographical position remained at the top of West Hill overlooking the city and Cathedral, a ten minute walk from the centre of town. The further development of a former boys' prep school, West Downs, saw the business school, conference centre and a student village expand the physical presence of the College, although the recognisable local landmarks of water meadows, Cathedral and King Alfred's Statue, in the High Street, provided a familiar backdrop to those returning after an absence of some years. In this chapter we have drawn spatial rather than chronological boundaries to mark the areas of discussion in order to highlight the meanings that two areas – town and gown – city and institution had for our respondents across time. In drawing attention to the centrality of place we highlight the significance not only of the buildings of an institution but of its physical belonging in the landscape and in doing this we draw on developments in feminist and human geography, illustrating the interdisciplinary riches that writing an institutional history can provide. As Doreen Massey notes, 'in trying to understand the identity of places we cannot – or, perhaps, should not - separate space from time, or geography from history'.[4]

As we included a spatial dimension to our historical analysis so we also added a further reading within our use of Mauthner and Doucet's voice relational analysis, that of the 'spoken visual', to further enhance our understanding of the centrality of the whole higher education experience to the composing of self.[5] In this fifth reading we focus on the way in which individuals choose a detailed visual description of what might be a relatively inconsequential event in order to explain something of their experience. While the descriptions here are necessarily of the University of Winchester and the city of Winchester, this approach can be applied to other institutions and organisations.[6]

The countryside around Winchester invites hyperbole. Many of the interviewees, particularly at the second stage of the project which asked for comments on life in Winchester, referred to well-known local features. They spoke of walks by the river on summer evenings, drawing on familiar discourses of university life but in a way that also spoke of personal growth and maturing relationships. The sense of growing personal identity was reflected through the experience of being - on campus, by the water meadows or in the Cathedral. The resulting narratives, invoking as they do the 'dreaming spires' of Oxford and Cambridge, following Virginia Woolf, might be termed an Oxbridge myth of higher education.[7] Almost all the interviewees had a view of 'their Winchester' which was clearly fixed in their minds and enough of the current landscape remains unchanged for memories of their student lives not to seem to be part of a long-vanished world, and therefore of little relevance for today. However much pubs and cafes may have altered, in this chapter we also explore how the student relationship and engagement with the City has also changed. Many students remain living at home, have part-time term time jobs and family responsibilities and come only to the University for lectures and a visit to the library. They no longer expect the institution to provide for all their social as well as educational needs although, as is discussed later in this chapter, the role and reputation of the Student Union has increased substantially over the last forty years.

Winchester, in common with most universities, has seen a steady increase in the number of students who choose to stay at home rather than on site.[8] Indeed current policy excludes students who live less than twenty-five miles from the university from the first round of accommodation applications. The location of Winchester as a 'nice place to be' was one of the constant themes of our interviews. One of the problems with oral history is that it invites the production of a seamless narrative between past and present based on the continuity of space. Respondents see the Winchester of today as similar to the Winchester of their youth, essentially the same, despite superficial changes. Inevitably there is a tension here for current policy where the emphasis, especially for an educational institution, is necessarily on the new. An institution, however illustrious its past, has to move with the times. As Gemeinschaft gives way to Gesellschaft, what is the place of an oral history focusing on past student experience, rather than a documentary narrative celebrating progress and growth? What benefit is it to add a nostalgic recollection of an evening walking along the water meadows to a more formal history? Massey states that 'the identity of places is very much bound up with the histories which are told of them, how those histories are told, and which history turns out to be dominant'.[9] In writing this oral history we seek to offer a different, although complementary, history of an institution where, in order to examine the changes that have taken place, it is necessary to see these recollections as 'temporal and not just spatial: as set in time as well as space'.[10]

Oral histories allow a nuanced sense of the historical record and offer an insight into how staff may be more forward looking than their students: 'I think in the sense that they saw it as a sort of quiet, genteel institution in a Cathedral town when in fact we were having to sort of take our place, you know, in a much wider context, really with other institutions of higher education which weren't like that'.[11] Those returning for the reunion weekend at which we filmed interviews as part of the second stage of the project, spent much time reflecting in detail on the nature of familiar buildings and those no longer in existence, except as part of a remembered experience of learning which shaped their lives. The campus was almost unrecognisable to those who had studied at King Alfred's in the 1950s, while the surrounding city and countryside had changed less. This chapter therefore explores the nature of the relationship between the meanings of space and place in campus and city, often defined as 'town' and 'gown', rather than a chronologically changing landscape. In doing this we are able to draw conclusions of the meaning of place in the student experience of higher education more widely, as well as for Winchester itself. Interviews which reflected on the role of place and space located individual memories within a wider cultural memory of what a university environment should look like, and the gravitas associated with elite universities was carried into the gravitas attached to the role of learning within the composition of an individual's sense of self.

The Campus

This section, in part, highlights the extent to which the nature of its physical environment contributed to the sense of community and its Gemeinschaft characteristic, which we have already noted in the earlier chapters. Unlike many universities the institution has been restricted in its ability to expand its physical boundaries as the student population has grown from a few hundred to over six thousand. The greatest change has been in the provision of student accommodation. In the early days, as previously described, this was all within the main building. Later it included various houses and hostels, including the Carfax Hotel mentioned in the opening quote, within walking distance of the main campus. By 2013, the accommodation provided by the university included three student 'villages'. The award-winning architecture focuses on maintaining the notion of a community of scholars within easy reach of the main campus. However, as many students return home at weekends, making a clearer demarcation between work and social lives, these flats now perhaps will provide more of a location for a Gesellschaft community than the close-knit camaraderie of hostels in previous decades.

Echoing the Gemeinschaft nature of the earlier community, both students and staff remembered the days when the College was smaller and many tutors as well as students lived close to the institution. They used descriptions of student housing to ground a deeper sense of how the staff built up close relationships with their students ensuring that the community was run as a large family. The notion of family and its implications for caring is discussed in more detail in the following chapter. It appears significant that the physical boundaries of home and college were permeable; students and tutors were invited into each other's social spaces, reflecting a deeper mutuality of purpose than may be expected today when the introduction of fees has brought with it different expectations of tutor/ staff relationships. One member of staff remarked:

> John Stripe took [this] very seriously. He always entertained, he entertained the students in rotas I think I'm right in saying, he used to have them up to his house in groups and I don't know whether it was just for a drink or a meal or a coffee.[12]

Students in turn reciprocated, as one member of staff noted:

> I was going to say we mothered them, we fathered them [. . .] there was a feeling that you know they were our brood [. . .] people would invite them to their house [. . .] and then you would be invited to engagement parties, 21st birthday parties, weddings, those sorts of things, and the student residences down Christchurch Road would typically have a garden party in the Summer. It says something about the tone of the place, and they ... all the people in the residence would invite their personal tutors and their

> partners to a luncheon garden party and we'd stand around and drink in the garden of the houses down Christchurch Road.[13]

Massey writes of the relationship between imaginary spaces and physical places and this is particularly notable in interviews which invite interviewees to go back to their youth and their time as students. Massey notes that space is 'always in the process of being made. It is never finished, never closed'.[14] She emphasises the relational nature of space, and for our purpose this enables us to trace the ever-changing relationship between students, the city and the campus. Neither moves physically but their meaning is both significant and changing across time for each generation of students. The passing of time affects remembered place and with the benefit of hindsight the less desirable aspects of buildings become an occasion for a wry comment rather than a representation of a less well-endowed institution.

As the institution has grown from teacher training college to a university so it has invested heavily in the campus infrastructure, reflecting its increasingly high profile in the university rankings. It impresses itself on the landscape with a new modern entrance in front of the nineteenth century main building, with the Chapel a few yards to the east, which remains at the heart of the campus. The University also deliberately invokes the distant past in emphasising its relationship with the long history of Winchester as a seat of learning. A recent addition to the artwork around the campus is a wire statue outside the Reception area which echoes the well-known statue of King Alfred at the entrance to the city. Some of the teaching buildings are named after medieval saints also associated with learning; St Grimbald, St Alphege and St Edburga. These links also serve to underline the Christian foundation of the College. Of course in comparison with Winchester College, the boys' public school founded in 1382 by William of Wykeham a short walk away, the University is a very recent addition to the educational landscape of the city and the two institutions today have little in common.[15] Also, in contrast to larger universities whose buildings are named after industry sponsors,[16] several Winchester University buildings are named after twentieth century academic staff and governors, for example; the Martial Rose library, the Stripe lecture hall, Tom Atkinson, Herbert Jarman and Kenneth Kettle. As one alumnus remarked informally, 'all my tutors have turned into buildings'. Naming buildings after staff demonstrates the symbiotic nature of person and place and the longevity of personal association with the College. It also denotes a specific, perhaps more parochial, phase in the College history. New student residences locate themselves firmly onto the landscape of the present; 'Burma Road'[17] and 'West Downs'. Some resonance with the past can be found in the futuristic invert V shape of the Union roof which is a deliberate reference to the 1960s-built neo-Gothic refectory which it replaced.

Student Union Building

With the increase in fees, and competition amongst universities for students, the initial impression of place is as significant as the courses on offer to an increasingly consumer-oriented undergraduate population. Top of prospective students' lists as they work their way around various Open Days is the Student Union which at Winchester has not always been as imposing as it is now. The increasing importance of the student voice is reflected in the changing nature of the building as it has progressed from tin hut to modern flagship. The 1960s loom large in histories of student unrest but the main focus of the Student Union in Winchester at that time appears to have been the cheap beer, the opportunity to socialise and the provision of washing machines. The following extract demonstrates perhaps how, in oral history interviews, sometimes a prompt is necessary in order to elicit some long-forgotten insight into student life:

> We didn't have a Student Union building. If there were any meetings they generally used the Great Hall and we used to have year lectures there. But there was no Student Union building. I have a feeling that when I first went to college we had to pay student union fees, which was about 30 shillings or something. Then I think after that we got the money back because it was some government thing. I'm not sure.

People have talked about a building that was some sort of a hut.

> Oh just a minute. Now you're talking about it I have a feeling there were some huts. I think they were once used for science, but I'm not quite sure, and [. . .] then when we first had washing machines, the washing machines were in there because I can remember going over there. I used to wash my things out by hand and then put them in the drying rooms but I can remember going over to the washing machines and helping Tony do his washing. I think we had the twin tub then. But it was definitely in those wooden buildings. I'd forgotten about that completely.[18]

Another alumnus noted the very basic provision of entertainment offered by the union, yet students told us that the College provided all the entertainment they needed in the form of sports and societies. This gives us additional insight into the changing role that provision for extra-curricular activities has played in higher education:

> There were two other rooms as I remember in the hut, one of which we used to use for informal mid-week hops I think they were called, essentially bringing down a gramophone record, three Beatles LPs and the place shook to the extent that I think

> there was beginning to be some serious concern that it would fall to bits. Have you seen any photos of the inside? It was the sort of huts prisoners of war had and it was divided up into sections.[19]

The respondent here brings the interviewer into his narrative, asking if we have ever seen photos; he is, at one and the same time, telling us what the Union was like but also asking for evidence to support his account. Perhaps as the interviewer shook her head he felt able to embellish the tale by likening it to a PoW hut.

Other students from the 1960s were equally hazy about the role that the Student Union played in their campus life. We might conclude that the physical nature of the building reflects the significance that students attached to their union:

> We wondered what you meant by the Students' Union because nowadays people say 'I'll go to the Union' and it's the building. We didn't have a set building but there was a little old hut along the Burma Road which was initially some science room or something and then it became a place where the Students' Union would organise hops and things like that. The union itself didn't have a set place from what I can gather. They all met in various rooms like History Room 2 or something.

With no real physical centre it seems that there was little sense of student politics engendered by the Union. One respondent in hindsight recognised that 'it was the sixties' but observed 'I don't remember anything controversial that we got involved in'.[20] A few years later a purpose-built Union symbolised the centrality of student sociability to the life of the College but it could also act to marginalise students who were not part of the in-crowd:

> I think when I was there it really was central to everything going on because of the building. Even people who perhaps weren't in clubs and societies all got their cup of tea there in the coffee breaks. I think it was always seen as a bit of an exclusive group or a clique that could happen. I know some people were actually almost frightened of going into the building sometimes. I think we obviously all mix with our own type and forget sometimes where other people are in it all. Really they ran the bar and organised all the events and the weekend discos. Some people just found it intimidating going into the building where there were some confident, brash people I guess. Also before I started it was completely smoking and that put people off. We did get it changed to make it a no-smoking area. We fought hard to get that and I think that probably was significant for people as well.[21]

Again, in the extract above, the way that the respondent moves from talking about 'I' to 'we' to 'they' is interesting. She distances herself from those in charge who had perhaps unwittingly but inevitably made some students feel uncomfortable, but then as an active member of the Student Union she acknowledges that 'we' fought to get the smoking ban introduced.

At times the Student Union does appear to have been involved in student politics, enabling its members to move beyond the close boundaries of King Alfred's. It seemed to depend on individuals rather than a long legacy of radical student activism, as one student observed:

> There were a couple of characters who steered it. There was one person who was very active politically and had a lot of contacts beyond the College and the wider NUS. So I think he was quite active in promoting us being very involved in national student

> politics which we were and I think we used to...we always used to go to the national conferences and we used to have motions and we used to stand up and debate them.[22]

Part of this might have been due to the historical roots of the College in teacher training as some students noted issues round NUT/NUWT tensions.

The Old Student Union
'The student union was small enough to feel that you could meet and get to know people and after 12 months I did feel that I really belonged at KAC.'

If it is possible to generalise about comments made about the Student Union, once there was a specific building, it would be to highlight the amount of time that students in the 1970s were able to spend chatting after lectures and relaxing in the evenings when it was the only space available to watch television. There were comments about the different groups that used the Union with several reflections on the 'PE lads' and the changing gender ratio, discussed in the following chapter. The final comment in this section really highlights how memory alters how we view our student lives. Of course a building is going to suffer from wear and tear over the years, but the following comment does indicate how the physicality of a building viewed now[23] affects the way that memory constructs the past and how sometimes tales of the past tell us more about ourselves in the present:

> I had to drop a friend off to the Student Union and we walked through the bar and I couldn't believe how shabby it looked. I thought it looked really sad and I used to love going down there every Friday and Saturday night, it was the best place to be and I walked through and I thought, 'Oh, it looks horrible!' (laughs) but I guess most places when you ... at your student days probably end up feeling the same so ... it definitely looked different to me. Probably wasn't any different at all, probably just the fact I am more of a snob now (laughs). I am used to going, I can afford to go to more expensive places and drink![24]

Senior Common Room

In the third stage of the project the staff highlighted the importance of the Senior Common Room as their dedicated physical space. We were told very precisely that it was 'the room which is now the porter's lodge at the main entrance into the College, that was where all the staff sat and had their coffee'.[25] The role of the Senior Common Room in the creation of a Gemeinschaft community, with its overtones of Oxbridge, has already been touched upon in Chapter 3; here we reflect on the significance of the physical space itself. Massey notes how an understanding of space as relational, highlights the political nature of physical space. When a new Student Services Centre replaced the SCR a temporary replacement room generated the following comment: 'I think the SCR has been successfully killed off, and I would be surprised if there ever is a replacement SCR because we have created a new space people don't want to go to'.[26] The demise of the SCR signalled a changing, perhaps more democratic, relationship between students and staff once social space was shared in a Learning Cafe and the Dining Hall. The space may be open to staff and students but it is less conducive to the casual conversations mentioned in many interviews; as one current member of staff put it 'it's friendly, but not over friendly, I think we miss, I miss the SCR because you could always go in there and say hello to somebody, and that was quite nice'.[27] However, it may be that the SCR itself symbolised the old order in which small is not always beautiful, as a member of staff remarked 'And there was a Senior Common Room [. . .] It was very nice and twee, but it was very parochial and inward looking'.[28]

The significance of the staff room in school as a professional learning space has recently been highlighted. Similar claims could be made for the mentoring and maintenance of academic subjectivities in the university SCR.[29] Initially the timetable worked so that everyone stopped for coffee and tea at the same time, reflecting the timetable of a school day that would become familiar to those students preparing to become teachers:

> Everybody went to the Senior Common Room, and it was technically a club, so we paid a subscription and we had newspapers and tea and cakes in the afternoon, very nice cakes, and coffee and biscuits in the morning. But it was run as if it were, a members' club, I was going to say a male club, but I think male club might not have been too far away, and you could sit with anybody, and did sit with anybody.[30]

As the institution expanded the SCR retained its central position, enabling staff across departments and programmes to get to know each other and also to maintain established boundaries. With the recruitment of the first major cohort of research students in the late 1990s, the decision that they should have the privilege of using the SCR clearly marked them out as a distinct group. It provided 'a social space in which certain behaviours, attitudes and dispositions are sanctioned and reinforced while others are perhaps marginalised, dismissed or ridiculed'.[31]

Oral history interviews enable historians to identify the significance of small objects in charting institutional change. The SCR provided the backdrop to a number of reflections that we might analyse in terms of the spoken visual. For example the location of the pigeonholes and 'the' telephone may not be noted in any official documents, but their wider significance is clear in the following passage:

> People had the habit of going to the Common Room for those times, and the pigeon-holes were in the Common Room, so everybody came in to collect their mail, you actually very seldom went through an entire day if you were in the College where you didn't sit down with somebody.[32]

The change in size, as well as the change in modes of communication, is reflected in something as simple as a detailed explanation of the telephone location:

> The staff notice board was there and THE staff telephone, not telephones all over the [. . .] THE staff telephone.
>
> Only one phone?
>
> Yes if you wanted to make a phone call you went there in the [. . .]
>
> So you wouldn't have had a phone in your office?

Oh no, no, no not unless you were very senior [. . .] no. And the door which had been originally intended as being a kind of main entrance had been blocked up [. . .] I think there was a security thing and the phone was in that porch way and the main entrance then became almost a back entrance you know. But as the time changed, you see the Senior Common Room was moved to where it is now but this came along with an increase in student numbers and therefore an increase in staff. So the whole administration of the Senior Common Room became different. It did play an important part because that was where you went to find people, and you went at certain times. You went at coffee times or tea times because you'd try and catch people. [33]

Once the Junior Common Room, then the Senior Common Room, now Student Services
Three great rooms that began as teaching spaces have evolved new uses over 175 years.

Again, the change from a Gemeinschaft community to one more attuned to Gesellschaft is evident here. Having lost its centrality as the only location of coffee, cakes and a telephone, staff working lives now are more centred in the faculties than the Senior Common Room. Although earlier members of staff commented on the opportunities for personal contacts and professional relationships that the SCR provided, once the pigeonholes, the telephone and the coffee and catering were taken away, so too the impetus to find time to visit a common space dwindled. The new SCR opened in 2013 occupies a different physical space on the campus and bears no traces of an early teacher training staff room. It remains to be seen how staff will utilise this space as a place away from students, but also very much part of the new order and not a remnant of the past.

Medecroft

Before moving to discuss the leafy environment of the meadows and hills of Winchester recollected in the interviews, it is worth considering interpretations of the building known as Medecroft across time. A research project carried out by Winchester academics Tansy Jessop and Angela Smith examined the meaning of place within the campus.[34] This research has been used by those reflecting on their experiences in other universities.[35] Writing of their experience of academic space and place at the University of Sheffield, Andrew Cox, Tim Herrick and Patrick Keating considered the layout of their own offices in the light of Jessop and Smith's notion of the 'symbolic hierarchy in the campus layout'.[36] It is not only in Winchester that the iconic buildings at the centre of the campus bear little relation to 'the teaching spaces which are frequently marginal, temporary and in various states of maintenance'.[37] Cox and others discuss how the feeling of belonging and comfort affects students (and staff). Their research explored 'multiple ways in which spaces, bound together under the common heading 'the university', could be used, interpreted, and experienced to engage or alienate users from the institution'. Many Winchester students were, and are, first generation entrants to higher education. The role of the physical space in providing an environment conducive to learning is vital, and that might not always be provided by state-of-the-art architecture. This might go some way to explaining why Medecroft, originally a private house and, until recently, an old, and somewhat dilapidated building right on the boundary of campus and town, has been interpreted so differently by staff and students, with students perhaps seeing Medecroft as a less challenging space in which to encounter the unfamiliar environment of higher education.

In our reading of the interviews for their general narratives Medecroft served a purpose both for explanations of community and marginalisation, demonstrating how oral history can highlight differences within accounts and a multitude of interpretations of place within an institution's history. In the 1960s, when King Alfred's was a teacher training college, the placing of the art building away from the centre of the institution held a special affection for one student:

> It was like a little oasis down the road 100 metres or so and that was just the Art Department. We worked there and spent a lot of time there, not just in lecture or contact time with lecturers but in pursuing our art or pottery or whatever and after hours, evenings, weekends, we would set up kilns and stuff like that and it was almost like a little club.[38]

Ten years later this affection was still there but somewhat modified:

> There was a real sense of community down in Medecroft that first year. It was like a foundation year of art, which I'd already done, but it did gel us as a group. It made us very isolated, even though it

> was just slightly down the hill. There was Medecroft and then the rest of the university.[39]

By the time the History department was moved to Medecroft, isolation had lost its charm:

> History having to move from St James' [. . .] down to Medecroft which was in a terrible state. You know paint peeling off the walls and rooms were horrible... you wouldn't want to show anyone around and say look at this, given that the campus has a lot going for it I don't think that there was a single building you would have been proud of.[40]

In these reflections Medecroft provided the focus for staff narratives concerned at the status of their subjects, isolation (perhaps also from the SCR) and banishment to the boundaries of academic life. In student interviews Medecroft acted as a vehicle for explaining the role of the campus and its buildings in their experience of higher education. Each of the comments is, in addition, made in retrospect, so again we can see how buildings and their descriptions serve to act as metaphors of belonging or rejection from the growing community. The next section of this chapter moves beyond the campus boundaries to discuss the changing relationship between town and gown and the ways that unchanging geographical landmarks enable us to chart both continuities and changes within the undergraduate experience.

The City of Winchester

The notion of the separate nature of 'town' and 'gown' harks back to the origins of Plato's academy situated outside the city. Over time it has come to represent something of a tension between those temporarily studying and working in a university and the permanent inhabitants of the city in which the institution is situated.[41] When the training course at King Alfred's only lasted two years and students lived on site and did not seek employment in town during term time, this distinctiveness might have been more marked than it is now. Students in the early days covered by our project were distinguishable by the wearing of a university scarf or blazer. Today the visible boundary between student and resident is less clear, rag week has disappeared, and it is perhaps only in Freshers' Week with its late-night noise that student revelry strains relationships.

Over the period covered by this book, Winchester has itself changed. It can no longer be described, by any stretch of the imagination, as 'tatty', as one interviewee suggested.[42] Today there is a proliferation of trendy boutiques and eating places reflecting the increasing number of affluent commuters who choose to live in a cathedral city. House prices have remained almost immune from the problems of the economic downturn. Inevitably fewer staff, or students, can afford to buy or rent property in Winchester, and so the boundaries of the university 'catchment' area move ever further afield. Against this momentum of change, the water meadows, the Cathedral and its Close have remained the same and enabled respondents to think themselves back in time more easily than when faced with the new university buildings and halls of residence. The permanence of the geographical contours provided a useful contrast for reflection on personal and physical change.

Feminist geographer Linda McDowell notes the 'awkward relationship between the economic and the cultural' in driving new theoretical frameworks which emphasise 'questions of meaning and representation as well as material cultures'.[43] In taking these ideas forward for our voice relational reading for the overall narrative or plot, we can begin to identify how alumni and staff use recollections of changing economic circumstances or material conditions as representations of the role that their time as students or staff played in their developing identity. For example, very few of the students had cars in the early days and money, even for those on full grants, was scarce as so few worked during term time. This inevitably meant that rest and relaxation away from college life was in the near environs of the institution and revolved around walks and picnics, visits to local pubs and, most famously, Ken's Fish and Chip Shop. We noticed that as students increasingly engaged in paid employment, the town was related differently within their accounts of college life, as a source of employment and income as much as expenditure and leisure. This reflects Massey's notion of the ever-changing meaning of a physical place. Alumni clearly see themselves as 'Winchester' students, encouraged perhaps by the change of institutional name, as much as 'King Alfred's' the highly respected but self-contained college on the hill. At Open Days today prospective students are given bags proclaiming 'The Winchester Experience' which clearly emphasises the significance of place to the experience of higher education at this institution. The change of name from King Alfred's was mourned by some and is retained in the name of the main campus, as opposed to West Downs campus which houses the Business School and the Conference Centre.

Winchester's physical sites of interest were frequently used as the background for anecdotes that explained more about the educative process than might at first appear. In the following short reflection our respondent summarised the busy-ness of small college life and the consequent sense of duty to one's fellow students. The surrounding countryside offered an escape from 'the place', however convivial it could be, and provided the opportunity for quiet study, although the rather abrupt reference at the end perhaps suggest that studying was not always recalled as a pleasurable occupation:

> There was one particular place where there was a seat and I used to go and revise. There was never anybody else there and the big problem with college is that you sit down to do some revision and somebody bursts into your room and you could say

> 'Clear off, I want to get on with some work' but you don't. So I used to try and get out of the place to revise and went up there. I would say St Giles is a place I went to think and read and revise and so on. I learnt to read and love reading while I was here and that was very important to me and that was a place I went if I wanted to kill a book off.[44]

As referred to in the introductory chapter, this passage also highlights the dilemma of the oral historian in selecting beginnings and endings to quotes and demonstrates why, in this book, we have deliberately chosen, in many cases, to include quite long extracts of narrative. Should we have chosen to cut the quote off after 'very important to me' we would have lost the richness and inherent ambiguity of the last phrase where he 'kills the book off'.

Given the nature of Winchester as a cathedral city in the leafy countryside of Hampshire it is unsurprising that the city itself plays a substantial part in the telling of student life:

> You did go into the shops because it was such a lovely walk into town, whether you went by the water meadows or just went straight down all those streets. That was the bit I loved, the whole bit of being in amongst those beautifully historic buildings.[45]

In our analysis of the responses to our initial questionnaires, the city, as in the response above, was largely remembered for its greenery and historic buildings. The Cathedral was mentioned, although only the music students talked about it as part of their educational experience 'At that stage there must have been fifty to sixty in the Chapel choir and we sang in the Cathedral and did services there and he introduced me to composers I'd never heard of. I'd been a boy chorister in church but he loved Vaughan Williams and I loved Vaughan Williams'.[46] Another student also mentioned links with the Cathedral: 'In fact I sometimes used to play Evensong for Alwyn Surplice, the Cathedral organist, at the time as he used to lecture at King Alfred's'.[47]

As overseas students increasingly choose British universities to continue their studies, the physical location becomes vitally important in a competitive market. Winchester Cathedral as a tourist venue provokes immediate recognition. The University of Winchester celebrates its long term links with historical sites in the city with the Cathedral featuring prominently as the image on the university logo, emphasising the close relationship between the two. The University has built close links with Japanese colleges over the last decade and, following the general trend, has seen many students applying from all over Asia.[48] The location of the university in such an historic city can only enhance its attraction for those living overseas, so while the trend for UK domicile students is to attend universities closer to home, at the same time institutions are packaging their prospectuses to appeal to those from much further afield. Our interviews confirmed how the place was as important as the academic reputation of the College when making choices:

> The Bishop's Palace, the College itself, obviously the Cathedral and its surrounding parts and St Giles Hill at the other side with a lovely view of Winchester from the top. I think [this] was probably quite important. I was born and bred in the country and had come from a very small village, so to live in a town was very attractive to me and I found it a very pleasant town to live in. I don't think I'd have wanted to have lived in Birmingham.[49]

In the oral history interviews it was more the sense of history that the Cathedral invoked and the gravitas that it gave to students' chosen city of study, as well as its significance as the place of graduation, as much as the building as a site of worship that was recalled by alumni. Of course not everyone agreed, as one member of staff noted:

> I've never been and I never will [to graduation] because it's in the Cathedral, but partly also because I think as I said I've never quite understood the contradiction by which we could claim to be about widening participation, but that's measured in dressing people up and having them parade around Winchester?[50]

The Cathedral grounds also acted as a space for relaxation. At about a ten minute walk from the campus and adjacent to the High Street, the green space in front of the Cathedral provided space to play all year round 'We used to play Frisbee in the summer in the Cathedral grounds and snow fights in winter'.[51] Robert Anderson highlights how universities 'reflect the political, social and intellectual conditions of their time, and so does writing their history'.[52] We might add that for oral history participants, so does telling their history. In telling us of their student life individuals effectively retold their youth. The quotation above tells of the close physical location between institution and the city, but more than that, it also explains how, for that individual, the irresponsibility of youth demonstrated by snowball fights and Frisbees is inextricably linked with the sense of place and the role of the Cathedral gardens.

Public space, even in the surroundings of a cathedral, is not always welcoming, as one student told us: 'I had a major incident where I felt the bigger community didn't support me when I was attacked in the Cathedral grounds. One of the most wonderful places in Winchester that people talk about, and yet in broad daylight I was attacked'.[53] Comments such as this one can disrupt the tendency within institutional histories to make inevitable generalisations about the surroundings, which need moderation; after all an institutional history should not read like a prospectus. Juxtaposed with the following extract we can perhaps only draw the conclusion that experiences differ but that the city location proved central to the recollections of undergraduate years:

> I can't remember getting involved in much in Winchester, other than one enjoyed being in Winchester and walking down into town. It was just the general atmosphere of the place, which is a very pleasant atmospheric city. It's just pleasant enough to walk around the shops and the water meadows and the Cathedral Close or up on St Catherine's or St Giles Hill.

Students seemed to have memories of St Giles Hill and St Catherine's Hill at all hours of the day and night, using it for reading, walking and no doubt the inevitable romantic tryst:

> St Catherine's Hill – everybody walked up there and saw the sun come up there. I don't know anybody in my particular group who hadn't at some point. It was just something that one did. It was like Everest. It was there, so you had to walk up it.[54]

Winchester's climate also caused one of our respondents to remember his time as a student in terms of the social life of the College:

> Yes, Farley Mount [. . .] We used to go camping there and have barbecues and cook-outs there. We used to go for the night at weekends, just friends, not in an organised way, but we used to drive out there. St Catherine's Hill was a hill the other side of Winchester before that new controversial bypass was constructed. We had a particularly bad winter I think in '63 and there was heaps of snow and we used to take tea trays from the refectory and sledge on St Catherine's Hill. Hundreds of people were out there.

> Fantastic time. Purely recreational because it was such a snowy winter.[55]

An older alumnus also remembered a cold winter but couched his sledging more in terms of explaining King Alfred's separation from the wider local community once he was a student. This reflection perhaps offers us an insight into how students may view their university differently as a learning space, even if they have grown up in the surrounding area:

> The winter of '39 was a very cold, snowy one and those of us who were doing craft work knocked up some sledges, so we had a whale of time sledging down or skiing down St Catherine's. My previous memory of Winchester as a boy, I had enjoyed the Cathedral and museums and the recreation ground and St Giles and the river, the meadows, but not so much as a student. I was very much more within the College.[56]

A significant proportion of those we interviewed wanted to stay in the area once they graduated, which suggests that there were emotional as well as intellectual links with the city. One alumna noted how the sense of place was integral to their time at King Alfred's, as she explained in detail the route of her walks:

> the lovely walk along the river and canal and up to St Catherine's Hill was a regular, popular and along to St Cross and from my point of view and a few friends were like-minded, it was a very much an important part of our life there and I still do it (laughs).[57]

But not all alumni life was spent musing along the water meadows, singing in the Cathedral or climbing St Catherine's Hill. In discussing the importance of sociability with our respondents, the regular and vivid memories of pubs and cafes and their locations suggests that, together with the Student Union, time spent out of lectures was easily as important as time spent learning the trade of teaching or studying for a degree.

In terms of continuity, the place of the pub in student life appears to be fairly constant. We were regularly regaled with stories of the seventy pubs in Winchester. In the filmed interviews it was during the discussion of pubs that the respondents became most animated about actual locations, waving their arms in the general direction of 'The County', 'The Green Man' and 'The Battery' (now no longer in existence.) With Winchester city in easy walking distance of student halls and residences it was probably in the pubs that they were most visible to the local community. 'So typically I used to hang out with a group of people who were on either part of my course and we used to go to the pub together and into town'.[58] Some places were less student-friendly and again time intersects with place in creating a sense of belonging: 'I think if you went down to the Wykeham Arms as a student you'd probably be made to feel slightly less welcome than going into the Exchange'.[59]

A noticeable change in student socialising over the years of this study is linked to the general demise of the coffee bar, although if we were interviewing students now we might have more comments relating to the numerous coffee shops that have sprung up in the last half dozen years. Overall the winner from the early years of our study was Ken's Fish and Chip shop, now no longer in existence, but clearly it is held very dear in alumni memories as the high spot of an escape from, or an addition to, the rather poor meals originally provided by college catering. 'It was the only place really if you were fed up with the meals at college and you wanted to go out somewhere different, even if it was just beans on toast'.[60] Ken's was one of the most frequently cited venues outside college, indeed we were told 'Yes, sadly, Ken's Fish & Chip shop was only a folk memory when I was a student. I heard about it because it was legendary'.[61] An alumnus from the early days commented 'It wasn't at that stage a fish and chip shop. It was rather like a transport café'.[62] The visual image of students drifting from meadows and Cathedral to the local transport caff demonstrates how eclectic our memories are of the past and how we need to pay attention not only to the number of times a venue is mentioned but also why. When King Alfred's was a smaller institution it followed the tradition of formal dinners which require students to 'bow in' to top table if late, and 'bow out' should they wish to leave early. Latin grace before and after meals was remembered vividly and affectionately by former students. While a more conventional history might note the formality of the dining rituals, oral histories add further, more nuanced details. While such a practice might suggest that King Alfred's was behind the times in the 1960s, our oral accounts show that students, while appreciating tradition, were quite prepared to make alternative arrangements:

> That was a place that was regularly invaded by students who were on a particular occasion dissatisfied with college food. That's what happened. I'm talking about the evening meal and if it didn't look good, a lot of students would get up and leave and half an hour later they'd appear in this café.[63]

In the case of Ken's right at the bottom of town, not such a short walk as Cathedral or pub, it perhaps evokes a carefree time when money was short but memory suggests that sociability was more important than sophisticated venues. An analysis of the readings identified by voice relational analysis in the following extract raises some interesting points:

> But Ken's Fish & Chip Shop, yes, because you could go there and buy your fish and chips in paper if you wanted and they had these scraps which were made out of batter and you got those free. But occasionally we would celebrate and when we got engaged we

> went to Ken's Fish & Chip Shop for chips and sausage or something like that. You wore your college scarf when you were having a sit down meal and you could have a slight reduction. There was a take away but also a sitting down place in the back and that was a treat if you could afford to sit down. You used to get your cup of tea and bread and butter. You know where the water mill is, it's just up the hill as you start to go up St Giles Hill. It's on the left. I could show you on a map. But it's not there anymore. It was the best fish and chips in town, worth walking over the other side of the town for those fish and chips. But they were shut on Mondays.[64]

First, in terms of the interviewer's reaction, the place under detailed discussion is no longer there so there is little to enable us to relate our experience of studying at the institution to that of our respondent. Its location is clearly important to the respondent, as she goes to some length to ensure that we know exactly where she is talking about. But she is talking about an unfamiliar time, and the more detail she offers, the less we have in common. As we move to the second reading, the narrative, we can see the story recounted at the distance of time is of poor, but respectable, students, tough financial beginnings with a successful career behind her evidenced by the comfortable surroundings of the home where the interview took place. The detail of Ken's precise location and the opening times highlight its significance in the narrative of student life. Then we are told of the engagement supper as the reading for wider relationships comes in, although interestingly that one incident appears to be of less importance 'sausage or something like that' than the wider place of Ken's throughout her college days. If we trace the changes in 'I' and 'you' and 'we' we can identify the distancing over the years of the student she once was to the woman of today, 'You wore your college scarf when you were having a sit down meal and you could have a slight reduction'. She clearly remembers her college days with fondness, noting the college scarf that marked them out as members of the college community whom the proprietors of Ken's recognised as financially limited. There is little 'I' in this passage except in terms of her as the raconteur, 'I could show you where that is'; she positions herself as an observer and always as part of the student body 'we', never the solitary 'I'.

Conclusion

Although the University of Winchester has grown exponentially in status and in the size of its student body, it is still a small institution when compared to Russell Group Universities, advertising itself as 'A university on a human scale, with around 6,000 students studying a broad range of programmes at both undergraduate and postgraduate level' and emphasising the positive aspect of this: 'The culture of the University is informal, with an emphasis on providing a supportive community for students to unlock their potential and become the best they can be in their chosen careers'.[65] The physical appearance of the university buildings and surroundings and the range of provision for students' work and leisure are integral to the successful recruitment of national and international students. First impressions count. In this chapter we have considered how oral history narratives of place and space can offer insights into the way that institutions present themselves to the outside world and how those within them use metaphors of place to explain their higher education experience.

The oral histories help us to chart the changing relationships that students have had with the city itself. Although, as Gifford notes, relations between town and gown 'are an ancillary activity in that it is neither teaching, nor research, nor service to the public', such relations are central to the eventual reputation and success of an institution.[66] As students have increasingly lived and worked outside the campus boundaries, so they have taken more part in the commercial life of the city as well as seeing the town as a place for leisure activities. Students perhaps spent more time in pubs and less in cafes, especially once Ken's closed, but the narratives of making entertainment on a budget remain constant. Members of staff are less likely to live close to the university and their work and social lives have become more separate than their predecessors' who regularly shared social activities with their students.

The naming of buildings after retired staff, and new building shapes reflecting those of their predecessor, serve to create a representation of continuity in a changing institution, although recent naming of student halls according to location rather than personalities further links the institution within its spatial location as much as within its intellectual heritage. The surrounding countryside is still recognisable, and accounts of student experience linked with meadow walks and Cathedral graduations also remain remarkably similar. Where buildings such as the Student Union have changed beyond all recognition, so has the place of the Union in student memories. In the early part of our story we were presented with an image of a collegiate and active Senior Common Room and a tin hut of a Student Union whose main purpose appeared to be the provision of washing machines. As we pay close attention to the way that spaces and places on campus and in the city are described, the identification between 'I' and 'we' and 'they' enables us to chart how individuals place themselves within some aspects of their narratives but, sometimes with the benefit of hindsight, manage to distance themselves from the excesses of irresponsibility associated with student days.

Notes to Chapter 5.

---

[1] Questionnaire 59, Stage 2 (1965-1968).

[2] Sue Hawkins, '"Whose Story is it Anyway?": The Challenges of Conducting Institutional Histories', *Journal of Conservation and Museum Studies* (2012): www.jcms-journal.com (accessed 5 January 2013).

[3] Pierre Nora, 'Between Memory and History: Les lieux de memoire', *Representations* 26 (Special Issue: Memory and Counter-Memory, Spring 1989), 22.

[4] Doreen Massey, 'Places and their Pasts', *History Workshop Journal,* 39 (1995): 182-192. See also Doreen Massey, *Space, Place and Gender* (Oxford: Polity, 1994) and Linda McDowell, ed., *Undoing Place?: A Geographical Reader* (London: Arnold, 1997).

[5] Stephanie Spencer, 'A Uniform Identity: Schoolgirl Snapshots and the Spoken Visual', *History of Education,* 36.2 (2007): 227-246.

[6] This raises an intriguing question, for example, as to whether the experience of attending a university that is spread throughout a city, like Bristol, is in any way different from that of attending a campus university, such as its near neighbour outside Bath.

[7] In 1928, in *A Room of One's Own,* Virginia Woolf used what she called the 'invention' of 'Oxbridge' as the setting for a polemic. She imagined a college, complete with a river, where 'one might have sat the clock round lost in thought'. The college had well-established buildings and grounds, and clear traditions where the 'spirit of peace descended like a cloud from heaven, for if the spirit of peace dwells anywhere, it is in the courts and quadrangles of

Oxbridge on a fine October morning'. See Virginia Woolf, *A Room of One's Own* (London: Penguin, 1945), 8.

[8] In 2011, Lucy Tobin noted that Higher Education Agency Statistics charted a rise in students living at home from 8 per cent in 1984 to 19 per cent in 2011. See Lucy Tobin, 'Rise of the Stay-at-Home Students', *The Guardian* (12 August 2011): www.theguardian.com. See also Chapter 3 for further discussion of this aspect of change.

[9] Massey, *Places and their Pasts,* 186.

[10] Massey, *Places and their Pasts,* 186.

[11] Interview 12, Stage 3 (1973-1996).

[12] Interview 18, Stage 3 (1960-1967).

[13] Interview 17, Stage 3 (1973-2006).

[14] Doreen Massey, *For Space* (London: Sage, 2005), 9.

[15] Membership of the governing body has included teaching staff, and the headmaster of Winchester College.

[16] For example the Rootes building at Warwick University.

[17] We were told that the Burma Road was named by students who had been Japanese Prisoners of War, See Interview 23, Stage 3 (1953-1965).

[18] Interview 3, Stage 2 (1962-1965).

[19] Interview 7, Stage 2 (1963-1966).

[20] Interview 13, Stage 2 (1963-1966).

[21] Interview 19, Stage 2 (1977-1981).

[22] Interview 9, Stage 1 (1975-1979).

[23] This student was talking of the Student Union built in the 1960s, not the new Building which graces the entrance to the University in 2013.

[24] Interview 7, Stage 1 (1989-1992).

[25] Interview 8, Stage 3 (1969-1998).

[26] Interview 20, Stage 3 (1987-current).

[27] Interview 15, Stage 3 (1976-current).

[28] Interview 20, Stage 3 (1987-current).

[29] Lisa Hunter, Toni Rossi, Richard Tinning, Erin Flanagan and Doune Mcdonald, 'Professional Learning

Places and Spaces: The Staffroom as a Site of Beginning Teacher Induction and Transition', *Asia-Pacific Journal of Teacher Education* 39. 1 (2009): 33-46.

[30] Interview 17, Stage 3 (1973-2006).

[31] Lisa Hunter and others, 34.

[32] Interview 18, Stage 3 (1960-1967).

[33] Interview 1, Stage 3 (1962-1984).

[34] Tansy Jessop, Laura Gubby, and Angela Smith, 'Space Frontiers for New Pedagogies: A Tale of Constraints and Possibilities', *Studies in Higher Education* 37.2 (2012): 189-202.

[35] Andrew Cox, Tim Herrick, and Patrick Keating, 'Accommodations: Staff Identity and University Space', *Teaching in Higher Education* 17.6 (2012): 697-709.

[36] Cox, 'Accommodations', 698.

[37] Cox 'Accommodations', 699.

[38] Interview 13, Stage 2 (1963-1966).

[39] Interview 1, Stage 2 (1974-1978).

[40] Interview 16, Stage 3 (1993-2004).

[41] See Giles Pickford, 'Town Gown Relations', *Journal of Tertiary Educational Administration* 11.1 (1989): 201-210.

[42] Interview 6, Stage 2 (1963-1966), 'Winchester wasn't the place it is now. It was quite a depressed and tatty place'.

[43] Linda McDowell, 'Acts of Memory and Millennial Hopes and Anxieties: The Awkward Relationship between the Economic and the Cultural', *Social and Cultural Geography* 1.1 (2000): 15-24.

[44] Interview 9, Stage 2 (1964-1967). St Giles Hill is at the opposite end of the city to the main campus.

[45] Interview 19, Stage 2 (1977-1981).

[46] Interview 9, Stage 2 (1964-1967).

[47] Interview 8, Stage 2 (1956-1958).

[48] Higher Education Statistics Agency notes that the fall in applications to British universities is due to UK domiciled students and that there is an increase in applicants from Asia. See HESA, Non-UK Domicile

Students', *Products and Statistics*, HESA: htwww.hesa.ac.uk (accessed 20 July 2013).

[49] Interview 10, Stage 2 (1962-1965).

[50] Interview 20, Stage 3 (1987-current).

[51] Interview 17, Stage 2 (1999-2003).

[52] Robert Anderson, *British Universities, Past and Present* (London: Continuum, 2006), 183.

[53] Interview 1, Stage 2 (1974-1978).

[54] Interview 10, Stage 2 (1962-1965).

[55] Interview 13, Stage 2 (1963-1966).

[56] Interview 5, Stage 2 (1939-1946).

[57] Interview 8, Stage 1 (1969-1971).

[58] Interview 14, Stage 2 (1993-1996).

[59] Interview 14, Stage 2. The Wykeham Arms, located just outside the walls of Winchester College, is more usually frequented by Winchester residents and staff of Winchester College and therefore less attractive to undergraduates.

[60] Interview 6, Stage 2 (1963-1966).

[61] Interview 2, Stage 2 (1974-1978).

[62] Interview 7, Stage 2 (1963-1966).

[63] Interview 13, Stage 2 (1963-1966).

[64] Interview 3, Stage 2 (1962-1965).

[65] See the entry for the University on the SI-UK Education Council's website (SI-UK, *The University of Winchester*, SI-UK: www.studyin-uk.com).

[66] Gifford, 'Town and Gown', 201. While Gifford's remarks were originally made with reference to the Australian experience, his overall conclusion demonstrates the importance of finding ways to explore how this relationship changes across time. Oral history provides one such insight.

6.

GENDER AND 'THE CULTURE OF CARE'

> In the second year we had the proposal that those dreaded of all people, women, were going to come to the College. As you know we were involved in the three-legged walk to Bargate in Southampton and it was such an unusual thing that it quite hit the press headlines, much to our amazement [. . .] But we were really quite upset at the thought that the special sort of feeling one had in college with all the chaps together sort of thing was going to be spoilt by these 'dreaded women' coming and changing everything.[1]

Introduction

In this chapter we explore whether the advent of women into the institution did 'spoil' the sense of community that had previously been seen as created by the notion of 'all the chaps together'. Although the statement above made by a student alumnus ended in laughter at the memory of the protest march against the advent of women students, and a rueful acknowledgement that the arrival of women was ultimately 'all for the benefit', it does reflect the anxiety that was felt over the arrival of women students into the College in 1960. King Alfred's was not alone as the 1960s and '70s saw coeducation, usually, but not always, in terms of women joining male institutions sweeping across the higher education sector. Oxford and Cambridge men's colleges began to admit women from 1972 and the change was largely complete by 1988.[2]

We also draw on Joan Scott's much rehearsed observation that 'gender is a signifier of power'.[3] The all-male power structure of King Alfred's was under threat once women joined the institution and it may have been concern over this loss of power that worried male staff and students as much as the potential loss of any camaraderie. The very fact that the community was all male had been seen as a bonding mechanism, cemented from the late 1940s by the inclusion of those students who had completed two years' National Service. However, the advent of women could also have been expected to soften the more austere aspects of that community. Once we begin to examine the complex construction of gender as social behaviour expected of a sexed body we can gain insight into the nuanced way that such assumptions are driven by social conventions of femininity bound by historical context. In turn this highlights just how significant was women's increased participation as students and as staff in higher education in the second half of the twentieth century for understanding wider changes in attitudes to employment and family policy and practice.

In a single-sex institution it is all too easy to overlook the social constructions of masculinity or femininity at work. The respondent whom we quote at the beginning of this chapter assumes that the interviewer will understand what he means by a masculinity represented by 'all chaps together' and confirms Scott's emphasis on gender as a relational concept. Masculinity is just as complex a mix between physiological and socially imposed factors as femininity. The arrival of women was going to 'change everything' implicitly because women were seen as everything that men were not. The performance of masculinity described both before and after the arrival of women is one that R.W. Connell recognised as 'hegemonic' in 1982.[4] Connell's theory, which sought to explore the socially constructed nature of male behaviour, defined as masculinity, suggested that at any one time there is an agreed model of dominant masculinity within a society. In addition there are other constructions of masculinity, which may be accepted but remain marginalised, for example that of gay masculinity. Connell argued that the recognised form of hegemonic masculinity in the mid to late twentieth century was overtly heterosexual, physically powerful and effortlessly successful. In Connell's model all forms of masculinity dominate all forms of femininity. Our respondent at the start of this chapter implicitly confirms the dominance of, and the wish to maintain, such a model. It should be noted that even though Connell's model is flexible, and what is today's hegemonic masculinity might not be that of tomorrow, his theory has been challenged. Michael Moller for example argues, based on Susan Bordo's work, that Connell's model is persuasive. It can be recognised at work in a range of settings, but he suggests that it equally might be possible to consider masculinity as vulnerable, and its performance as a protection from that vulnerability rather than a manifestation of dominance. Eric Anderson notes that there is now a move to what he terms a more 'inclusive' masculinity.[5] In our interviews we have recognised descriptions that might be understood through either Connell's or Moller's perspectives, but either way it became clear that gender as an organising concept played a large part in the formation and development of the Winchester community. This emphasis on the performance of gender roles amongst students as representative of wider change was not restricted to Winchester but has been identified as also evident in larger institutions such as the University of Liverpool.[6]

In parallel to this we also focus on the development of primary teacher education within the institution, given its primacy at the time when women were first admitted and its being a factor in the change in the ratio of female students to male at the institution. We also link this to the long association of women with the care and teaching of young children, and explore this concept of 'care' that is frequently recognised as both part of the primary teacher's role and a natural female characteristic. We reflect on the multifaceted nature of care including 'care over' and well as 'care for' drawing on the work of feminist philosopher Nel Noddings and educationist Jennifer Nias. Extracts from interviews enable us to trace the subtle changes in the way that gender brought about alterations in the institution but also helped to maintain aspects of a Gemeinschaft community at a time when wider policy changes made a move towards a more Gesellschaft institution inevitable.

In 1967 the *Plowden Report, Children and their Primary Schools*, was published, recommending changes in primary pedagogy to a more child-centred progressive theory and practice. Following the general trend to secondary comprehensivisation, primary schools were released from the onus of spending time preparing pupils to take the Eleven Plus exam. In the early 1960s King Alfred's' primary teaching course was ahead of most colleges' and already promoting teaching methods endorsed by Plowden:

> We were talking about things like working in sets and integrated days and project work and all sorts of topics and it was just something that seemed to capture the essence of the time in the early '60s and seemed to be the way in which we should be going.[7]

As we have noted, women have long been associated with the care and teaching of young children and the Plowden era, building as it did on a more holistic view of the education of the young child, also enabled educationists to revisit the assumption that women were 'naturally' suited to be primary teachers given their capacity for nurture and care of the very young.[8] Alongside this, while primary teaching may appear to be particularly attractive to women, the move to a progressive pedagogy did not mean a move away from professionalisation and recognised that children up to the age of ten required more than substitute mothering during the school day. Once the doors were opened to women, King Alfred's may therefore have been particularly attractive to those considering primary teaching, increasingly seen as a female occupation, but also one which required specialist training. Over the same period provision of training of secondary teachers declined at King Alfred's as teaching moved to a graduate profession and the two year Certificate of Education, seen as preparation for teaching in Secondary Modern schools, was phased out. The consequent growth in primary provision is likely to have attracted more young women to the College. The ratio of women to men increased rapidly so that fears that women were going to 'take-over' the institution were well founded. Alongside the increase in women students, the 1960s saw the advent of more lecturing appointments for women including Jennifer Nias, whose work informs this chapter, and the first woman vice-principal, Robina Macintyre, also discussed later.

In drawing on and extending Nias's discussion of primary teaching as a culture of care we suggest that the notion of teaching in higher education can also be understood within this discourse. This is especially appropriate for those who taught in an institution such as King Alfred's, given its long legacy of preparing its students to work in the elementary or primary sector. Shortly after leaving King Alfred's, Nias wrote a reflection on the role of the Church colleges in general and observed, 'One of the most striking features of colleges of education is the tenacity with which they have clung throughout expansion and modification to their peculiar institutional values'.[9] One of those values is a concern for individual well-being. Across the period alumni praised the care shown to students by the staff, and on the whole the staff also commented on the collegiate working environment.[10] Even as a male institution the ethos of the institution built on the idea of a Christian family, itself a gendered concept. Caring is central to our understanding of a family and indeed the phrase 'culture of care' was used by one of our respondents in the earlier phases of the project reflecting on how they felt nurtured and part of a strong Christian community.

Nias discusses the nuanced meanings of care, developing Nel Noddings' observation that when she started her work on caring she was not aware of the gendered nature of the term. The creation of a caring community at Winchester derived from Christian principles may have justified the approach to elementary and primary teaching at a time when the student body was exclusively male. This would have enabled a distance to be created from the physical aspects of caring more usually associated with women, specifically mothers. Noddings observes pertinently 'It seems to me quite natural that men, many of whom are separated from the intimacy of caring, should create gods and seek security and love in worship'.[11] We might expect an educational community to be, by its very nature, a 'caring community' but unless we understand exactly what that implies it becomes a somewhat empty term. It is more productive, and perhaps more helpful to our understanding of what drives the development of such communities, to explore which aspects of care are dominant at any one time. Nias identified six meanings of care, several of which are in tension with each other. She argues that such tensions are useful in that they highlight the complex 'educational significance of the beliefs and values which lie at the heart of particular cultures'.[12] In the extract below one of our respondents uses the concept of care to reflect on whether it was the fact of being a Christian college that created the ethos of the institution. Although they use an analogy of care in the institution with one of the primary teacher for their children it is not articulated as an exact parallel, allowing for some flexibility in our interpretation of the nature and origin of care within the institution itself:

> I think, but I don't know, but I think that possibly the care that's evident in that institution came from its established cultural patterns just as much as it did

> from people, active Christians saying this is what we ought to do, I think it's kind of unquestioned in the same way that primary school teachers would feel they had to care for their children.[13]

Nias explains that three of her understandings of care are derived from feminist relational theorists such as Noddings. Two she argues explain 'care' as social conditioning identifiable in socio-historical roots and the last 'stresses personal investment and self-esteem'.[14] Nias comments that for teachers, from Augustine onwards, 'their relationship with individual learners lies at the heart of what they do',[15] reflecting her expectations for teaching in the training colleges as much as in the primary classroom itself. The socio-historical roots of teacher education at Winchester offer an insight into how wider changes may have their origins in the move from an all-male community to a predominantly female one. This was at a time when wider society has been seen as moving from a Gemeinschaft to what might be seen as a less caring, more individualistic Gesellschaft community.

The move to a more individualistic society has also seen an increase in single female-headed households which has in turn led to concerns that many young boys lack a male role model. This has led to a public demand for more male primary teachers to provide this model of masculinity which again extends the caring professional role of the primary teacher beyond that of delivering an academic curriculum. It appears that primary teachers are expected to perform, and implicitly teach, the gender roles of wider society to their young pupils. It seems that the professional identity of the primary teacher includes a public performance of their gender role which for men should include some, but not all, aspects of hegemonic masculinity recognised by Connell. [16] This becomes increasingly difficult if we recognise, in line with Eric Anderson, that multiple models of masculinity are now accepted within wider society.[17] Whatever model they offer it seems that this aspect of care for their pupils, which extends beyond formal teaching hours, is still central to the role of the primary teacher. Nias notes that the expectation of care for their pupils beyond formal contact hours is one of the tensions inherent in primary teaching as a culture of care. She was similarly committed to her students following Noddings' injunction that becoming a teacher means entering a 'very special relation'.[18] Nias's former pupils at King Alfred's remembered her entertaining them socially in order to get to know them, and each other, better.[19]

The next two sections of this chapter explore the way that gender was used by our respondents to explain how they saw the community 'before' and 'after' the advent of women in the 1960s. The final section considers the reflections of women who worked at Winchester as lecturers and administrators. We argue that the alumni voices show remarkably little change over more than sixty years in their overall impression of a caring community where staff and students alike, as we have noted in Chapter 3, 'looked out for each other'. The change from a single sex to a coeducational institution served to re-emphasise some of the characteristics associated with a Gemeinschaft society, as well as generating an awareness that an institution such as King Alfred's had to engage with wider changes to survive, and embrace the progress towards a Gesellschaft view of the role and purpose of higher education.

The monastic community

'He liked it to be a men's college with services every Sunday morning'.[20] This statement on the attitude of the Principal of King Alfred's College in the late 1950s reflects the relationship between gender and religious practice at Winchester prior to 1960. Even before the arrival of women, the College drew on gender constructions in the performance of masculinity as part of its daily routine. The idea of a 'monastic community' was also embedded within the College traditions which sought to emulate the model of the Oxbridge colleges or the elite public schools.[21] Once women students and female academics arrived at King Alfred's it was feared that many traditions would be lost, even though these activities were not in themselves exclusive to men but signalled a single-sex community where camaraderie, discipline and loyalty, all of which can also be interpreted as aspects of care, were identified as part of this male ethos.[22]

What became clear in our interviews was that, although the fears about women 'taking over' were to a great extent confirmed in terms of the number of women present on campus, the arrival of female students does not seem to have altered the overall ethos observed in the quote which begins this chapter. Traditions which seemed so central to a single-sex college, and which were perhaps also under siege in larger universities, changed with the move to coeducation, but are more likely to have been compromised by the rise in student numbers than by the change in the gender ratio.

The most vocal objection to the inclusion of women came from the students. As noted in Chapter 3 the 'manliness' of the student body in the 1950s was confirmed by the large number of National Servicemen who arrived for training having completed their military time. Although some of them might not have been further than a quiet backwater of Scotland others would have seen active service in Korea, Malaya, Cyprus and Suez:

> I think most if not all of us had just done our National Service. There was a feeling of camaraderie within the group itself so that I think we had a feeling that we owed something to others besides ourselves. So we went out and did things within the community and within the College…I knew one person who I actually served with in the army. He was an officer and I was in the ranks, but we became the best of pals and actually we were inseparable and

> we seemed to go around together. But although we didn't as a body know one another I think we had this feeling that we were all in the same boat and we'd all experienced life in the Army, Navy or Air Force and basically took it from there. We had a common starting ground really.[23]

Settling into college life for these ex-servicemen, with all the restrictions on student behaviour, must have been irksome although of course in many ways college rules may simply have replaced the discipline of Service life. In this example we can see the hierarchy of care at work; the student notes the change in relationship as he and a previous superior officer 'became pals', but there is also the aspect of care which is manifested within the statement 'we owed something to others', a reflection on the Gemeinschaft nature of the community at that time. As one of the principal's secretaries remarked:

> They were all coming in at the age of about 20+, some of them having served in Korea, Germany, Malaysia, all over the world, and they'd gone straight from school into doing this. So when they came here, they were very disciplined ... I know the staff always used to say ... oh their bedrooms are so easy, they've all made their beds as though the Sergeant's going to come in.[24]

The students came from a wide range of social and regional backgrounds but the common cause of a teaching career enabled them to bond and to cross class boundaries. However, crossing gender boundaries was a step too far:

The First Mini-Skirt
'I remember the first mini skirt I had - my mother bought me in Brighton, and I remember wearing it.'

'You get a group of men together, whether they're fighting a war or playing a game of cricket, they all watch out for each other, whatever their personal likes or dislikes'.[25]

The prospect of the presence of much younger women, who had not had to complete two years in the Services, could not fail to compromise the male club atmosphere of a small teacher training college. Fears about the changing gender balance in higher education were not restricted to King Alfred's. Carol Dyhouse has emphasised the concerns voiced by male colleges beyond Winchester that the arrival of young women would diminish their status.[26] They also worried that any increased link between teacher training and femininity might lead to a reduction in the status of teaching, especially at primary level. While male teachers might have been preferred within the wider age range served by the working-class elementary schools, once the 1944 Act brought in the primary/secondary divide at eleven the very nature of primary teaching demanded what were seen as more feminine characteristics. Distrust of the caring/mother substitute role performed by women as primary teachers had been voiced as early as 1927 in the National Association of Schoolmasters' misogynistic pamphlet *Making Our Boys Effeminate.*[27] By the 1950s, demands for equal pay for men and women teachers were hotly debated within the 'Joint Four' especially within the Association of Assistant Mistresses who were equally damning of the assumed link between care as teaching and care as mothering. The Association, representing many single teachers who had a lifelong commitment to their profession, was very reluctant to agree to the recruitment of married women back into the profession on a part-time basis, feeling that this might compromise the Association's ability to claim equal professional status with the Association of Schoolmasters.[28]

The dedicated vocational nature of teaching which had been championed at King Alfred's since its inception was not a model that allowed for the inclusion of girls who might view their teaching role as a temporary occupation before marriage, to be returned to part-time after time out for raising a family. Kelsall, Poole and Kuhn present a convincing case that for girls in the 1950s and '60s entry to higher education increased their prospects of a lucrative marriage quite as much as it provided them with the means to earn their own living.[29] Students arrived from predominantly exclusively male spaces of National Service or single sex schools.[30] One of our interviewees for the second stage of the project explained:

> It was the whole being of the place. Not having experienced a mixed campus I can't really comment on that, but certainly from our point of view we were

> all lads together, so this was another thing that held us together, besides having served our bit for two years.[31]

R.R. Dale's research in the 1960s identified similar comments by those favouring single sex schooling; he quoted one teacher's reflection on, 'The good atmosphere of boys enjoying life together. Girl friends were always out of school and much more forgotten during working hours'.[32] However, Dale's conclusion came down firmly in favour of coeducation: 'it would seem wise to enable the two sexes to grow up together, so that they might get to know each other's outlook' suggesting that the changes at King Alfred's were part of a wider change in society's expectations for education as preparation for adulthood.[33] Nonetheless, assumptions of natural female and male roles in the teaching profession were deeply embedded. In a letter to the project an alumnus noted 'women did a good job [but] men were needed to keep a good discipline on the young males [in the classroom]'.[34]

Concern at the possible arrival of women generated a student protest in the form of the three-legged race, noted at the beginning of this chapter, between Westgate, Winchester and the Bargate, Southampton, a distance of about 12 miles. They carried banners proclaiming 'No Women Please' and 'Why This? Keep King Alfred's as it is. Clean Living'. We have suggested elsewhere that perhaps this student protest should not be taken too much at face value although it was not an isolated incident. *The Wintonian*, the student newspaper, used equally heavy humour when discussing the advent of women:

> A lady asked me recently what views I held about the forthcoming invasion of this College by one hundred and fifty females.
> 'Well', I replied, 'they're coming, so we may as well make the most if it - academically that is!' So armed

> with this opinion, and firmly convinced that 90 per cent of the students would think similarly, I started some personal investigations.
>
> The horrifying results of these investigations left me shaking with terror at the thought of so many hard-hearted soulless male animals! Gentlemen! How can you say these awful things about our future female associates! You do not want women (ladies, I mean) at King Alfred's? I am amazed at the apathy! Just think, gentlemen. Morning porridge will have a new scintillating effect upon you; you will discover hidden beauties in your sausage and mash when a slender white hand places the steaming dish in front of you. Will you sleep during lectures? I fancy not when you are sitting next to the nearest thing to Brigitte Bardot since Roger Vadim! No longer will the sheer fascination of your subject and lecturer keep you awake: other things will assist. No longer will the familiar 'We hate KAC' notices adorn the college walls after dissolute bands of female adventurers have departed from a Christmas Ball. Christmas, Easter - all year round will hold pleasure in store for all. Geographical field trips (official and otherwise) will be a delight; history will spring to life; madrigal groups will abound; Health Education lectures will be cancelled; sporting interests will double.
>
> Life will begin again for the College. Maybe Winchester will be overcrowded, maybe the Chaplain will have his work cut out with marriage ceremonies; nevertheless gentlemen let us welcome the advent of a mixed King Alfred's College.[35]

The issue of coeducation was not a nine-day wonder, as a year later the outgoing president of the Students' Union wrote of his concerns, with less humour, again in *The Wintonian*:

> Gone will be the monastic flavour of the life of preceding generations of students. In its place will reign a life in which the opposite sex will figure in ever increasing numbers... Years of tradition have passed, and a new era is beginning. Co-education has reached the hallowed domain of the College, a sacred retreat for men over the past hundred years.[36]

Although there is an element of 'tongue-in-cheek' in these reflections there is also an undercurrent of unease at the changing character of King Alfred's. The secular/sacred dichotomy where the sacred is signified by the male and the secular by the female is striking and suggests a very real concern at the change that female students represented, although the discourse of 'family' had been employed in earlier times to describe the all-male college where the most significant female figure was the matron in charge of all things domestic.[37] The notion of a monastic community was used both for and against coeducation and was clearly a metaphor in common use. Dyhouse has noted that by 1970 the JCRs in Oxford were using it as part of their campaign for accepting women: 'Exponents deplored what they saw as unnatural, unhealthy, unbalanced "monastic/army camp atmosphere" of the all-male college'.[38] It may have been that the Winchester students knew that the decision had already been taken; it is of course impossible to get an accurate insight into how the students who took part in the protest really felt at the time about the proposed change. Mediated through both the vagaries of time and the benefit of hindsight that the College did not collapse into an immoral heap once women arrived, oral accounts are to be viewed with caution.

Women students arrive

The first set of interviews for this project specifically addressed the theme of gender as an organising concept in discussing the alumnae experience of life in Winchester. This demonstrates the power and the responsibility attached to the oral historian in framing interview questions. While recognising the role that we played in directing the focus of interviews, our respondents did not offer any comments that they felt we were over-emphasising the role that the changing gender ratio played in the development of the college community. In the previous section we emphasised the rhetoric of the 'monastic community' prior to 1960. Although they may not have welcomed female students onto the campus our interviews confirmed that the monastic community referred only to the all-male living and working space. When it came to socialising there were 'three main sources' of women: the hospital 'Nightingales'; Salisbury St Michael Training College; and Chichester, Bishop Otter.[39] Rules were there to be circumvented but in the regulations 'lady friends' had to be out of rooms by 10.00 pm.

The 1960s was an interesting decade in terms of the adult status of the student population across the country. Until the lowering of the age of majority in 1969 the College acted in loco parentis, charged with policing student morals and social behaviour, a serious responsibility when pregnancy outside marriage was unacceptable.[40] This was especially relevant to the reputation of King Alfred's as one of the Church colleges where student morals might be expected to conform to well-established standards. One of our respondents reflected how, in most cases, the authorities need not have worried: fear of being found out was a strong deterrent in itself:

> So strangely enough, when we went back for forty years (reunion), perhaps it was ever thus, but you always have the impression that everybody else is experimenting a lot more than you were prepared to, but in fact it wasn't the truth. Most of the women I spoke to had gone to the College virgins and left in the same state. We were all terrified of getting chucked out and having to go home. [41]

While students may have recognised the care of friends for each other, those in authority had to view care very much in terms of looking after those who were placed 'in' their care. Additionally they were charged with caring 'for' the College's reputation, highlighting the complexity of the apparently unproblematic 'culture of care' observed by our respondent.

The headache of policing the sexual activities of students prior to 1969 was not limited to King Alfred's or indeed the Church colleges. As the move to coeducation gained pace Dyhouse notes how institutions sought advice from each other. The warden of Crombie Hall in Aberdeen for example was 'deluged' by requests for advice. He observed that there had in fact been less 'horseplay' once women had arrived 'if there was some loss of "male camaraderie"', he confessed, 'there were much better opportunities for Scottish country dancing'.[42] When we interviewed one of the earliest female students we asked her whether she remembered the College authorities monitoring sexual behaviour. She confirmed that this was indeed the case:

> The girls had to leave, absolutely no question about it. They left, one of them I know has done very well since she left - the one who was pregnant actually married the man involved who did stay at the College but was severely chastised and I think it was only because his Finals were coming up, that he in fact was allowed to stay but I have the feeling things were just as hard for him as they were for the girl involved but clearly she couldn't stay because it was going to set a bad example (laughs) whereas it didn't show with him...but yes both suffered over the whole business, yes. And the other one who was caught in bed, she had to leave and the man was an outsider anyway.[43]

We also asked this student whether she had been aware of the animosity towards the inclusion of women in the community or whether she was told of the protest three-legged race, as the overall narrative reading of her interview reflected a very positive and enjoyable college experience. She dismissed what has become one of the much rehearsed events of King Alfred's history:

> We did hear that there had been some protest march or something, but I didn't know it to begin with and I certainly had absolutely no nasty incidents with men who appeared not to want us. I didn't see anything happening; I didn't see men avoiding women. I didn't see any signs of hostility whatsoever from that second year, as it would have been, because that year only stayed two years, it was us started to stay three years. I had no nasty feelings, experienced absolutely nothing about animosity. I think that if they didn't want us, they soon got round to the idea that it was, it was OK because some of those who were supposed to have been most against women were the ones who took up with women most readily and most quickly. [44]

Carol Dyhouse suggests that the new universities of the 1960s were particularly attractive to women students with broader curricula and 'no tradition of gender segregation or discrimination against female students'. Photographs of this new generation of university students were used as publicity, using gender as a representation of 'the new'. Dyhouse cites a photograph used at Sussex University of 'three long-haired girls with high boots and even higher hemlines descending steps near the library.'[45] Once women were admitted to King Alfred's they also featured strongly in the prospectus, often against the background of the original main building demonstrating the meeting of the old with the new. Alternatively publicity focused on the new student union with groups of young men and women relaxing between lectures or sitting together in the open air.

The well-established strong sporting tradition of the male community continued once women arrived at the College, at a time when most students stayed on campus for their leisure as well as for studying. For many female students sport became an important part of college life, as this student from 1964 reflected when asked about her sporting activities:

> Just everything! Tennis, squash, badminton, I've forgotten now, table tennis, anything that was sporty, ladies' football. I was a hockey supporter, I didn't play, my main winter sport had been lacrosse, netball. All those things. Did lots because there was the big PE department there for the men. So there was a huge focus on PE and that just suited me down to the ground. So you had teams and all your fun games and whatever. So it was brilliant.[46]

This respondent clearly enjoyed the change from an all girls' school to an environment where women were outnumbered by the men. In her interview she reflected on the close friendships that arose and the underlying assumptions about future gender roles that were embedded in the social and working life of the College:

> [My friend] reminded me that I had to do some physics at one time, which was way beyond my mental capacity, so in exchange, he did my physics homework for me and I ironed his shirts, so we were all very happy in our modest little way (laughs). I honestly can say there was never any problem with male/female thing at all. Everybody mucked in, you know. I was doing the pure infant education course and I am sure there were far more, that was much more a female based group, but in my music course, and in other areas we had to do, it was all mixed up and there were far more men than women in the

College, although a huge number of those were attached to the PE course. It was 3:1, three men to one woman which is why I chose the College (laughs) I had been to a girls' school and it was brilliant because there was just crate loads of social life and we just had a wonderful time. We really did. Brilliant![47]

Studying and Leisure on Campus
'Once women arrived at the College, most students stayed on campus for their leisure as well as for studying.'

By 1967 the gender balance was more even and the women's narratives reflected on some of the traits that Connell identified within hegemonic masculinity. For example, in terms of the work ethos, one female student noted: 'They were typical Beatle look-alikes with long hair and moustaches and wonderful lovely blokes, super blokes but couldn't be bothered to do anything to get work in on time'.[48] This alumna eventually met her husband through the College. Her choice of words in describing her social life is interesting, she is clearly aware of the tension between judging her contemporaries' behavior by the standards of the day and according to today's expectations 'There were one or two who had boyfriends and stayed with them but most of us were very promiscuous, promiscuous is the wrong word because we didn't do "that sort of thing" but we had lots of boyfriends, lots of boyfriends'.[49] She observed a clear gender divide within the courses 'most of my seminar groups were in age-related [i.e. groups that were arranged according to the intended pupil age group] and I was 4-8 and we didn't have any men'. She added the by now familiar comment on the sporty men 'I am afraid the PE group got blamed for all sorts of things. Some of them were very pleasant really'.[50] Within the interviews the 'PE lads' were frequently used to describe the male students who were clearly not caring in their attitude towards their female contemporaries. The performance of masculinity sought to confirm a gender hierarchy based on physical strength and overt heterosexuality.

Having been so concerned at the future disruption of their monastic life many respondents commented on how the sports specialists displayed their heterosexual identities as the number of women students increased exponentially. This seems to have caused amusement rather than irritation amongst the women:

> The men became far better known for good or bad reasons (laughs). There was, there was a sense that the blokes could get away with murder almost because in the social life side because there was a huge, huge pool of women to choose from and the blokes were fought over to some extent. The kind of very high profile, high profile teams like the Football, the Rugby and the Hockey, everybody knew the guys out of those teams and because there weren't many guys going into the teams so the ones who did choose to were very well known, very popular…the

> guys were elevated in their status ...it's safe to say! (laughs).[51]

We asked this respondent if she agreed with a previous reflection that the male students were not interested in non-sexual relationships with the women students. Again her response indicates that the traditional male culture of drinking and sport was asserted within an increasingly female environment:

> I think there was a point made that guys who started off as nice guys here didn't last very long because they suddenly realised there were plenty, plenty of women to pick from and that wasn't always the case but certainly I think a lot of blokes who would, if they'd been in a more gender, more an equal gender split scenario wouldn't have behaved and wouldn't have got away with behaving in the way they did (laughs). Because far more women [were] vying for their attention.[52]

The culture shock of coming from single-sex schools into a coeducational community was not limited to the male students. A woman who had been at the College between 1979 and 1982 commented 'I think my first experience of coming to college was the fact that it was a mixed college. I had come from an all girls' school, a convent school, and so actually coming into a mixed hall of residence was unusual and quite a new experience for me'.[53] Her reflection offers us an interesting insight into how a culture of care can also be seen as a performance of gender, that is, care is manifested differently by men and women but in relation to each other. She went into a mixed hall and spoke of the camaraderie that built up between the male and female students, free from sexual undertones. Her comment about the gendered division of labour in mixed halls, even in the 1980s, was not uncommon: 'because it was a mixed hostel as well, the men at the time were quite happy to walk the girls home if they wanted to at the end of the evening um or you know help them with shopping or whatever. And we helped them with their washing (laughter) No...nothing changes really (laughter)'.[54]

The alumnae interviews reflect the changing values in society and changing expectations of student life over the last sixty years. For these women students their college years occupied only three years of their life, in the brief period of independence between school, career, and marriage. We might argue that their comments reflect changing youth culture generally quite as much as they relate to the 'Winchester experience'. Apart from the overt antics of the PE boys the alumnae were not aware even at first that women were not a welcome part of the student body, although in happily taking on traditional female caring roles such as doing washing and ironing for their male peers they seem to have confirmed rather than challenged the gendered status quo. The first women students may have contributed to the maintenance of some Gemeinschaft characteristics of the institution at a time of change, however as women became more prevalent on the staff we can see gender acting as a signifier of changing power dynamics within a community that may have been seen as caring but was also having to manage the changing nature of higher education in a wider context.

Women on the staff

We were told that in 1953 the female staff consisted of a newly appointed principal's secretary, a matron and her sister, two part-time lecturers, and three cooks.[55] Changes in the staff gender ratio have been as dramatic as changes in the student population. Although the ratio of male to female lecturers is not as unbalanced as in the student population, in 2013 the Chancellor, Vice Chancellor, Senior Pro-Vice-Chancellor and two Faculty Deans are women. One of the characteristics of both lecturing and administrative staff at Winchester is that they have tended to remain in the institution for a number of years. Unlike the students their reflections include their middle-age and the years approaching their retirement as well as the days of their youth. Inequalities due to assumptions over gender roles were less likely to be laughed off, and it is fair to conclude that it took longer for women lecturers to be fully accepted into the institution than the students. Secretarial and administrative work was a well-established female occupation: women employed in this capacity reflected on the gendered dynamics of a predominantly male workforce but unsurprisingly did not comment on any discriminatory behaviour. The nature of their role did not challenge accepted gender boundaries: 'Yes, I suppose half the time I've been a PA, and what makes a PA, the ability to think ahead and to smooth the path of the person you're working for in whatever way that is necessary'.[56] Neither did they challenge the gendered hierarchy of the institution: 'Well, the academics were here and we were ... there. Quite a long way down there'.[57]

Reflecting this hierarchy, the secretarial members of staff were initially not allowed into the Senior Common Room and although this was put down to the role they performed, their sex may well have contributed to their exclusion. Indeed the Senior Common Room provided the backdrop for several comments about day-to-day attitudes to female lecturing staff as well. Discrimination can be quite subtle as the following quote demonstrates:

> Oh quite a serious effect, a lot of the original members of staff were really quite resentful of the change particularly with the coming of the women. I mean there was a feeling in the Senior Common Room.[58]

In terms of recruitment and career advancement in the early days there were worries about tokenism and also a number of reported incidents which hinted at entrenched sexist attitudes by the older staff which emphatically did not reflect any sense of a caring community. Using voice-relational analysis to consider these transcripts it is useful to reflect on the way in which these comments were framed in relation to wider events. Many of the narratives were recalled in terms of reported incidents and this leaves open the question of the extent to which they have been composed and refined over a space of time. It is worth taking a little time to analyse in more detail the way that the member of staff quoted above continued her narrative. We already know that she was of the opinion that there was a feeling of resentment against women, but initially simply describes this as a 'feeling'. She continued:

> Well I can tell you the Head of Department that I worked for took on a young, very intelligent young woman and before she knew what had happened he had turned around and said, "do my marking for me", and she was wise enough to say, "no, I won't do it, that's your job". It was that sort of a problem.

This incident, which would have taken just a couple of minutes in real time, becomes an exemplar of a more deeply perceived problem. It was a reported incident; unless of course the 'she' in question was the respondent herself and she chose in the interview to distance herself from the narrative. Then the interviewee takes on the role of the researcher and analyses the incident for us:

> Well gradually, but there was just a sort of hanging on feeling that while those older men were there, there was still that feeling that they still resented the change, not in an unpleasant way but you were aware of the fact that they were feeling it.

Again, the respondent talks in terms of 'feeling' without any real evidence and the reported incident finally becomes a vehicle for explaining change:

> Well I think it gave them a sense of insecurity but there really was no fear of that really. You see if you're in a college where it's a small community and in that case all men, and then suddenly you import a lot of young women and start expanding the premises, and start expanding the numbers of students and so on, and the staff, and developing different ways of working, I think somebody who has, who thinks themselves as well-established and in a very small community does feel insecure.

In the space of a very short time, the respondent uses gender as the focus for an explanation of an incident that effectively describes the initial marginalisation of women in the community. This then changed to a narrative of the successful challenge that women and the new order brought to the old-fashioned and out-dated ways of the male community of the 1950s, taking forward rather than softening, the move to a Gesellschaft institution. At the end of this section of the interview an additional sense of frustration comes into the narrative; that of a hierarchy of status attached to previous experience. Gender begins to intersect with class (as represented by an Oxbridge degree). She concludes:

> I once raised this with the Principal and he said I was talking nonsense because look at the people who had been promoted in the College who were women but he didn't quite get the message. I mean I told you about the young member of staff who was asked to do the marking, there was always this feeling that the men, particularly the men from Oxford had priority, if you watched the promotions, Oxford had a priority, there was a feeling against women there, I'm convinced of it.[59]

Gender becomes a powerful signifier of difference that extends beyond the traditionally accepted division of labour.

A member of staff from 1975 was less concerned at the inequality of opportunity but did refer briefly to possible tokenism during a period of change:

> I suppose it was at the level, "Oh yes or you know let's have a woman doing this job," and I suppose … probably some of the first women who got top jobs…might have thought, "Oh I wonder if I got it because I was a woman," you know. They just wanted to see a woman in a particular job, whereas obviously you'd hope as things went on that it would be that people got a job because they were going to be good at doing it you know, regardless of who they were. But I suspect, you know, there's bound to be a bit of tokenism just to start with, to sort of please, you know, all sorts of people including governments, statisticians.[60]

We had heard some comments about a women's group amongst the staff that had been established, but detail of its activities proved elusive either in archival research, the questionnaires or in the interviews, indicating how easily day-to-day activities disappear from the historical record. One long serving member of staff remembered it in more detail after observing that when she arrived from a larger institution, 'Winchester had a sort of old boys' cosiness about the institution I thought which was a bit 1920s … it had that, you know, hangover feel of not really being in the 20th century'.[61] She described the women's group as dealing with rather 'trivial' issues and was rather vague about its purpose. Eventually she told us that the group collapsed in the early 1990s over the proposed introduction of a cross faculty/school gender studies programme. The respondent hinted that there was opposition to the proposals that did not come from senior management, but would not be drawn as to the extent of the opposition.

Another interviewee noted that the group was very informal although she described herself as 'the convenor', 'we weren't just political we used to invite women writers and women in public life to come and give us talks and things'. However there was an awkward moment when the Vice-Principal completed a questionnaire that had been sent from Chester College about the role of women staff:

> I went and tackled him about it. He was annoyed with me. I was seen as a stirrer (laughs) and I didn't see myself as that at all really, but I did feel that we were not informed about this but we did have a view…So we were very angry about it and they were angry with us and it was a bit of an interesting dramatic moment (laughs) but you see that was the kind of thing that we were concerned about really.[62]

The interviews seem to suggest that the introduction of female academic staff onto the campus took longer to be part of accepted everyday life than the arrival of women students. However the tensions are related as isolated incidents of irritation within a community that was largely supportive, welcoming and prepared to take on the gender changes in the workplace, albeit at times with a reluctance to abandon the gentlemen's clubbiness of the previous era.

Joan Scott has noted that women's history itself has evolved through a number of stages including the introduction and promotion of 'women worthies' into the historical record. This quickly extended to recognition that their significance is not just in their addition to the record ('add women and stir') but how they change the record itself. Earlier in this chapter we discussed the contribution that Jennifer Nias made to King Alfred's while she was gaining the experience that informed much of her later research. Robina Macintyre, another woman worthy of note in the history of Winchester, came to King Alfred's much later in her career. She was appointed as the first female Vice-Principal of the College in 1960 when women students arrived. A short exploration of her career to that point offers an insight into how progressive methods, often associated with the culture of care identified by Nias, were introduced into the syllabus. Macintyre had previously been a Senior Lecturer at Homerton College, Cambridge and then Vice-Principal of Maria Assumpta Roman Catholic Training College in London. She took up her post there in 1946 just as the Montessori school attached to the college was re-opened after the war. Maria Assumpta had been the site of the first Montessori school and training course in England in 1921.[63] This link with Montessori may explain the reflection earlier in this chapter that King Alfred's was ahead of Plowden in its inclusion of progressive methods on its training course.

It does not seem to have been easy for Miss Macintyre or her ideas to be accepted into the male environment. Her force of character and the originality of her approach to her role were remarked upon by many of our respondents, both male and female, across all stages of the research. One retired member of staff whom we interviewed referred to her several times as a 'firebrand' and it must have been a challenging task to take on a high profile academic leadership role in such a male dominated institution. When she was appointed there were two Vice-Principals, but one member of staff described her as 'junior to him, she was second, she was always, never as important'.[64] He reported an incident where the students picked up her mini car and threw it into the bushes 'because she was a woman, they didn't want the women there'. Of course there might well be other interpretations of this event; it might have been part of a general student stunt as related by Dyhouse.[65] Miss Macintyre's reputation as somewhat subversive might also have encouraged the students to feel that she would be less likely to complain at being the centre of a rag than the more reactionary members of staff. This respondent concluded 'She was quite popular in the end but she was very wily'.[66] He did not elaborate on what she did to make him form that conclusion. However another respondent commented 'Oh well now Miss Macintyre really did have a rough passage, I mean she was very unpopular'. They continued 'she was a bit distant but she was very approachable. She was a character and she wouldn't stand any nonsense, and I think she probably stood up for herself'.[67]

Miss Robina Macintyre on the Drums
'Miss Macintyre was called onto the stage to play the drums, everyone cheered as she went up.'

Miss Macintyre's previous jobs included time as a journalist on *The Sunday Express.* Her features involved her spending time in a travelling circus, running a menagerie at a fair, and working in the notorious Mrs Meyrick's Night Clubs.[68] Her engagement in these activities as part of her journalistic role is usually missed out from accounts which simply suggest that she had a rather exciting curriculum vitae, without explaining that they were part of her employment as a reporter. There is also a photograph of her playing drums in the Student Union.[69] Firebrand or not, as the first female Vice-Principal at the time when women were admitted as students, Miss Macintyre might be seen as the representation of the new order.

Alongside such strong characters as Robina Macintyre and Jennifer Nias making their way in the male domain of the lecturing staff, women were present, and welcomed, as administrators. While lecturers tend to remain within one department the administrative staff moved around and changed jobs as they were needed. This enabled them to gain an insight into wider changes in the institution, and in interviews the reading for wider relationships provided a useful lens for analysis. In the following quote we can see how a well-established female administrator picked up and managed unforeseen problems, and articulated her narrative in terms of characteristics associated with women in terms of caring and nurture:

> We had some teachers come from Uganda and to study for a year. And they were delightful, the first two were men and well they had no idea what they were coming into at all, and no-one else really knew what they were coming into either because they were spending the week with us and the weekends with various people. They had a base in Winchester or surrounding but they had no money, so we had to provide that and we had to make arrangements for it to be … how it was to be paid you know to them and how they were going to eat in college and where they were going to be based and what their schedules were like because they had no idea about time.[70]

This respondent has enjoyed a number of roles within the institution and identified two ways in which it allowed women to participate more fully, either as a result of individual ability or the changing nature of course provision:

> Janet Trotter, she became Vice Chancellor of Gloucester … Gloucester and Cheltenham and I mean obviously really good and she came up through the ranks, as it were quite quickly, and then went on. So there were women with talent that did rise in the

> '80s, '90s but as a proportion of the total, they were probably quite a small percentage of people who headed anything [. . .] probably the beginning of [change] was when we had the School of Nursing and then we had the Director of Nursing was a woman, and it brought in a very female dominated subject. .. that was one of the times when women became as prominent in the subject more than men whereas almost all the other subjects were dominated by men, not all, Maths we had a Head of Maths [. . .] but I can't think of too many.[71]

We have digressed from the general to the particular in discussing details of individual women at Winchester. It does however highlight the way that gender acts as a significant aspect of change in one institution. Understanding the role that individuals play within wider change, such as the move from single-sex to coeducation, is difficult. Is it change that drives the appointment of strong personalities, or do those personalities enable change to be more rapid? Janet Trotter, Jennifer Nias and Robina Macintyre were each singled out by our respondents without any prompting from us and therefore it seemed appropriate to consider in more detail how these 'women worthies' contributed to a gendered perspective on change within the institution.

Conclusion

In this chapter we have focused on the role that the changing gender ratio has played within the college community at Winchester. Understood as the social role attached to a sexed body, concepts of gender help us to understand the way that 'caring', whether by the community, the faculty or the student body, remained significant within the interviews at all three stages of the project. Once we place the very meaning of care under the spotlight it becomes apparent that the gendered inflections that it carries enable us to explore why, or perhaps how, the alumni voice has consistently articulated the caring nature of an institution that has changed so substantially over sixty years.

In addition the discussion has highlighted the inflection of gender within so many areas of the corporate life of the College. The discourse of family as central to the formation of a community, with its specific gender roles, was overt even within the virtually all male environment of the post-war institution. The notion of the principal as a 'father figure' was highlighted in more than one interview from the early period. It would, however, be surprising to see the current Vice-Chancellor described as a 'mother-figure', and this apparent absurdity perhaps highlights how useful representations of gender are in exploring change within an institution.

Carol Dyhouse recognised how the increase and change in the provision of teacher training courses in universities in the 1960s contributed enormously to the rise in the number of women in higher education. In turn the increase in the number of women with degrees contributed to social, cultural and economic change in the latter part of the twentieth century. Discourses of gender offered our respondents a tool with which to reflect on the nature of their day-to-day experience at Winchester and the way in which a caring community developed.

This chapter has reflected on the way in which oral history enables individuals to express their experience in terms of specific incidents. So the role of sport, the Wednesday afternoon football match, takes on a wider meaning in terms of expressing social change in young people's behaviour. At the same time it is clear that the power held by the male hierarchy (student and staff) was not relinquished without a struggle. This enables us to add a more nuanced understanding to the quantitative data of changing gender ratios in higher education at Winchester and beyond. A simple increase in numbers is not sufficient to change

hierarchical gendered practices and assumptions; there is inevitably a time lag between the arrival of women into a hitherto physical or conceptual male space and their acceptance and participation on equal terms.

Notes to Chapter 6.

---

[1] Filmed Interview 8, Stage 2 (1958-1960).

[2] Carol Dyhouse, *Students: A Gendered History* (London: Routledge, 2006).

[3] Joan Scott, 'Gender as a Useful Category of Historical Analysis', *American Historical Review* 91.5 (1986): 1053-1075.

[4] Raewyn Connell, *Masculinities* (Cambridge: Polity, 1995). Connell notes that she first used the term in 1982 following research into hierarchies of masculinity in school settings. See Raewyn Connell, *Masculinities* www.raewynconnell.net (accessed April 19, 2013).

[5] Michael Moller, 'Exploiting Patterns: A Critique of Hegemonic Masculinity', *Journal of Gender Studies* 16.3 (November 2007): 263-276; Eric Anderson, *Inclusive Masculinity: The Changing Nature of Masculinities* (London: Routledge, 2011).

[6] See Sarah Aiston, '"A Woman's Place ...": Male Representations of University Women in the Student Press of the University of Liverpool, 1944-1979', *Women's History Review,* 15.1 (2006): 3-34.

[7] Interview 4, Stage 2 (1962-1965).

[8] Johann Heinrich Pestalozzi (1746-1827) and Friedrich Wilhelm August Froebel (1782-1852) are just two educators who championed the role of the mother (and implicitly the female teacher) in the holistic education of the young.

[9] Jennifer Nias, 'Value-persistence and Utility in Colleges of Education', *Education for Teaching* 89 (1972): 29.

[10] We should also, however, note that those involved in subjects other than teacher training put forward similar views when we asked about the significance of the gender ratio during their time at Winchester. As we have discussed earlier despite the changes in size, shape and course provision our analysis of interviews and questionnaires suggests that the alumni voices have been remarkably consistent in their recollection of a small, friendly and collegiate institution.

[11] Nel Noddings, *Caring: A Feminine Approach to Ethics and Moral Education* (California: University of California Press, 1984), 97.

[12] Jennifer Nias, 'Primary Teaching as a Culture of Care' in *School Culture,* ed. John Prosser (London: Sage, 1999), 66.

[13] Interview 18, Stage 3 (1960-1967).

[14] Nias, 'Primary Teaching', 66.

[15] Nias, 'Primary Teaching', 69.

[16] Francesca Vogt, 'A Caring Teacher: Explorations into Primary School Teachers' Professional Identity and Ethic of Care', *Gender and Education,* 14.3 (2002): 251-264.

[17] Nel Noddings, *Educating Moral People: A Caring Alternative To Character Education* (New York: Teachers College Press, 2002); Eric Anderson, *Inclusive Masculinity: The Changing Nature of Masculinities* (London: Routledge, 2011).

[18] Noddings, *Caring,* 175.

[19] Interview 9, Stage 2 (1964-1967).

[20] Interview 8, Stage 2 (1956-1958).

[21] In the editorial for the *Wintonian* in 1960 the editor bemoaned the passing of years of tradition, citing the 'monastic flavour' that was part of college life.

[22] Letter from PW, student 1958-60 to Andrea Jacobs, 1 August 2004.

[23] Interview 12, Stage 2 (1954-56).

[24] Interview 23, Stage 3 (1953-65).

[25] Interview 8, Stage 2 (1956-58).

[26] Carol Dyhouse, *Students, A Gendered History* (Manchester: University Press, 2005).

[27] Marjorie Bowen, 'Making Our Boys Effeminate', National Association of Schoolmasters, Warwick Modern Records Centre, MSS.38C/4/2/2. The Joint Four comprised the two Associations of Headmasters and Headmistresses and the Assistant Masters and Assistant Mistresses.

[28] See Stephanie Spencer, *Gender Work and Education in Britain in the 1950s* (Basingstoke: Palgrave Macmillan, 2005), Chapter Three, 49-78.

[29] Roger K. Kelsall, Anne Poole and Annette Kuhn, *Graduates: The Sociology of an Elite* (London: Methuen, 1972).

[30] With, of course, the exception of the occasional female tutor or matron.

[31] Interview 12, Stage 2 (1954-56).

[32] Reginald R. Dale, *Mixed or Single-Sex School?* (London: Routledge, Kegan Paul, 1974), 3:235.

[33] Reginald R. Dale, *Mixed*, 233.

[34] PW to Andrea Jacobs.

[35] *The Wintonian,* 13.2 (Lent 1959): 15.

[36] Editorial, *The Wintonian,* (1960).

[37] Michael Roper and John Tosh, 'Mummy, Matron and the Maids: Feminine Presence and Absence in Male Institutions 1934-63' in *Manful Assertions*, ed. Michael Roper and John Tosh (London: Routledge, 1991) 168-190.

[38] Dyhouse, *A Gendered History,* 178.

[39] Interview 12, Stage 2 (1954-1956).

[40] However, prior to 1960 most (male) students were already close to twenty-one when they arrived at the College after National Service, two years older than the boys who arrived after National Service was abolished in 1963, or the girls who arrived at the same time.

[41] Interview 10, Stage 2 (1962-1965).

[42] Dyhouse, *A Gendered History,* 178.

[43] Interview 2, Stage 1 (1960-1963).

[44] Interview 2, Stage 1 (1960-1963).

[45] Dyhouse, *A Gendered History,* 100.
[46] Interview 3, Stage 1 (1964-1967).
[47] Interview 3, Stage 1 (1964-1967).
[48] Interview 4, Stage 1 (1967-1970).
[49] Interview 4, Stage 1 (1967-1970).
[50] Interview 4, Stage 1 (1967-1970).
[51] Interview 7, Stage 1 (1989-1992).
[52] Interview 7, Stage 1 (1989-1992).
[53] Interview 1, Stage 1 (1979-1982).
[54] Interview 1, Stage 1 (1979-1982).
[55] Interview 23, Stage 3 (1953-1965).
[56] Interview 15, Stage 3 (1976-current).
[57] Interview 15, Stage 3 (1976-current).
[58] Interview 1, Stage 3 (1962-1984).
[59] All quotations taken from a single passage in Interview 1, Stage 3 (1962-1984).
[60] Interview 10, Stage 3 (1975-2003).
[61] Interview 14, Stage 3 (1987-current).
[62] Interview 12, Stage 3 (1973-1996).
[63] *Maria Assumpta Centre*, 'Maria Assumpta', www.mariaassumpta.cswebsites.org (accessed 14 May 2013).
[64] Interview 12, Stage 3 (1973-1996).
[65] See Dyhouse, *A Gendered History,* Chapter 10.
[66] Interview 12, Stage 3 (1973-1996).
[67] Interview 1, Stage 3 (1962-1984).
[68] With thanks to Peter Cunningham for his help in accessing material in the Homerton archives.
[69] Interviewee 10, Stage 2 (1962-1965) advised us: 'Oh she played the drums. I've got a photo of her playing the drums. Yes, she interviewed me when I went to the college for my interview and she was very straightforward and obviously, although she came across as quite austere in some ways, she obviously wasn't because the drum playing was amazing!'
[70] Interview 15, Stage 3 (1976-current).
[71] Interview 15, Stage 3 (1976-current).

7.

MANAGEMENT, LEADERSHIP AND CHANGE

> I can still see it very clearly now, it was unthinkable that we would be turned down [by CNAA], it just didn't enter people's imagination, and when Martial Rose came in, and we were all gathered in the what was the then SCR and he said "it's all gone wrong", we were just stunned, and people can't say this to us, but they did, and it was the saving of the institution [. . .] but that was salutary, it wasn't just over the shock it meant that changes had to happen, and changes did happen, and we were much stronger because of that, it was necessary, uncomfortable but necessary, it did us good.[1]

Introduction

The following discussion reflects on the literature on change management as a way of highlighting the changing role of leadership and its relationship to management within higher education, using the Winchester experience as an exemplar. There is a rich source of available archival material in terms of reports, committee minutes and policy documents that can give accurate data about the process of institutional change. While the addition of oral history narratives does not alter events, it can provide a nuanced understanding of how that process affected everyday working lives, and how that change was successfully led and managed. John Kotter usefully distinguishes the difference between these two related but distinct terms; he notes that management 'is about coping with complexity [...] without good management, complex enterprises tend to become chaotic in ways that threaten their very existence', whereas leadership 'is about coping with change'.[2]

In this chapter we consider, in the light of Kotter's analysis, how our respondents discussed change.[3] At the time of writing the University of Winchester is well-established as an institution that consistently achieves good rankings in national surveys, and looks to the future with confidence. In this chapter we discuss how our interviews highlighted the rather bumpy nature of the road to progress and the significance of individual personalities and leadership styles which culminated in the awarding of taught and research degree awarding powers. A major focus of the chapter is an extended discussion of the move to CNAA validation at Winchester. This was an example of a significant change point in the history of an institution as national policy change affected the survival of institutions originally constituted for a different purpose. Our discussion responds partly to Harold Silver's observation of the difficulty of charting how institutions experienced the change that CNAA brought: 'The ideal range of experience and insights would include those of course teams and the various participants' views of institutional review visits, college members of CNAA committees and their perception of their roles and the experience of academic registrars [. . .] '[4] The chapter concludes with an exploration of the resistance to change that was presented by the activities of staff Unions.[5] Waddell and Sohal have noted how effective resistance can positively enhance the successful implementation of change, and resistance is most likely to be found within discussions of Union activity and its role in enhancing or resisting leaders' attempts to implement their vision for the future.[6]

As noted in Chapter 2, the chronology of change at the institution records a diocesan training college progressing from providing two and three year courses for sub-degree qualification to offering Bachelors' degrees, initially validated by the University of Southampton, then by the

CNAA. It then returned to being overseen by the University of Southampton, before eventually achieving the independence that today entitles it to award, in its own name, Bachelors', Masters' and Doctoral degrees in a variety of academic and professional subjects.[7] In this long trajectory of change there were plenty of opportunities for failure. The spoken reflections of those who experienced or observed those processes can offer some insight into how this was avoided. Although the vagaries of memory might, if anything, give a more inaccurate ordering of events, the emotional impact of change is rarely forgotten.[8]

There is always a danger in oral history interviews with members of staff that those whose careers were adversely affected by change see an opportunity to air long held grievances. Conversely some individuals' positive contributions might be overemphasised. Anonymity, both of respondents and of individuals discussed within interviews, at this level is also impossible to maintain the minute, for example, that a Principal is mentioned in relation to a specific year or event. Arguably the attitudes of the powerful are already present within official histories and a view from leaders and managers in a study such as this could be seen to add little to the existing narrative provided in the conventional histories. Yet in writing a history using the voices of those who worked and studied at Winchester, it would seem strange to leave out some reflections on the constitutional changes that have driven the growth of King Alfred's College into the University of Winchester.[9] This chapter therefore focuses primarily on the voices of the academic staff we interviewed in Stage Three of the project and also includes reflections from those who worked in a support, or administrative position as well as those who worked in Registry.

In being asked to recall changes in organisation, many of our respondents articulated their concerns for accuracy; we were told either 'you can check that' or more definitively 'you'll have to check that'. The oral historian is left with a conundrum. Without specific references a section such as this could become a succession of free-floating unrepresentative observations on sixty years of constitutional and administrative change, yet the precise details of change are already well documented in existing histories of the institution. However, an oral history does offer senior personalities the opportunity to offer their recollections on their decisions with the benefit of hindsight, so adding a further layer to the record. In this chapter our analysis focuses on the voice relational reading of the interviews for the narrative and for the wider relationships. While individual students can tell us of the 'I' in their experience, the use of 'we' 'I' and even 'they' in terms of understanding management and leadership can begin to illustrate how leaders and managers performed their distinctive roles, with varying degrees of success.

The literature on leadership is extensive and it is not possible in a short chapter to consider in detail the vast array of leadership definitions and explanations that are available. Even a brief foray into the many debates over the nature of leadership does help to illuminate and contextualise the detailed and sometimes ambiguous narratives presented in our interviews, providing an example of the wider implications for the use of oral histories of higher education more generally. Central to definitions of effective leadership are the nature of the relationships built between leaders and those within and outside the institution.[10] Martial Rose emphasised the Principal's role as negotiator between the demands of the outside world and as defender of established practice:

> Mr. Stripe had been marvellous and he took me on occasions, for he was a wise man to do this. In those days the Principal had, acting on the advice of the Department of Education and Science, appointed an adviser, or administrator, and we would go up to the DES and say, 'These are our plans for building.

> These are our plans for staffing. Are you going to agree? And you had to put these pretty firmly, pretty clearly, with the Church support, you see. I think it was a 20 per cent contribution from the Church for capital building in those days. And this is what mattered then: this is what matters now. How many staff have we got to teach? How many students?'[11]

Gary Yukl offers us a useful definition of leadership as a result of 'the evolving social order that results from interactions, exchanges and influence processes among many people' to work alongside our reflection of Tönnies's work.[12] Yukl observes that 'leadership cannot be understood apart from the dynamics of the social system in which it occurs'. Considering the institution as one where the ethos moved from one of 'Gemeinschaft' to one that might more readily associate with 'Gesellschaft' helps to explain change in the way that leaders in the institution interpreted their role. Taken with Yukl's observation this again highlights the significance of individual reflections in conjunction with the official documentary record.

During the period covered by our research, higher education has become increasingly seen as a 'business', driven by economic change and a service-user focus and it is therefore appropriate to consider our interview transcripts informed by some of the literature more usually found in an analysis of commercial organisations. In drawing on business theory we consider why, at moments of change in higher education provision, some institutions managed to survive while others disappeared from the landscape. As well as managing change, the resistance to change, which was evident in some of our interviews, can itself be highly significant in the success (or otherwise) of the change process.[13]

The Church colleges may have faced additional problems given the tensions inherent in managing change. As

Chapter 4 noted, the role of religion or religious observance in the institution has evolved significantly over the last sixty years. Yukl has observed the controversial nature of leadership if it is seen to involve changing the 'underlying values and beliefs of individual followers'.[14] This is particularly pertinent in the evolution of a Church college and may have contributed to the demise of other institutions. We have already noted how one Principal of King Alfred's was tragically unable to reconcile the changes that were being imposed with the existing ethos of the institution and took his own life. John Stripe and Martial Rose were singled out as being leaders who were able to turn King Alfred's College round. Interview transcripts can offer some insight into the way that change was led by those who 'have a responsibility to implement major changes in an organisation to ensure its survival and effectiveness'. Yukl notes that the process of change 'may (or may not) result in the emergence of a new set of shared beliefs and values'.[15] This was all the more difficult in the case of a Church college as it sought to maintain its distinctiveness while complying with increased centralisation of higher education policy. One of the first initiatives taken by Joy Carter, the most recent Vice-Chancellor of Winchester, was to revise and articulate the mission and values of the institution after lengthy discussion with members of staff.

We recognised a considerable difference in interviews completed for this project between the students, who spent a short part of their early adulthood in higher education, and the staff, many of whom remained working at Winchester for a long period of time. The members of staff who we interviewed were either in retirement or had been employed at Winchester for over twenty years. While student alumni were invited to look back to the beginning of their professional lives, members of staff were asked about their professional profiles and, in the case of senior management and leaders, about their personal role in driving change at King Alfred's, Winchester. The benefit of hindsight is therefore especially poignant when one's actions and opinions have impacted not only on one's own career but on the very existence and survival of the institution itself.

A common dilemma faced by institutional oral historians is that of being 'insiders' as well as 'outsiders'. This was certainly an additional dimension to the interviewer / interviewee relationship in our interviews with long-term existing members of staff as they were also our day-to-day colleagues. There was a great deal of tacit knowledge understood, or expected, that underpinned some of the interviews. Equally, by sharing some stories, retired staff demonstrated their growing trust in us as an interviewing team and in the purpose of the project. While as academics we were able to understand colleagues' discussions of course development and student/staff relationships, when it came to interviewing those who had been in senior management positions the power dynamic between interviewer and respondents changed again. Support or administrative staff offered an additional perspective on the dynamics of leadership and management, demonstrating how individual voices highlight the complex interactions and relationships that give an institution its distinctive profile within the sector.

In our introduction we posed a number of questions that we hoped to answer in the course of our research, including 'How can the ethos of an institution be defined?' This question is part answered within our conversations with members of staff, past and present, and addresses the fundamental and much debated issue of the purpose of higher education to the individual and the community. Indeed, do institutions change in order to survive within an existing climate, or are they responsible for fostering change and preparing their students to face a swiftly changing society, such as that of the last sixty years? It would be disingenuous to assume that there was just one approach. This is the strength of oral history in that it can delve beneath the corporate story to the individuals, the subject groups and the faculties that make up the staff of even a small institution such as the one under consideration here.

Survival is not too strong a word to use when considering the history of King Alfred's. As several respondents noted, at one point a headline on King Alfred's closure in the Times Higher greeted staff over their breakfast tables.[16] It is especially difficult in this section to use quotations which, out of context, might suggest criticism by interviewees who often noted that, despite some lows, on the whole they had enjoyed their professional lives and were concerned that their narrative would suggest that that they had 'moaned'. Certainly the staff narratives were more ambivalent, there was indeed some criticism either that the institution did not move quickly enough or that it advanced too rapidly. On the whole comments were made with the acknowledgement that the institution survived and grew, despite any misgivings over the initiation of change. Criticism was sometimes directed at specific groups. One member of staff who changed department spoke of 'tunnelling out' from what they saw as a very self-sufficient group of colleagues and in some cases personal antipathy between individuals or departments, inevitable in any workplace, surfaced.

Managing change

Chapter 2 laid out the somewhat chequered history of the Diocesan Training College that became first King Alfred's College, then a University College and finally the University of Winchester. The institution is not alone in this trajectory. Others that have followed a similar path include Liverpool Hope, Chichester, and Canterbury Christchurch. Far more has changed in the institution than what might initially be seen as cosmetic changes of name. For example the academic and administrative head of the institution is now designated as 'Vice-Chancellor' rather than 'Principal'. Departments first became schools, then restructuring collected departments within Faculties. Even the original core business of King Alfred's, that of teacher training, changed to teacher education and then to teacher development. Recent changes in funding for undergraduate courses and changes in the provision of teacher education have further contributed to the evolution of the original remit and ethos of the institution that is the focus of this book.

Although some may have regretted the changes that occurred, a majority of our correspondents recognised that change was inevitable. However, change is not something that happens spontaneously. Theorists have identified a number of stages in the implementation of change. Initially, in 1958, Lewin identified three stages: 'Unfreezing the present level of behaviour [. . .] , movement [. . .] taking action to change the organisation's social system [. . .] the third step is called refreezing. This involves establishing a process that new levels of behaviour will be relatively secure against reversion to prior modes of operation'.[17] These stages have been elaborated upon and John Kotter's eight step model is now widely recognised and implemented within change management.[18] While of course they cannot be taken as representative, individual voices may highlight why some institutions successfully moved with the times while some fell by the wayside. Returning to our discussion of the move from Gemeinschaft to Gesellschaft it is pertinent to note that Kotter's final point in change management is to anchor the changes in corporate culture – what we might see as the final shift to a Gesellschaft institution.

The first step to successful change management has been identified as creating a sense of urgency so that the entire organisation recognises that change is not only inevitable but also necessary. Many of the interviews did look back to a golden time when institutional practice and policy was not so tightly controlled, but also admitted that moving with the times had enabled the College to stay solvent, as our opening quote demonstrates. It was recognised that while old systems may have generated a community spirit they were not fit for purpose in a more bureaucratic age:

> It was cliquey, it was slightly non-professional. It was you know not where the place ought to be, but it was all very friendly. Things got done because people owed a loyalty to the collective, rather than because they were told to do it [. . .] I think it came from getting things, wanting to get things done, wanting to kind of muddle through and make it OK when we were wildly under resourced, didn't have the technology to do it, had very little planning to sort things out and therefore it was about, well we'll just roll from one task to the next and get it done, not wanting to let the students down, not wanting to let the College down.[19]

Secondly change management requires a gradual acceptance by the majority that change is necessary, and several of our respondents told us of the reluctance to accept how changes in the outside environment drove changes in the College. This has already been noted in our discussion in the previous chapter with regard to gender.

Managing change requires strong leadership and this was recognised within the interviews. Kotter identifies his third step in managing change as that of the ability to create a vision of that change. Official documents cannot record how dependent the direction of change is upon the individual leadership of the institution, but the detail in oral history interviews can go some way to filling in those gaps, as one vice principal reflected:

> In my day Martial and I would say ideally 'well of course Winchester, lovely old place, just like Oxbridge really, we could become a University couldn't we?' and then we'd go onto the question of who might have to be made redundant because of this that or the other, that was the reality [. . .] I think

> they were quite right to go for some … well, [he] wasn't right … but the next man Dickinson did know because he came from a University background, that was the person they really wanted [. . .] and then like Paul Light … and like the one they've got now, that was the right thing to do.[20]

Vision for change was not always shared:

> I think there were staff who felt that it was hopeless to try and get university status. I mean I think people who thought that have now been proved well and truly wrong but there was a period when it did look unlikely because we hadn't got what people called critical mass. You know there weren't enough students and we were so close to a major university. It would have been a nice little conference centre really.[21]

Step four for Kotter involves communicating the vision, which, if underpinned by fears of redundancy, can be fraught with problems, and step five involves removing obstacles to change. This inevitably took the form of redundancy and challenges to much loved and revered traditions and this can be difficult. Not everyone welcomed or could be won over to change and removing obstacles to the development of the institution required some tough decisions by those at the top. The period covered by this project saw two phases of redundancies which were recalled in very different ways.

The first, in the 1970s was government-led and known as 'Crombie'. It became apparent, given the demographic and economic conditions of the early 1970s, that there were too many colleges of education training too many teachers. Consequently plans were made to shut down a number of colleges and to award compensation to lecturers through a system known as the 'Crombie Code', initially designed to deal with local government redundancies. Other small colleges affected by closures included Mary Ward, a Catholic college in Nottinghamshire and the Athiny Training College in Kingston-Upon-Hull. In what appears to have been a lively House of Commons debate on 11th March 1975, Kenneth Clarke observed that he supported the move which was 'reducing the number of teacher training places in colleges of education and amalgamating the reduced colleges of education with other institutions of higher education to give a wider range of subject-matter and syllabus in the amalgamated larger polytechnics and other institutions'.[22] Ernest Armstrong (Under Secretary for State for Education and Science) responded that:

> It is the Government's policy that, wherever possible, colleges should develop new courses outside teacher training in order to make the fullest possible use of the places no longer required for the training of teachers. Changes of the magnitude that we have in mind, involving a major reorganisation of the teacher training system, will unfortunately, but inevitably, mean that some individual members of staff will be displaced.[23]

Clearly King Alfred's was one of those colleges affected, and the vivid memories of those who were working at the College when the scheme came in demonstrate how the survival strategies of those leading the institution were not always supported by those lower down the hierarchy. Crombie however, provided a good package and one member of staff described being 'tickled pink' when he was awarded a Crombie settlement.[24] Others were more ambivalent:

> People who were made redundant if they were under fifty I think … you got a proportion of your salary which would be inflation linked and probably a lump sum and [. . .] you had to apply for jobs every so often, it didn't matter what sort of job, so people

> would leave college and get Crombie which was a very good deal, and apply to be a garage attendant or something and they wouldn't get it. And I remember the Head of the RE department got a Crombie on a Principal Lectureship and within five years he was earning or pensioned more money than people who were on Principal Lectureships at that time in college [. . .] some people were borderline cases, so there was worry about that, people had mortgages and children and you know it was a worrying time.[25]

Although the closures as a result of government policy suggested that it would not be easy for those who were made redundant to find new jobs, on the whole there was a recognition that the College's survival depended on change. Mergers with bigger institutions such as polytechnics and colleges of higher education as well as universities were considered:

> It was a time of great anxiety and I suppose that was inevitably one of the motivating forces for diversifying the institution, and I mean from time to time there was talk about merging with what was then Southampton Institute and other institutions ... but for good or bad well, hopefully good on the whole, this place survived as an independent college and ... it was an anxious time actually right from about '76 through to about the early '80s, and then, I don't know, things settled down a bit in that respect.[26]

Later, in the 1990s, the situation changed as the management structure grew, to the dismay of the teaching staff who did not share or understand the vision for change into the twenty-first century:

> Well, the mass sackings were in 1996 actually and I didn't go until 2000, and so there were people who

> went at the same time as me but a lot of subjects were closed … 1996 well, I think basically the College wanted a lot more money to employ a lot more 'men in suits', you know. They had Directors of this and Directors of that and the administrative side of the College was quite small until about the mid '90s and they actually got rid of a lot of people in Teaching Studies who were on very high salaries and all that money probably went nicely to 'men in suits'.[27]

However, having decided in 1992 not to move with many of the polytechnics to university status Winchester was then faced, with several other Church colleges, with later application for university status; first with taught Degree Awarding Powers and finally with Research Degree Awarding Powers. Again oral evidence demonstrates the complex nature of these applications and the amount of administrative work that was required, together with discussion with other institutions, highlighting that KAC was not an isolated example of these changes in higher education:

> The beginning was extremely interesting because we were corresponding with other Universities or people that had tried and failed and just to get some feel [. . .] I know we were never refused, we never had to start from scratch, it was always, 'well this is quite good, and that's good, and yes we like that but', and it was never, 'apply in six months', it was always 'apply in two years'. Yes so it wasn't an easy row to hoe. It was really difficult, and a bit like research degree awarding powers in a way because again you know they don't want a dilution of quality do they? That's not what they're about.[28]

Following Kotter's framework, it is necessary to build on change once it has been established. Given the rapidly changing nature of the higher education climate, driven by external forces, managers and leaders have not always had time to fully implement one set of changes before government policy has moved on. Kotter's final step is that of 'institutionalising new approaches' which involves 'developing the means to ensure leadership development and succession'.[29] 'Change sticks' he notes 'when it becomes "the way we do things here".'[30] Our student interviews ranged across forty years of enormous change in the institution, yet the similarities in the way that the institution was described as 'small and friendly' despite the huge growth in student numbers would seem to indicate that change, at least from the point of view of the student, has been managed so successfully that in each decade the distinctiveness of the 'way we do things' has been recognised.

Reacting to change - the move to CNAA

The move to academic validation by the CNAA, finally approved in 1975, provides an example of a critical change that, while it may have helped the institution to survive, encountered some opposition and relied on strong leadership for its introduction, followed by careful management for its implementation.

As Tom James notes in Chapter 2 and as highlighted in the quotation with which we begin this chapter, the move to CNAA came about at a time when it seemed that whatever students might recall, staff worked in an atmosphere of uncertainty and fear for the future. Harold Silver explains that correspondence indicates that the College 'regretted' turning to CNAA after all other avenues had been explored and highlights Martial Rose's comment on the 'salutary' experience of the initial rejection. While Silver notes the changing view by Rose of the initial rejection by CNAA as 'crushing' to recognition of it as a 'significant achievement' this change of heart was not necessarily universal.[31] The following quote clearly illustrates how fear for the institution as a whole permeated down to individual departments:

> Ah now, I think […] I don't know why they changed to CNAA to validate our degrees, I couldn't answer that. But they did … I think it was partly that … it's connected with a constant fear there was then that the College was going to close down. A lot of colleges were closing down then; and a fear that different departments would be closing down; and almost every year, perhaps even every term, there'd be a terrible whisper going around … "They're going to close down the Drama Department" … "They're going to close down the RE Department"
> … and then there would be a panic you know. How could we preserve that department?[32]

On the one hand this respondent declares ignorance of the reasons for the unpopular move, but in the next breath shows a clear insight into the context of the problems that drove the move. At the same time as understanding the need to move and survive there was a sense that the move to CNAA took the institution to another level and moved away from the cosiness and family feeling (which some felt rather old-fashioned) that had characterised the earlier institution. In doing so, there is a sense of regret that the old values that had been enough to preserve the integrity of King Alfred's were being overtaken by bureaucracy, reflecting our earlier discussion of the move from Gemeinschaft to Gesellschaft in this and other small institutions:

> And so the move when we went to CNAA for the first time we had to calculate [. . .] workloads of members of staff, something that had never been attempted at King Alfred's before, you just didn't think to compare how hard someone else was working because you didn't know. Suddenly under the CNAA arrangement we had to calculate how much time must be spent on this and that and the other and the whole thing became far more of a calculated environment in which to work, you could measure things, you were required to measure things that previously as in a

> family you don't measure ... well in most families you don't actually measure the amount of time that people spend on things and the relative worth of what they do. So I never knew how the different departments operated but under the CNAA arrangements suddenly all this had to be tabulated and laid bare, and a necessary move as I say but a change in climate.[33]

The use of the 'I' 'we' and 'you' is intriguing in the quote above reflecting the very ambivalent attitude to the changes imposed by CNAA, 'we went' implies general involvement and unity of purpose, modified by 'you' didn't know, the difficulty of what 'we' had to do and the final distancing of 'I never knew' implying respect for colleagues in other departments but swiftly followed by an authoritative statement about knowledge of change in the whole institution. This was not a lone voice. The sense of change and the vivid memory of the extra detailed work that CNAA required is quite palpable and as can be seen in the following quote, the memory is still vivid and, perhaps unsurprisingly, highlights the problem that still exercises academic staff today when workloads are under discussion:

> No, I don't think I had any difficulties through CNAA. You had to do things in a certain way but if I'd had to find a way of doing things for myself that would have been much worse wouldn't it, than having a nice set of regulations, you know, and I had to sit in at all the examination boards and make sure that they were all run properly in that sense. CNAA made it easier because there were guidelines. No I don't think CNAA made my job difficult. I remember we had to have a ... we had to describe work, individual members of staff's workload in units of work, and I can't remember the details but I know some colleagues had great difficulty working this out for themselves, particularly people who did practical

> work, and I had to go, and that was a job ... I can't remember whether that was the CNAA or the Ministry but I really had to struggle with that one because I had to send the returns in, and some people had real difficulty and I had difficulty in helping them ... but it was just that sometimes you know it's quite easy to say well I do ten hours a week, ten one hour lectures a week. But some people supervise this, supervise that, they don't appear to be doing anything really but they're there, it's work, it's a responsibility.[34]

There have been substantial turning points in the college administration, and CNAA validation was seen by staff as one of those defining moments. It demanded a clear management structure, and emphasised the difference between those who led and those whose job it was to manage. This was a sea change in an institution that had been likened so often to a 'family'. As one respondent put it 'Well I think there's always resistance to change isn't there, I mean we were all fairly busy and then if you know there's a great change like for example the move to CNAA, you know everybody thought ... oh Lord you know how much work is that going to involve ... just a general resistance to change I would say'.[35] Resistance to change might well be particularly strong in a small institution with a low turnover of staff. While this may lead to continuity and common purpose it can also lead to stasis and, as one less enthusiastic respondent put it, a 'moribund' atmosphere. [36]

Several staff put the changes in King Alfred's down to the move to CNAA and in doing this were able to locate the blame for unpleasant events as falling outside the control of the college hierarchy. This has two effects, first that it unites a community in adversity against a common difficulty and second, it removes blame for any of the unpleasant consequences from those who have power in the institution itself. In the quote below the respondent draws the interviewer into his commentary, adding a third dimension or layer to the analysis by bringing the history into the present and demanding a partial/biased view from the present:

> But when CNAA would visit us of course, they would address the entire staff including all the subjects that wouldn't be immediately involved and so there was already the beginning of a division between where the College would diversify and what would happen to the part that didn't, so that was an anxious time I think, and I mean only you can tell how it has finally succeeded or not because you are the growth from those shoots I take it.[37]

The outcome of CNAA was such that it caused some people to change direction in their careers as they felt that the centralisation of policy-making resulted in management from outside the institution and undermined the expertise or the autonomy of the individual working within the institution. Increasingly those who had been employed to teach saw the amount of time they spent with students being eroded, as their careers developed and responsibilities changed:

> CNAA … it was all done in these units that you had to produce, I mean that was … it killed teaching as far as I'm concerned but I mean I didn't last long in that because I moved on to this admissions work, and I was there … I did just a little bit of it [. . .] and then I was out in school as well.[38]

Change was also reflected in changing expectations of staff qualifications. This did not always sit easily with the long-serving members of the teaching faculty, as one newcomer reflected:

> I was appointed if you like as a sort of academic, I don't know, obviously to boost the credibility of the

> College in the eyes of the CNAA the then degree awarding body, and you know I came as a sort of, if you like, as in a sense of an academic, I suppose, rather than someone who had perhaps, I don't know, maybe had ten or twenty years' school teaching experience and then you know did an MA in education and then came to teach here. So my background for a start was very, very different I think.[39]

What is striking about the comment above is the reticence of the more highly qualified speaker, which is even more pronounced in the voice recording. Whereas an analysis of staff CVs as they joined the institution would provide evidence (if these were available) of changing qualification profiles, it would not offer such insight into the nuances of staff relations. The short paragraph is full of caveats 'I don't know', 'if you like', 'I suppose' and finishing with 'I think'.

Juxtaposed with the stories of Common Room cliques noted in Chapter 5, we can begin to build a picture of an institution at a time of change and specialisation, and perhaps the build-up of tension or rivalry between departments, exacerbated by increased reporting and observance from external validating bodies such as CNAA. 'I was given a free rein in the Drama course of the BEd, I was given absolutely tight rein on what CNAA would accept for a BA, so there was clearly a difference there. Having said that, once they'd been accepted, the way they were taught was not interfered with'.[40]

The move from Southampton to CNAA validation was a major topic of discussion by our staff correspondents. They used strong language when talking about the CNAA, clearly the shock of the failure in the first application was felt deeply and still rankled after a gap of many years. In many ways the history of small institutions is Darwinian with a sense of battle lines being drawn on several occasions, as the extract below reveals. Again the respondent wants to make it clear that they are not talking factual detail, 'you can probably get hold of' the official guidelines, but explaining the success against all odds and against competition from other small colleges. Our respondent had a difficult time composing a coherent narrative, even to the extent of being unsure whether to use the all-embracing 'we' or whether to suggest to the interviewer that 'I' made the decisions. Yet again, the unease and tension felt as a result of an outsider coming in and dictating terms is emphasised:

> CNAA that was a fraught time for all of us having to make certain restrictions but … you can probably get hold of the restrictions of the CNAA at that time, but I'm thinking of initially again from the subject point of view and that we … I had to argue the case for my area of study against sometimes the restrictions of attitudes of people outside the institution towards Physical Education you see, so that in a sense was a restriction … but if we argued our case very well accepted. So in a way, not a restriction, but were made to look at oneself and look at one's area of study and what was going to happen.[41]

Undoubtedly increased accountability and changes in government funding, as a higher proportion of school-leavers has entered higher education, have resulted in an increase in bureaucracy. The origins of this increase might be found in the CNAA guidelines, and there were occasions when such accountability was relished:

> Oh yes, you know they were rigorous and they didn't give us an easy ride, I mean I think in fact when Drama went back for revision it was failed and we didn't recruit for a year, and the students that we had recruited had to wait for a year while the programme got its act together really. So it wasn't easy to get things validated and we spent enormous amount of time putting the documents together with a specific

> requirement but that was fun and all the better when we got them.[42]

King Alfred's was not alone in finding the relationship with CNAA challenging. Westminster College, which later became part of Oxford Brookes University, faced similar trials which kept 'staff at full stretch for several years to come and affect(ed) college organisation, deployment of resources, arrangements for staff development and research, and support services for students'.[43] While the students continued to tell of the informal relationships that what they saw as a small institution was able to provide, there was a contrast in the observations by staff members. While some may have seen increasing bureaucracy as an attack on their professionalism, others identified more positive aspects of the changes from the informality of a focused teacher training college:

> Clearly we had on paper a scheme, I and my colleagues said "this is how the course will be" and we did it, but we did it with very few meetings, perhaps one a term … we knew what we were doing, went ahead and did it. The CNAA work, we had detailed programmes for each stage of the course, what would be done, how it would be examined, when it would be done, how long it would take, and we had to stick to those very rigidly, so obviously the informality turned into a much more required formality of teaching and preparation.[44]

The proliferation of committees and policies that the CNAA generated has irritated staff across the years, especially when workloads were seen as becoming top-heavy with administration and less time for teaching and research. At the same time, as the institution grew there were fewer opportunities for staff to talk across faculties. This was acknowledged by one respondent who noted:

> When we went to CNAA, that was staff conference and there was an academic board without staff representation [. . .] when we went to CNAA I remember Martial saying after we were turned down the first time [...] and they don't like our paternalistic way of doing things, and so we're going to have to make the formal processes more democratic by having staff reps on lots of committees, so we'll have lots of committees and there will be staff reps on them and that will make it more democratic.[45]

If read at face value this would appear to suggest that changes were welcome and the staff were increasingly invited to see the value of their roles within the organisation. On the other hand it might be read as a frustrated analysis of the amount of time spent in formal meetings and discussions. The next section discusses the role of the union as an influential factor in change.

Reflections on Union Activity

We conclude this chapter with a reflection on the way that our interviewees spoke about Trade Union activity in Winchester. In doing so we were informed by Dianne Waddell's argument that resistance, rather than being seen as antithetical to change, is in fact integral to its successful implementation.[46] The lack of real engagement with the union as it sought to challenge some innovation might go some way to explaining why King Alfred's College took so long to start its application for university status, which, once started, quickly gained momentum. It might in part be the origins of the institution but the reflections by our correspondents about union matters were often quite vague, and frequently voiced in terms of how others had participated, perhaps linked with a reflection that the individual felt that they should have had more engagement with first ACTL and then NATFHE.[47] Again the advent of CNAA seems to have sparked interest in union activity:

> Yes, and you say here the University has always had a vocal union branch, I don't think that's true, I don't think the union started getting really powerful and outspoken and sometimes very difficult probably until the CNAA and the question of redundancies. [48]

Our respondents were, on the whole, rather ambivalent about their role in the union and the effectiveness of those who were active. The policy at Winchester has been that staff opt in to union membership rather than, as in other institutions, having to take the step of opting out. As a result union membership has never been very high, although as the institution grew the cosy family atmosphere clearly gave way to some resistance and an increase in union activity.

Waddell cites Zaltman's definition of resistance as 'any conduct that serves to maintain the status quo in the face of pressure to change the status quo'.[49] The retreat into a nostalgic reference to less bureaucratic times by some of our respondents might indicate a more passive resistance to the changes that were embraced by the institution. On the whole, analysis of the structure of responses to questions about the union does suggest some ambivalence or tension within narratives that were usually very positive. The following is a good example of the difficulty our respondents had in explaining the role of the union in college life. It is reproduced at length in order to demonstrate the uncertainty of the place of union activity in the life of the College. They chose to refer more to general trends and were clearly not inviting further questions:

> Yes, well as I said, I think partly because people, not everyone felt they wanted to join the union so NATFHE couldn't really speak for all members of staff any more, the teaching staff that is [...] but I suppose into the '80s into the '90s it was just a reflection of the times really whereas unions had had a higher profile and probably more power in the late

> '60s and the 1970s, I mean that had been reduced generally in the country as a whole into the '80s and '90s you know depending upon your perspective, for good or bad, and I think that was just reflected in a diversity of opinions, and to new staff who came in [. . .] I don't know if that really answers that.[50]

However, the opportunity to speak about union activity did seem to disrupt some of the more halcyon narratives of working at King Alfred's that the interviewing team were offered. In each case those being interviewed offered their observations as one detached from the proceedings, as in the following extract:

> Well both on principle I couldn't see what the point of it was, and secondly of the four people who were being virtually ostracised, I can remember some very nasty incidents in the SCR where when some of them walked in other people walked out. Now I found that quite indefensible, particularly as two of the people had been very long standing and very good friends of mine, and I hadn't got the slightest intention of either voting against them or making life difficult. So, there were stresses with what I regarded as the, not resurgence, but the development of a militant tone to the union, which I really couldn't go along with [. . .] it would have been I suppose [. . .] 1980s I suppose, 1980s.[51]

It may be relevant to note here the wider national concerns over educational policy and provision that were apparent at that time, and as were articulated in the Black Papers, ultimately resulting in the 1988 Education Act which increased centralised control and led to some concerns over the de-professionalisation of teachers.[52] Looking back, one member of staff clearly saw changes in union activity at this point in relation to external events 'I just think it's the time of Mrs Thatcher and the miners' strike ... Yes indeed which of course might have promoted hostility amongst some people to unions, on the other hand it might have sort of promoted solidarity with others'.[53] It might well have been that, as the close community atmosphere that had been deliberately fostered in the early days gave way to a bigger student body, more diversity of programme provision, and a change in the political climate, union activity amongst staff became more noticeable. Waddell recognises three components of resistance: rational factors, i.e. personal opinions on change; non-rational factors such as uncertainty of the likely outcomes, changing offices or practices; and finally, political factors such as 'point scoring' 'against those instigating the change effort'. [54] Each one of these can be identified as part of our conversations over union involvement. On the whole union resistance to change was not remembered as being terribly effective, as the two comments below illustrate:

> No, I don't think we did really use that in those situations. I don't know [. . .] it is all beginning to get rather hazy in my mind, that is the trouble, but I know there were, there was a bit of conflict really and I think it partly had to do with the changing pattern, you know, patterns of work within the College and the fact that we did feel fairly pressured. We were very pressurised really.[55]

> Two or three times we picketed the place, all of that. I remember a wonderful occasion in the '90s when we marched down the High Street with a banner saying something like "No to the 12 hour week" meaning class contact [. . .] and we wondered why the population of Winchester were not that sympathetic.[56]

A member of staff who worked at Winchester during the 1980s and 1990s drew some contrasts between Winchester and a previous workplace. The extract highlights how difficult it is to generalise from one institution to another, and at the same time reflects how the union did not appear to challenge the prevailing ethos of the institution:

> I wasn't aware of that really, I mean there was a strong union at the college in Luton where I worked and I thought in a way, there's quite a strong union in the place here really, and they were very, very different institutions in other respects, but like most people my experience is very limited [. . .] I think the sort of shared values and communal interest that a lot of people perceived rightly or wrongly when I first came to college [. . .] I think joining the union was something you did, you know, I think there's a lot of wanting to conform really, and [. . .] it wasn't seen as particularly good, bad, threatening, unthreatening being a member. You just sort of went along with it and, you know, I don't think people were particularly anti or particularly radical really from my experience of it.[57]

Those staff we interviewed did not appear to have played a major part in union activity, but appreciated that it was there at times of crisis. We were told:

> No the union was there and I think the union was very helpful. You had the one or two hot heads [. . .] I think one of them even led some sort of a strike whether that was in my time, yes it was. There was a withdrawal of labour at one time. But in the main, it was there to help us and you see I was there at the time when there was a lot of redundancy talk and the union helped us a lot over that.[58]

Those involved in administrative and support work also had the opportunity to join a union but as the extract below demonstrates it does not appear to have been very active:

> Yes I was a union member at some time. They didn't operate very well really. If we had a problem, we all used to go up, all the support staff, the secretarial, PAs to the room now which is the Director of HR's room, and there was a kitchen next door which is now not a kitchen but somebody's office, I think it's where the photocopier is [. . .] and we all used to go up there if we could about 10.30, and if we had a gripe then we used to get together and we used to go to the Bursar and say [. . .] look, this is not fair [. . .] One thing was our holiday allowance if you were part-time and he always used to say it was terribly good you know it was generous, but when you worked it out it wasn't generous at all. In fact it didn't even cover what we were supposed to have but he was fine, I mean did he like it [. . .] no, probably not but [. . .] and that's the way we did it. So the union wasn't quite the same because we were doing it ourselves [. . .] but then the union did become stronger and I think it did support a number of support staff who were having problems.[59]

Members of staff we interviewed were more likely than those who had been students to be critical in their evaluation of their time at Winchester, and inevitably these reflections highlight the changing climate of expectation within the tertiary sector. Interviewing provides an opportunity for those in retirement to see their working lives in a wider perspective and as we consider change within higher education more generally it is also worth considering how expectations of the lecturer role have also changed. Discussion of union activity prompted a number of self-reflexive comments which perhaps tell us more about expectations today than they offer insight into earlier times. For example, this respondent who worked at Winchester between 1970 and 2008 noted:

> I feel rather bad about it and I don't think I played, I only joined it latterly, and I think I should have taken

> a more active part you see. Here I've been moaning to you about poor management, and I think maybe that might have been part of a way of trying to put a bit of pressure on the management to say "Oi! We're here, don't actually forget us and don't forget our point of view, and let's try some you know bottom up as well as top down planning", but I didn't, I think that was a shame because as is often the case if the sort of middle of the road woolly people like me don't join the union then it tends to be taken over by perhaps rather more radical people who are very splendid in their own way but have quite particular strong views that then come to represent the whole body.[60]

Equally concerns over change fade over time and so oral history fails to capture the intensity of feeling when institutional change affects one individual negatively. The extract below captures this and presents the oral historian with a layered interpretation of events:

> For what it's worth, I didn't particularly like being made redundant in 2000 you know but [. . .] I mean without boring you about that, I hoped I could have been redeployed you know [. . .] it seemed a great shame that apart from me alone you know that they couldn't somehow use my experience or background that I had [. . .] but anyway it wasn't to be. There were all sort of internal politics and all sorts of things and it's easy to speculate why they didn't want me to carry on there but who knows, but anyway, no I would have liked a few more years to carry on.[61]

The impression left by those we spoke to who worked at Winchester over a number of years was that union activity has not played a very large part in the day-to-day life of the community, although there were individuals who spoke up regularly; as one respondent noted, at Academic Board there were 'Union officers arguing vociferously for a long time'.[62] It is difficult from our interviews to ascertain the reason for this as there have been significant periods of uncertainty and concerns over redundancy. A wider study might offer some insight into whether similar antipathy might be found across the Church college sector. Even those who held positions in the Union were quite non-committal about the legacy of union activity within the history of the institution:

> I was its membership secretary once - I remember discovering that one member of staff had actually been paying for two subscriptions for a decade, which sort of tells you something about the place back then. Again the English Department tended to take the lead in that, as their left critical theory politics tended to push them in that direction. I was quite keen, less so today but that's just middle age and climbing the greasy pole a little bit.[63]

Conclusion

In ending our exploration of Alumni Voices with reflections by those who worked at the institution we have considered how long-standing members of staff reflected on how change was led and managed. Over the sixty years covered by our research the institution has changed dramatically, both in the number of students and the courses provided, and also in its relation to the wider provision of higher education. We chose to focus largely on the change point to CNAA for two reasons, firstly because our respondents themselves identified it as a momentous point of change in the evolution of the institution. Secondly, in reading the interview extracts in line with some management theories of change and leadership, it becomes possible to put the history of one institution into a wider history of changes in the way that universities and colleges have been understood as increasingly aligned to business organisational models. Concerns over the move to CNAA were not limited to Winchester, as the Westminster history and Silver's research confirm. The particular concerns voiced by our respondents reflect wider changes as more institutions were brought within the definition of 'higher education' provision. The move from a Gemeinschaft to a Gesellschaft community identified by one of our staff alumni has been particularly pertinent in this chapter and will underpin our final remarks as we review the project as a whole.

Notes to Chapter 7.

---

[1] Stage 3, Interview 11 (1971-1992).

[2] John Kotter notes the distinctive difference between leadership and management in John Kotter, *What Leaders Really Do* (Harvard: Harvard Business Review, 1999), 52.

[3] John Kotter, 'Leading Change: Why Transformation Efforts Fail', *Harvard Business Review* (March-April 1995): 59-67.

[4] Harold Silver, *A Higher Education: The Council for National Academic Awards and British Higher Education 1964-1989* (London: Falmer, 1990), 166.

[5] Strictly speaking this was also Association activity as staff belonged to a range of bodies that included the National Association of Teachers in Further Education and Association of University Teachers. We have used 'union' as a catch all as that is the term that was used by respondents

[6] Diane Waddell and Amrik Sohal, 'Resistance: A Constructive Tool For Change Management', *Management Decision,* 36.8 (1998): 543-548.

[7] The authors would like to thank Professor Sir William Taylor for his advice and guidance in the writing of this chapter.

[8] A paper by Andrea Jacobs, Camilla Leach, and Stephanie Spencer, 'The Institution Changes but the Memories Live On: Alumni Voices on Higher Education', presented at the Oral History Annual Conference (7 July 2013) and based on part of this chapter, explored in more detail the way that oral history contributes to the history of emotions. In presenting extracts using the taped interviews, the authors were able to discuss in more detail the pauses, inflections and tones that are lost in the transcript but that

are vital in understanding the emotional memory of some difficult times.

[9] We were able to interview only one past Principal from the period covered by this history, and we would like to thank Martial Rose for the time spent offering his personal recollections and his support for the project.

[10] Gary Yukl, *Leadership in Organisations* (Boston: Pearson, 2010), 504.

[11] Interview 22, Stage 3 (1965-1984).

[12] Yukl, *Leadership*, 504.

[13] John Kotter, 'Leading Change: Why Transformation Efforts Fail', *Harvard Business Review,* (March-April 1995): 59-67.

[14] Yukl, *Leadership*, 332.

[15] Yukl, *Leadership*, 332.

[16] In one instance we were advised, 'there was an article in the *Times Supplement* which named three colleges that were going to be closed and ours was one of them'. See Interview 12, Stage 3 (1973-1996).

[17] Wes Siegal, Allan H. Church, Miriam Javitch, Janine Waclawski, Steffani Burd, Michael Bazigos, Ta-Fu Yang, Kate Anderson-Rudolph and W. Warner Burke, 'Understanding the Management of Change: An Overview of Managers' Perspectives and Assumptions in the 1990s', *Journal of Organisational Change Management,* 9.6 (1996): 54-80.

[18] See *Mind Tools*, 'Kotter's 8-Step Change Model', www.mindtools.com (accessed 19 June, 2013).

[19] Interview 16, Stage 3 (1993-2004).

[20] Interview 19, Stage 3(1969-1985).

[21] Interview 12, Stage 3(1973-1996).

[22] *Hansard* HC Deb (11 March 1975) 888: 468-80.

[23] *Hansard* HC Deb (11 March 1975) 888: 468-80.

[24] Interview 6, Stage 3 (1967-1988).

[25] Interview 3, Stage 3 (1968-1991).

[26] Interview 10, Stage 3 (1975-2003).

[27] Interview 10, Stage 3 (1975-2003).

[28] Interview 15, Stage 3 (1976-current).

[29] Kotter, 'Leading Change', 61.

[30] Kotter, 'Leading Change', 67.

[31] Silver, *A Higher Education,* 176.

[32] Interview 13, Stage 3 (1970-2008) The following three quotations are a good example of how the written transcript can only hint at the intensity of feeling that the spoken word conveys. These quotations were used in our session at the 2013 Oral History Conference, and we would like to record our thanks to the participants of that session for their comments and interest in the voice relational method.

[33] Interview 11, Stage 3 (1971-1992).

[34] Interview 4, Stage 3 (1964-1987).

[35] Interview 8, Stage 3 (1969-1998).

[36] Interview 3, Stage 3 (1968-1991).

[37] Interview 6, Stage 3 (1967-1988).

[38] Interview 1, Stage 3 (1962-1984).

[39] Interview 10, Stage 3 (1975-2003).

[40] Interview 6, Stage 3 (1967-1988).

[41] Interview 1, Stage 3 (1962-1984).

[42] Interview 6, Stage 3 (1967-1988).

[43] Jennifer Bone, *Our Calling to Fulfil: Westminster College and the Changing Face of Teacher Education 1951-2001,* (Tockington: Westminster College Trust Tockington Press, 2003), 106.

[44] Interview 6, Stage 3 (1967-1988).

[45] Interview 17, Stage 3 (1973-2006).

[46] Waddell and Sohal, 'Resistance'.

[47] ACTL (Association of College Teachers and Lecturers) NATFHE (National Association of Teachers in Fuether and Higher Education) Since the completion of the project the University Union has now become part of the University and College Union (UCU).

[48] Interview 3, Stage 3 (1968-1991).

[49] Waddell and Sohal, 'Resistance', 543.

[50] Interview 10, Stage 3 (1975-2003).

[51] Interview 11, Stage 3 (1971-1992).

[52] See for example Dennis Lawton, *Education and Politics in the 1990s: Conflict or Consensus?* (London, Falmer, 1992).

[53] Interview 10, Stage 3 (1975-2003).

[54] Waddell and Sohal, 'Resistance', 544.

[55] Interview 12, Stage 3 (1973-1996).

[56] Interview 20, Stage 3 (1987-current).

[57] Interview 10, Stage 3 (1975-2003).

[58] Interview 1, Stage 3 (1962-1984).

[59] Interview 15, Stage 3 (1976-current).

[60] Interview 13, Stage 3 (1970-2008).

[61] Interview 10, Stage 3 (1975-2003).

[62] Interview 16, Stage 3 (1993-2004).

[63] Interview 20, Stage 3 (1987-current).

8.

ALUMNI VOICES
PAST, PRESENT AND LOOKING TO THE FUTURE

> I think we all had a special, splendid time, which we certainly will not readily forget. I don't know why I came here specifically to Winchester or who I wanted to be – just a teacher [. . .] just a teacher. But I knew who I was when I left! King Alfred's gave us an identity. It moulded us, yet developed our own originality. I became a deliverer of enquiry. I taught primary age children for thirty-two years, the last fourteen as Head teacher. A short time after I retired I received a letter from one of my early pupils. She had just given birth to a baby boy and wanted to name him after me. She said 'it was because you gave me confidence and an enquiring spirit. You taught me to question and consider each answer, to value friendship and believe in principle. You gave me hope in the future. If my child can grow up with half those qualities, I will be happy for his future – Thank-you'. Well I had gained that from my life with the ethos that was King Alfred's College. You see the geography may alter, the buildings and the campus expand, and the name may change, but the ethos that created our past and gave us our future can and should remain. I hope it will.[1]

In the conclusion we consider how oral histories and individual questionnaires can enrich, challenge and offer new insights into ways of writing the history of a university or college. We discuss how a case study such as Winchester enables us to raise much wider issues around the process and production of accounts based on oral history methods. The book is multi-authored in the true sense of the word, and our regular guest slots at the alumni reunion weekends have confirmed our sense that those who contribute their narratives also feel an investment in the final piece. At a time when the purpose of higher education is under the microscope, it is possible, through oral history, to tease out the complex relationship between institution and individual, and to identify what exactly it is that creates a common ground between alumni who studied perhaps as many as sixty years apart and makes their choice of location for their higher education so valuable and significant a part of their life history. Individually, the interviews conducted for the Alumni Voices project reflect the lives and careers of the interviewees; together they help form a narrative of the development of the university and changes in higher education.

The past sixty years have witnessed a period of continual change for further and higher education in the United Kingdom.[2] Government changes in education policies, funding support and an expansion in student numbers have impacted on all higher education institutions. Oral history has been used as a research tool in this project to realise data able to show how these changes, using the University of Winchester as an example, affected not only an institution, its staff and its students but also an institution's interactions with the wider community.[3] Through the interviews it has been possible to gain greater insight into how changes arising from a government report, such as the *Robbins Report* of 1963,[4] or the institutional reporting requirements of the Council for National Academic Awards,[5] were implemented and the subsequent changes this led to in academic processes, staff leadership styles and management of the College. These two examples are reflective of the many changes that have taken place in higher education. Over the past sixty years, as in Winchester, many institutions have changed from single sex to coeducational, have widened the spectrum of subjects that can be studied and expanded. Former polytechnics have become universities and new universities have been opened. This has led not only into an enormous nationwide growth in student numbers but also a corresponding growth in the number of buildings that form the campuses.

Our research data were generated by questionnaires and interviews. The first were analysed using SPSS and the latter by VRM[6] which allowed for a deeper interrogation. In permitting the voice of the individual participant to be heard, VRM helps to uncover themes that may have been overlooked. VRM recognises that all interviewers and respondents bring to the interview their own preconceptions and value systems. Hence one of the aims of this methodology is to engage with, rather than negate, the problems of representing the subject. By using four readings to examine the interview data, VRM acknowledges that the voice of the researcher, as well as the interviewee, must be taken into account. Another reading requires the researcher to look at the way in which the overall plot or story is presented by the respondent and how these experiences are then portrayed in relation to other aspects of their lives. Occasionally the interviewees assumed the identity of, and spoke on behalf of, the institution as a whole. As noted by Sue Hawkins, this gives an additional voice 'to the mix, even if it is a proxy voice – the voice of the institution given expression through the words of its employees'.[7] For some, the alumni project provided a new forum for them to reflect upon and share their experiences of higher education in ways they had not previously considered. Whilst in general the interview responses were positive, this was not always the case and at times reflection led to the memory of, and re-engendering of, difficult or painful emotions for a participant. When the interviews were analysed using VRM the pain or difficulty of the respondent could be witnessed in the way their speech moved rapidly between the pronouns 'I', 'we' and 'they' as they tried to distance themselves from or justify a particular event. It was not the remit of the project to unsettle the respondents but to chart the changing face of higher education through individual voices. The ethical dilemmas inherent in this project are part of the oral historian's daily decision-making and while some who read this might feel we have omitted some details, the story we have endeavoured to present is a scholarly interpretation of recorded conversations.

Across the questionnaire and interview data, staff and students were asked to consider whether they felt part of a community whilst at the College. In their responses they frequently referred to the 'ethos of the institution', the 'community feel', or 'being part of one large family'. Predominantly, memories of being a member of the community produced recollections of the mutual support that was gained from membership, its help in enabling those who were students to complete their courses, and the life lessons that occurred contemporaneously with their academic studies. Memories of social and domestic life during their time in higher education produced a greater volume of response from the students than recollections of their areas of academic study. Whilst ethos, family and community were not used as defined terms and were occasionally used interchangeably by the respondents, there was an expectation from them that the interviewer would, without difficulty, be able to comprehend the sense of meaning they were intending to convey and its importance to them. This raised several analytical problems for the research team, as neither ethos, nor community nor family can be interpreted as fixed cultural constructs. The use of our data to address these questions was similarly not straightforward, as staff and students held differing hierarchical positions within the institution; the respondents spanned a period of sixty years; institutional structures underwent immense change; student numbers grew and increasingly it was not possible for all to share residency on campus. At the suggestion of one our respondents, we used Ferdinand Tönnies's sociological concepts of 'Gemeinschaft' and 'Gesellschaft' as a way of understanding the ideas associated with community and analysing the changes.[8] Gemeinschaft is associated with common beliefs in a community where the welfare of the whole has precedence over the individual, exemplified by the family. This compares with Gesellschaft which is associated with business or nation and where individual loyalty is of less importance. Tönnies is careful to note that the two are not exclusive and are to be 'found interwoven in all kinds of associations'.[9]

As the similarities between running a business and a university have converged, with students now viewed as 'service users' or consumers and the necessity to compete against other institutions to secure a share of the higher-education market, it seemed appropriate to draw on business theories to interpret the changes that have taken place in higher education. John Kotter's work seeks to look at the differences between leadership and management and the factors necessary for successful change management.[10] His eight-step model has been used to analyse and comprehend the changes that have occurred in higher education. The eight steps include: recognition of the need for change; communication of the vision; acknowledgement of the resistance to organisational change and the necessity for a subsequent 'buy in'; before concluding with the incorporation of change into the organisation's culture and traditions. Records of the institutional changes that have taken place at the University of Winchester are well documented in official archives through the retention of reports, committee minutes, policy documents and other official publications. These documents record the actions undertaken by the institution's leadership and governing body to implement changes which ensured its successful continuation, demonstrated by its progression from a Diocesan teacher training college to its current status as a university. Whilst the factual records are immutable, the oral history interviews are able to provide a nuanced understanding of how this was achieved and the impact that it had upon the working lives of staff and management as these changes were realised.

In conjunction with Kotter, the use of Tönnies's concept is continued to demonstrate how institutional changes in management, bureaucracy and leadership styles move an institution from operating as a Gemeinschaft community to one more akin to Gesellschaft. Whilst the structure and running of the institution at Winchester became more business-like, with some staff expressing the difficulties they experienced adapting to a more Gesellschaft community, students across the period of research continued to make reference to having experienced a Gemeinschaft community during their period of study. Although institutional cohesion was no longer possible in the way that it had been when the institution numbered 150 students, students and staff each found arenas in which they could continue to create or experience a sense of community and belonging, demonstrating Tönnies's belief that the two types of community are not mutually exclusive. For students a community or 'college family' could be created with those who shared their hall of residence. Staff reported finding community through membership of the smaller unit of their faculty or department. Community membership was perceived as an important part of the higher education experience and held by respondents as contributing to student retention and the greater likelihood of course completion. Those students who did not qualify for halls, or mature students who were combining academic study with home commitments, expressed a sense of loss that possibly they had not benefitted as much from their time in higher education as a result of fewer interactions with the resident community. With the widespread adoption of social networking and the blurring for students of the divisions between their academic and social environments, new types of community are being created. The virtual community is one that allows for synchronous and asynchronous contributions to be made, enabling all students, resident or not, to contribute to academic discussion outside of 'working hours' and also to the cohort banter. This is perhaps lessening the necessity for physical residency to constitute full membership of the community.

The purpose of the Church colleges when established in the nineteenth century was to train elementary school teachers to be Christian missionaries, with teaching viewed as a vocational duty. As these institutions continue to celebrate and recognise their faith foundation we investigate perceptions of the spiritual life of the community at Winchester and report on the changes noted by this research across the period.[11] The oral history interviews were analysed in historical context and in conjunction with contemporary debates, including the question of what role the Cathedrals Group Universities should continue to play in higher education.[12] Respondents were asked for their views on religion, their personal attitudes towards faith beliefs and what difference they felt this did or did not make to the life of an academic institution. Respondents were asked if they could recognise something distinctive about an institution with a Christian foundation when compared with secular universities. These questions link to larger debates, which question the place of religion in education at all levels, and the Anglican Church as the official state Church, particularly by those who would argue that Britain is now a secular society.[13] It was these questions that proved the hardest for participants to answer. The responses were analysed by date in three separate sections pre-1960, 1960-1976 and post 1976. Questions about religion became linked by the respondents to discussions of morality, personal value systems, and choice of career pathways, voluntary activities and the duties of good citizenship. Over the time period, fewer respondents described themselves as regular participants in organised faith activities, Christianity being the dominant faith. However, our results show this decrease in formal participation cannot be taken to automatically correspond with a lack of interest in religion or a de-valuing of religious beliefs. The language used in discussions expanded to include reference to a sense of spirituality, an inner personal belief, one not necessarily linked to a named faith.[14] Non-believers still expressed appreciation of the pastoral services that a dedicated university chaplain could offer staff and students, and valued the Chapel as a space for reflection and contemplation. As students are now drawn from a wider background the student body can no longer be represented as a single faith community. Consequently the campus now includes a Muslim prayer room and a multi-faith space is currently under development. Despite the inability of respondents to be precise in locating the differences between an institution with a faith foundation and a secular university, there was a perception that a gentler and more caring atmosphere was exhibited.[15] Some respondents felt that a Christian foundation permitted the staff to include a concern for the students' spiritual and mental well-being in addition to concern for their academic studies. Another respondent felt that Winchester's roots as a Christian foundation continued to shape its ethos as one that is caring and where the individual matters.[16]

In 1958, when the governing body at Winchester agreed that the college should expand to 400 students with a balance of 250 men to 150 women, this initially generated strong oppositional protest amongst the students.[17] In the 1959 edition of *The Wintonian* the outgoing student president stated that 'the opposite sex will feature in ever increasing numbers'.[18] His comments were prescient. By 1967, women comprised 40 per cent of the total student body, and in 2005 this had risen to 71 per cent. The inclusion of female students led, for the first time, to the employment of women lecturers amongst the College's academic staff, with Robina Macintyre appointed as the first woman Vice-Principal in 1960. Previously the employment of women was limited to the support roles of secretary and College Matron, resulting in a predominantly male staff. Students of this time described the College as one big family. The Principal, the head of the College, was described as a Christian father figure, in an institution which looked after its students academically and spiritually. Another student likened the atmosphere of the College to a monastic community, an atmosphere that would be lost once women were admitted.[19] These comments were illustrative of a culture of male hegemony but under the aegis of Christianity, one that enabled men to publicly exhibit care for each other: care acceptably described as 'male camaraderie'. Despite these protests, alumnae who entered the College at this time did not report experiencing feelings of animosity, and with the hindsight of years these male respondents laughed off their early fears. For the researcher their attitudes led us to question why those fears arose. What were the predominant social constructions of women in this period? What changed in society during the intervening sixty years that caused these respondents to reconsider and confess their fears as ridiculous or unfounded? The interviews were examined to trace these changes and question whether the concept of a culture of care, frequently mentioned in relation to the institution, also changed once the student body became predominantly female.

The increase in the numbers of female students at Winchester was reflective of a growth, across the country, of women accessing higher education which started in the 1960s and continues to this day. In particular the 1960s coincided with an increase in the population's birth rate and a corresponding need for an increase in the number of trained teachers. For women, long associated with care of the young, teaching was seen as an attractive and socially acceptable profession. As the educational ideology within teacher training and primary education shifted to a more child-centred approach, concerned with the needs of the individual child and endorsed in 1967 by the *Plowden Report, Children and their Primary Schools*, primary education was viewed by contemporary society as a 'natural' occupation for women, but one which still necessitated a professional training. Winchester was an early adopter of a child-centred approach into the curriculum, encouraged by a Vice-Principal who had previously worked at a teacher training college linked to Maria Montessori.[20] The alumni interviews identified that a culture of care could be linked to both men and women; it was not exclusively female, although it may have been manifested in different ways. The work of a former Winchester lecturer, Jennifer Nias, is used to explore aspects of care, and which aspects are dominant at any one time. Nias identifies six meanings of care, including one which looks to 'care' as social conditioning identifiable in socio-historical roots.[21] In her article Nias comments on how colleges of education clung to their 'peculiar' institutional values despite expansion, and academic and societal changes. In the case of Winchester these roots would include its Christian foundation and an adherence to these values may explain how an ethos of care continues to be recognised and transmitted across the generations of students.

Analysis of the oral history interviews allowed for changes in the discourse of gender between the cohorts to be observed. Gender was used by the respondents to consider what had, or had not, changed in the societal attitudes that surround men and women. Discussions of gender enabled the respondents to provide comment on: the continuing construction and reconstruction of male and female roles, the relationships between men and women as students, relationships between colleagues in the professional workplace, and the work of women to achieve parity of opportunity for appointment to senior management posts. The feminisation of teaching was noted, as were the more recent calls for a return of men to primary teaching and the reasons behind this. Whilst the numbers of women on the staff increased, our research uncovered opinions of a time lag between women's physical presence and their acceptance as equals with their male counterparts. However, by 2013, any time lag that may have existed had been dispelled by the positions of Chancellor, Vice-Chancellor, Deputy Chancellor and Dean/Pro-Vice Chancellor on the Senior Management Team all being held by women. Through the use of oral history, using Winchester as a model, we have been able to provide more nuanced understanding of the impact of the changing gender ratios in higher education.

Graduation in Winchester Cathedral
'The highlight of my studies was receiving my degree in Winchester Cathedral with a reception in the Guildhall - and parading around Winchester in cap and gown!'

The imprint of the campus and the location of the institution within the City of Winchester featured strongly in the memories of many of the interviewees. While the buildings constituting the campus have changed, in their recollections they had not, they were fixed at the point in time when they either studied or worked there. The respondents' efforts to describe in detail how things had looked were marked, as if in doing so we would be able to move with them, back through time, and experience it as they had, to see buildings and features that in some cases no longer exist. In their recollections of Winchester itself, the enduring geographical features such as St Giles Hill, or the position of the Cathedral enabled respondents to envision a sense of continuity between the past and the present. We have used the work of Doreen Massey to examine and interpret the interviewees' responses. Massey notes that in understanding the identity of places, it would perhaps be wrong to separate space and time or geography and history.[22] The visual descriptions provided by the respondents suggested that a fifth reading should be added to Mauthner and Doucet's voice relational analysis, that of the 'spoken visual'[23] enabling us to understand how the physical location of the students' experience of higher education contributed to their developing sense of identity. In our work we questioned to what extent physical surroundings affected a student's experience of higher education and what legacy it left. We wondered if students who study at an institution with geographically dispersed sites across a city have a different experience of higher education from those at a smaller campus-based institution. We questioned how important is the physical attractiveness of a campus and its locale in attracting students' applications. Certainly in their production of marketing materials, universities now highlight good transport links and local geographical and historical points of interest in their efforts to attract students from home and abroad.

In considering space and place, the links between the institution and the city, or 'town and gown', are examined to determine the nature of these links and how these links have changed or evolved over time. In terms of their location the institution and the city at Winchester are physically close, allowing for an easy fluidity of movement between the two sites and interplay between their respective populations. Students have been both consumers in the city, contributing to the success and maintenance of local businesses, and providers, in terms of their labour. This research has found that, with the advent of student fees and maintenance loans, the number of students at Winchester seeking to combine study with term time paid employment has increased. Winchester students, like others across the country, are now to be found contributing to the local economy by their work in the city's shops, bars, cafes and hospitals. This is in contrast to our earlier alumni for whom employment was largely confined to vacation periods and in the locale of their home residence. Many students engage in a formal relationship with the city and the local community by undertaking work experience as a part of their studies. Local schools have a long-standing relationship with the institution, evidenced by their hosting of students for school experience. As the number of subject degrees and other professional courses has expanded at the institution, so too has the number of students engaging in work experience across a growing number of fields in the city and surrounding areas. Our interview and questionnaire data showed that there has been a tradition of students undertaking voluntary work in the local area, providing another forum for 'town and gown' interaction. There has been a long relationship between Winchester prison and the institution. Currently, the Playing for Time theatre company presents a show each year where prisoners and students work together to produce and perform plays. In 2013 this company celebrated its tenth anniversary.

The mutual relationship between the institution and the city of Winchester is evidenced further by the fact that the university is itself a provider of employment opportunities for the local population. Its staff and students increasingly act as a resource for the development of joint business and research ventures, and its facilities are used to host university and city events. There is evidence of city and university members each giving of their time and knowledge to ensure the expert running of their respective local organisations and institutions. The Diocese has, since the institution's foundation, provided representatives to sit on the University's governing body and the current Vice-Chancellor is chair of the Winchester City Trust.[24] There is recognition of the benefits, in terms of continued growth and development, to be derived from a strong relationship between town and gown.

Interviews with staff enabled us to see how physical changes to the campus, changes in the use of its buildings and the siting of staff within the campus, chart the shift from a Gemeinschaft to a Gesellschaft community. Staff reported small incidents which, whilst appearing too insignificant for recording in an official history, are nevertheless indicators of that change. The Senior Common Room (SCR) acted as a central point for post, for lunch and tea breaks, and for use of the staff phone, consequently it was likely that all staff would at some point each day enter this space. When the institution had a universal timetable, with fixed stopping points for breaks, and only one location to obtain coffee or tea, staff from all subject areas had the opportunity to meet informally each day. As a result the SCR was used as a site for a quick clarification of points; it acted as a space for intellectual debate or informal mentoring between staff. Once the timetable changed and fixed breaks ceased to exist, it became harder to guarantee when, or if, staff could be found in the SCR. Consequently arrangements to meet had, of necessity, to become more formal. As the campus expanded, some staff found it easier to have coffee facilities in their own departments, again lessening the opportunities for the creation of a cohesive Gemeinschaft community. The interviews uncovered how the physical location of a department within the campus could be perceived by staff as indicative of their status within the institution. When one department was relocated further away from the main campus it was viewed as a cause for concern by staff. However, students reflecting on the same move perceived it as one that was beneficial to their studies. For these students the increased distance led to the department being viewed as an oasis, one more conducive to creativity

The interview and questionnaire data generated by this research have produced tangible results by increasing the resources of the university archive and enhancing the existing documentary and pictorial records. Additionally it has enabled us to discern answers to some of our less tangible, but nevertheless key, research questions. What are the connections that link students whose time in higher education spans a period of sixty years? How can the ethos of an institution be defined? And what do students gain in addition to their academic qualifications? Our data show, and the quotation at the opening of the chapter especially testifies, that students and staff across the generations have continued to make reference to the importance of being a part of the learning community at Winchester. Irrespective of the size of the campus or the growth in student numbers, they have described this as a caring community, one that helped them to grow academically and where they were able to develop and test out their adult identities and grow in confidence. They attribute the caring atmosphere they encountered to the ethos and guiding principles of the institution: an ethos generated by its foundation values and manifested in the positive interactions witnessed between staff and students. They have described the lasting impact of the values they gained from the institution and how they have taken these values with them into their subsequent professional lives, one aim of which has been to share these values with peers and future generations, helping them to similarly grow and develop. The university, in common with other institutions with similar histories, needs now to determine how it can face future challenges whilst maintaining its distinctive ethos and values into the next sixty years. An ethos considered responsible for its success in providing a holistic experience of higher education for its alumni.

The quotation which begins this chapter raises the questions that were central to our research. Carefully constructed interviews and questionnaires using alumni voices offer a way into writing a university history which explores the relationships between: students and staff; students and the institution; students and the wider world.

Notes to Chapter 8.

---

[1] Rob Pepper, speaking at the Winton Reunion, July 2007.

[2] See Derek Gillard, *Education in England: A Brief History:* www.educationengland.org.uk (accessed 19 October 2013).

[3] Harold Silver, *Tradition and Higher Education* (Winchester: Winchester University Press, 2007).

[4] Lionel Robbins, *The Report of the Committee on Higher Education*, known as *The Robbins Report* (London: HMSO, 1963).

[5] The Council for National Academic Awards, 1964-1993: archiveshub.ac.uk (accessed November 1, 2013).

[6] See Natalie Mauthner and Andrea Doucet, 'Reflections on a Voice Centred Relational Method', in *Feminist Dilemmas in Qualitative Research: Public Knowledge and Private Lives,* ed. Jane Ribbons and Rosalind Edwards (London: Sage 1998), 119-146.

[7] Sue Hawkins, '"Whose Story is it Anyway?": The Challenges of Conducting Institutional Histories', *Journal of Conservation and Museum Studies* (2012): www.jcms-journal.com (accessed 5 January 2013).

[8] Ferdinand Tönnies, *Community and Association* (first published as *Gemeinschaft und Gesellschaft* in 1887) (Routledge and Kegan Paul, London 1955), 18.

[9] Charles P Loumis, Introduction in Tönnies, xv.

[10] John Kotter, 'Leading Change: Why Transformation Efforts Fail' *Harvard Business Review,* (March-April 1995); John Kotter, 'What Leaders Really Do'. *Harvard Business Review* (1999).

[11] See Ewart Wooldridge and Eddie Newcombe, *Distinctiveness and Identity in a Challenging HE Environment: A Unique Opportunity for Cathedrals Group Institutions* (Chester: The Cathedrals Group, 2011).

[12] The Cathedrals Group, 'Welcome', *The Cathedrals Group*: cathedralsgroup.org.uk (accessed 29 October 2013).

[13] See Callum G Brown, *The Death of Christian Britain, Understanding Secularisation 1800-2000* (London and New York: Routledge, 2001). Callum Brown's current research project is 'Religion and the demographic revolution since c. 1960'.

[14] Robert Pigott, 'Is Christianity Shrinking or Just Changing?', *BBC News* (11 December 2012): www.bbc.co.uk/news (accessed 30 October 2013).

[15] Questionnaire 120, Stage 1 (1993-1997).

[16] Evidence of the University's Christian Foundation can be found on its website as part of its Mission and Values. There it states: 'The University celebrates its Christian Foundation, and welcomes people of all faiths and people of none. Together, we aim to explore the mystery of life and grow in wisdom and love.' See 'About Us', *The University of Winchester*: winchester.ac.uk (accessed 30 October 2013).

[17] Filmed interview 8, Stage 2 (1960-62).

[18] *The Wintonian* 13.2 (1959): 15.

[19] *The Wintonian* 1960.

[20] Maria Montessori was an occasional lecturer at Maria Assumpta Teacher Training College (founded 1946). See *Maria Assumpta*: www.mariaassumpta (accessed 20 October 2013).

[21] Jennifer Nias, 'Value-persistence and Utility in Colleges of Education', *Education for Teaching* 89 (1972): 29.

[22] Doreen Massey, 'Places and their Pasts', *History Workshop Journal* 39 (1995): 182-192.

[23] Stephanie Spencer, 'A Uniform Identity: Schoolgirl Snapshots and the Spoken Visual', *History of Education*, 36.2 (2007): 227-246.

---

[24] Until the 1990s, the Bishop of Winchester was traditionally the Chair of the Governors.

Appendix 1.

THE QUESTIONNAIRE AND INTERVIEW PROCESS

At each of the three stages of the Alumni Voices Project we drew up a questionnaire designed to elicit both quantitative and qualitative data. While we did not want to deter respondents, the questionnaires were, of necessity, quite detailed and required some time to complete. Many questions appeared at all three stages of the project and at each stage the questionnaire was piloted before being sent out to possible respondents.

To find respondents for the first two stages of the project, which targeted former students, we initially consulted the records of the institution's long established alumni association, the Winton Club. To broaden the sample and include those who had chosen to stay in touch with their social group but not necessarily with their alma mater, we also contacted other alumni through the social networking website, Friends Reunited.[1] This technology, which in 2004 was comparatively new,[2] had the advantage of being cheap and quick. It overcame geographical distance and, as members tend to use their 'original' names, it also overcame the problem of those female students who had changed their names on marriage.[3] For the third stage of the project, which targeted staff, the Alumni Office at the University approached former staff on our behalf.[4] We also 'advertised' on the college intranet for participants from among staff with more than fifteen years' service and made personal approaches to certain staff whom we considered had a special contribution to make and who might have already 'volunteered' to take part, but who had not always filled in the questionnaire. Those completing the questionnaires were required to confirm that they had no objection to the use of the material from their questionnaires or interviews being used for the purposes of research or publication. They were also required to confirm whether they were happy to be interviewed, as we had promised that all responses would be confidential and the respondents would remain anonymous. Although the majority were happy to have their names disclosed, we decided not to use real names although there are occasions where, by virtue of the position they held, it is not possible to disguise the identity of particular respondents.

The questionnaire we devised for the first stage of the project posed many questions about the student experience, enquiring about living in student accommodation, social lives, personal development and the relevance to future career of the course studied. There were also two especially important points that we wished to explore. The first related to any possible spiritual development connected to the institution's position as a Church college: the second to the relevance of the gender balance during their courses of study. In 1960 there were sixty women and 330 men but the tables gradually turned and, as described in Chapter 2, the female students at the institution now considerably outnumber the male.[5] At the second stage of the project specific questions were posed to ascertain the extent to which the students were involved with the wider community both in Winchester and beyond. These included questions relating to employment in the local area, joining local sports teams or local organisations and the number of occasions on which they travelled away from college during normal term time. We also set out to find what proportion of students remained in Winchester after graduation.[6] In addition to the data collected from these questionnaires and subsequent interviews, we had the opportunity to film some further interviews at the college annual reunion, the Winton weekend, in 2006. As a result fourteen more alumni were interviewed, resulting in about four hours of film, which required us to consider the addition that the visual made to our analysis. The questionnaire we devised for the third stage, the staff stage, was designed to complement those of the first two stages. Additionally, given that the participants may have spent many years, or in some cases the majority of their career, at the institution, it required respondents to reflect on how things might have changed over time especially whether there was a sense of shared beliefs and values between management and staff and the extent to which they were given freedom in what they taught.[7]

The questionnaire data generated by the project was analysed using a statistical social sciences software package, SPSS. This enabled the data to be interrogated against a number of variables including gender, year of entry, prior education and religious beliefs, and it served to highlight any significant differences or similarities between the three data sets. MaxQData, a qualitative data analysis package, was used to manage the volume of interview data, carry out the initial coding and identify themes.

For information we attach the questionnaire from the second stage of the project as an example, together with the draft document drawn up for this stage that was then sent to interviewees as a suggestion as to what they might like to think about in advance of the interview. As Chapter 1 has highlighted we refer to this as Participant Elicitation through Peer Comments. The items in italics represent the questions relating to the individual's own responses, the specific period when he/she was at the institution and an aide memoire to the interviewer as to the information to try to establish. The section concludes with a transcript of a complete interview, again from the second stage, which addresses many of the themes referred to in the book.

Notes to Appendix 1.

---

[1] We looked at the students' entries on the website and chose a cross section determined by their age and experiences since leaving college.

[2] It should be mentioned that in 2004 when the project started, this was the most used social networking website. If we were starting the project now, we would no doubt find participants through *Facebook, MySpace,* and others.

[3] As Sally Power, Geoff Whitty and Tony Edwards acknowledge, there were drawbacks at this time because of website regulations that stipulated that you could not include your direct contact details in the approaches made and those wanting to participate had to seek you out. See Sally Power, Geoff Whitty and Tony Edwards, 'Success Sustained? A Follow-up Study of the "Destined for success?" Cohort', *Research Papers in Education,* 21.3 (2006): 235-253.

[4] This was necessary because of stricter requirements regarding data protection.

[5] At this first stage we received some seventy-five responses (around 50 per cent of those we approached) and carried out ten interviews. The respondents varied from those who were among the original female cohort in 1960 and those who had only recently graduated. While we endeavoured to balance the responses from across the whole period, there was a particularly strong response from those who started their college course in the 1960s, with 37 per cent coming from this group. On completion of this stage we produced a pamphlet which was distributed at the celebrations for University College status. A little later, to share the results of our research, we held a seminar where

several of those who had been involved in the project were joined by some of the current students to share their experiences of higher education in Winchester.

[6] The data for this stage of the project was based on ninety-one questionnaire responses, again about 50 per cent of those approached, plus twenty audio interviews. The participants at this stage of the project ranged from a handful of alumni who had been students at King Alfred's College in the 1930s to those who had graduated fairly recently. As in the first stage, in spite of efforts to obtain a cross section of responses from different student cohorts, there was strong representation from those from the 1950s (20 per cent) and 1960s (30 per cent). We also produced a pamphlet from the data and this was distributed to all those who took part. We are grateful to the Winton Club for providing a small grant to fund the printing of the pamphlet.

[7] The date for this stage was based on fifty questionnaires and twenty-plus interviews. Participants had mostly been employed at the institution for many years: the earliest joining during the 1950s, many who joined during the 1960s and a small number who work at the University today.

Appendix 2.

QUESTIONNAIRE FROM STAGE TWO OF ALUMNI VOICES PROJECT (The Institution and the Wider Community)

---

1. ABOUT YOU

Are you male or female?	Male	Female
Dates of study at KAC	Start	Finish
What course of study did you attend?		
Did you complete your course?		

How old were you when you started your course?	Under 20	20-30	31-40	Over 40

	Single	Married	Other (please specify)
What was your marital status			

	Yes If so who and when?	No
Had/Has anyone else in your family studied in Winchester?		

Where were you born?

Place (Village/Town)	District/County	Country

Where did you live prior to attending KAC?

Within 10 miles of KAC	Within 20 miles KAC	Within 50 miles KAC	Within 100 miles KAC

South/South East	South West	North	North West
Midlands	London	West	Scotland
Wales	Northern Ireland	Overseas Europe	Overseas not Europe

2. COMING TO COLLEGE

Why did you choose to study in Winchester? (Tick as many as applicable)
Size
Course
Friends already here
Close to home
Good transport links to home
Church College
Good Reputation
The city itself
A cathedral city
Other (please specify)

3. STUDENT LIFE

(a) Accommodation

Where did you live while you were at KAC ? Tick as many as applicable
Student Halls
Which Hall(s) did you live in?
Rented private student accommodation
At home
Other

(b) Working in the area

	Yes	No
Did you have a part time job in the Winchester area * during your studies? (* Where we refer to the Winchester area in the questionnaire we are thinking of a radius of about 15 miles)		

If you answered yes, please tick where. Tick as many as applicable
Within college itself
Shop
Café/Restaurant
Bar/Pub
Office
Other (please specify)

	Yes	No
Did your course involve any placement /work experience in the local area		

If you answered 'yes', please reflect on your experience and advise us of any particular memories

(c) Social Life

	Yes	No
Did you join any societies at KAC?		

If you answered 'yes' what did you join and for how long? Did this involve you in playing local teams or becoming involved with local societies?

If you answered 'no', please tell us why not.

	Yes	No
Did you join any sports team at KAC?		

If you answered 'yes' what did you join and for how long? Did this involve playing local teams?

If you answered 'no', please tell us why not.

	Yes	No
Did you get involved in the organisation of any societies or the Student Union ...		

If you answered 'yes' which ones and in what capacity?

(d) College and the Community

	Yes (please specify)	No
Did you join any societies or sports teams in Winchester?		

	Yes (please specify)	No
Did you attend any joint college/community events while you were at KAC ... (, e.g. choirs)		

	Yes (please specify)	No
Did you get involved in any voluntary work in Winchester and surrounding area while you were at KAC? ...		

	Yes	No
Did you feel that there was a sense of community at KAC?		
Did you feel that you were part of it?		
Did you feel part of the wider Winchester community?		

Please comment on the sense of community (or otherwise)

(e) The Church

	Yes	No
Did you attend KAC chapel services on a regular basis?		

	Yes	No
Did you attend local church/cathedral services on a regular basis?		

(f) Beyond KAC

	Yes	No
Did you travel outside Winchester for sport/social reasons during term time?		

If you have answered yes, please tell us how often you left Winchester during term time, where you went and for what purpose? (e.g. to London for concerts)

	Car	Train	'Bus	Coach	Motorbike
What form of transport did you use? Tick as many as are applicable					

	Yes	No
Did you have your own car while studying in Winchester?		

(g) Reflections on Student Life in Winchester

Please reflect on your experiences as a student in Winchester, highlighting in particular any significant places or events that represent your experience (e.g. Cathedral, Water Meadows, Public Houses, Hat Fair)

4. WHAT DID YOU DO WHEN YOU LEFT COLLEGE?

(a) Career

What career /job did you enter after KAC?

Did you change career / job? If so, after how long and what did you do?

	Yes	No
Have you undertaken further study?		

(b) Where do you live?

If you stayed in the Winchester area after completing your course, please tell us why. (Tick as many as applicable.) Please strike through whole section if not applicable
Obtained job locally
Nice place to live and commute from
Friends and family here
Many of College contemporaries also stayed here
Good place to settle down (e.g. schooling)
Other (please specify)

If you were living in the Winchester area five years after completing your course, please tell us why. (Tick as many as applicable) Please strike through whole section if not applicable
Obtained job locally
Nice place to live and commute from
Friends and family here
Good place to settle down (e.g. schooling)
Other (please specify)

If you are still living in the Winchester area now, please tell us why. (Tick as many as applicable) Please strike through whole section if not applicable
Obtained job locally
Nice place to live and commute from

Friends and family here
Good place to settled down (e.g. schooling)
Other (please specify)

If you have stayed in the Winchester area, please reflect on how the relationship between the university/college and the community may have changed

If you moved away from the Winchester area when you completed your course or have moved away since, please indicate why you decided to leave the area. Tick as many as are applicable. Please strike through whole section if not applicable
Job
Housing
Finance
To join/rejoin family living elsewhere
College contemporaries all moved away
Too urban
Too rural
Didn't like Winchester
Other

If you live away from the Winchester area, please indicate how often you return to visit. (Tick the one that is most appropriate)
Several times a year
Annually
Every five years
Every ten years
Less than that

If you return to the Winchester area regularly, what is the principal reason for your visit? (Tick the one that is most appropriate
Visit the Institution
Visit old friends
Enjoy the area
Other (please specify)

(c) Maintaining contact

	Yes	No
Did you stay in contact with any fellow student or staff when you left KAC?		

	1year	5years	10years	Longer
If you answered yes, for how long did you maintain contact?				

	Yes	No	N/A
If you have remained in the Winchester area, do any of your College friends who have left the area return to visit you?			

Would you like to comment on maintaining contact/visiting with old friends from KAC?

(d) Voluntary work

After finishing your studies did you / do you undertake any local (i.e. local to where you live) voluntary work. If so please comment

Have you been / are you involved in local Church activities. If so, in what capacity?

5. YOUR OVERALL EXPERIENCE

And finally! Thank you so much for filling in this questionnaire. Please comment on how significant was the city of Winchester to :
(a) Your experience of higher education?
(b) Your future career and life?

Appendix 3.

DRAFT DOCUMENT FOR INTERVIEWEES
(Participant Elicitation through Peer Comments)

The formal interviews will be mainly based on the responses we have received to the questionnaires and focus loosely on three areas of enquiry:

1. The sense of community within the institution
2. Links with the local community
3. The effect (or otherwise) on future life/career of studying at/in Winchester

In many cases the questions will include specific quotes from other respondents. You will be asked to comment on these.

1. The sense of community within the institution

Almost everyone who has completed a questionnaire has agreed that there was a sense of community, an almost 'instant camaraderie' and almost all felt part of it. To what extent do you agree or disagree with the reasons that have been suggested for this?

Academic

There was a sense of common purpose

The Principal was an excellent figurehead

The staff was understanding and sympathetic: they all knew you and treated you as equals. *(How well did you know the staff and how well did they know you?)*

Nobody had jobs in addition to their studies

Social

It was a small college

Everyone was accommodated on campus and ate formal

meals together
The clubs and societies made the place buzz
Everyone called everyone else 'friend'
Hostel/Hall communities were satellite groupings of the larger College community.
The Students Union was the focal point for all
The work/socialisation balance was 60 per cent / 40 per cent.
You could experiment within boundaries.
I know that when my friends or friends of others in the group came to stay from other Universities etc. they always commented on how friendly the place was.
Spiritual
The College was a Church foundation
The Chapel was at the heart of the College and Chapel Services which were attended by staff as well as students seemed to provide the framework for our days.
We saw each other through good and bad times and common experiences within the same environment broke down barriers.
We were always there for each other
Principal Dickinson cared for the college as if it was his 'child'. *(Obviously only appropriate to those here in the 1950s but that in fact is quite a large number of the respondents).*
Tutors operated an effective pastoral system.
The institution championed giving everyone else dignity and respect when it is earned and having a humble compassion for the less fortunate.
It was motivating and forgiving.

2. Links with the local community
This second area is divided into two sections. First you are asked to comment on various quotations that suggest why links with the local community might have been limited. Second you are asked to comment more specifically on events and places that might have been relevant to your life as a student in the local community.
Please comment on the extent to which you agree with

these comments:

Section One

In the 1950s, Winchester seemed rather remote to the College

We led such a full and busy life seven days a week academically, spiritually and socially there was no time to get involved in the local community to any significant extent.

KAC did feel like a separate world inside Winchester

I rarely felt the need to go outside the college for activities as there was plenty to do already

We were peripheral – a group of outsiders stuck up by the hospital and prison and infinitely inferior to Winchester College, St Swithun's or the Cathedral laity. We were the respectable poor, like the poor bloody infantry in the barracks down the road, and the old chaps from St Cross marked out as paupers by their cloaks and hats.

Winchester struck me as a series of interlocking communities with which we came into contact.

Section Two

We were made to feel very welcome as we shopped and drank coffee and drank in the pubs

KAC did feel like a separate world inside Winchester but we certainly felt we were living and shopping/eating out/visiting cinemas etc. in the town. I certainly felt as if I lived in Winchester.

At Graduation, I did feel that the Wider Winchester community took pride in our achievements and appreciated our contribution to the diversity of Winchester.

The following places have been mentioned by more than one respondent as being significant to their life when studying in Winchester. How much significance do they have to you and why?

- Farley Mount, St Catherine's Hill, St Cross, the Water Meadows, the Cathedral and Close.
- Salisbury Diocesan College, Bishop Otter College, La Sainte Union, Avon Tyrrell.
- Ken's Fish and Chip Shop, Cadena Café, Kardomah Café, The Black Swan (The Mucky Duck?), Two

Bare Feet Coffee bar, The Elephant, The County Arms, The Vine, The Royal Oak, The Green Man, The Baker's Arms

- *(For more recent alumni – Louisianas, The Porthouse, The Guildhall Tavern, The Exchange, Greens, Muswells)*

General

How much would you agree or disagree with the following comments about Winchester?

- Winchester had an atmosphere conducive to study
- All the trees and other greenery, the ancient streets and buildings, the cathedral and close provided a backdrop to what was a pleasant place in which to live and study.
- Fantastic loved the College and its place in the city's history and the feeling of carrying on an age old tradition of learning in the city. *(How important is the sense of 'history' in Winchester to you?)*

3. The effect (or otherwise) on future life/career of studying at/in Winchester

As in the previous sections please give us your opinion on the comments made by other respondents:

- The city of Winchester enhanced my experience of higher education.
- KAC and Winchester gave me a vision for my life ahead.
- The city was an enjoyable place to live but I believe the in-college experience was the most significant influence on me.
- It was at KAC that I learned to be responsible for my work, output, both academic and social and those lessons proved to be my making
- Wouldn't change my higher education experience at all – thoroughly enjoyed it and gained so much from it!

Appendix 4

Interview from Stage Two

If you could start off talking about the sense of community within the institution and how you've found it.

I went to a boarding school when younger and then I was a day boy at what's now a public school, so it was interesting that there was a community immediately from the beginning of my course there. As soon as you arrived you were part of that community. It's very difficult to put your finger on exactly what it was. I was just looking at a photo here and I recognised the person in it. He was the senior student in the hostel I was in and he actually introduced himself to everybody who came to the hostel. He was in his second or third year I think and he introduced himself to all the first years immediately and made sure that everybody had everything and knew where they were going. Even though I'd been to boarding school, so had been through it several times before, it was very, very smooth as an entry into the place. Everything was being pulled down. It wasn't buildings because they were more or less empty. All the study bedrooms in the main building had gone. It was just a big, open space upstairs and downstairs I think there were a couple of classrooms left, so it wasn't the buildings. But it was the community.

In what way was it like an Oxbridge college?

I didn't realise that until later. It was only when I read Tom Brown at Oxford that I realised it was exactly what it was like there. I suppose everything was small and central enough in the same sense I imagine it would be in an Oxbridge College, and all the meals being taken together definitely and high tables. There were always staff, not all of them, but always staff at the high table so that if you arrived late you bowed in and if you wanted to go early you bowed out. There was a lot of that. All the staff, as they had at my school, wore gowns. All of them wore them all the time as far as I remember. So that was more or less the same. But really it was again that intangible feeling of being part of a community. There were no bits that you didn't know about.

How well did you know the Principal?

He actually lived in a small hostel at the time if I remember rightly and I went there a couple of times because I'd come from the same town as Royston Van Tromp, who a descendent of the Dutch Admiral who sailed up the Thames and devastated the Navy. But apart from that I was never really aware of the Principal apart from the fact that in the second year I was the entertainments secretary, which meant we went to meetings with the Principal. But he tended to leave a lot of what appeared to be more difficult decisions to the deputy principals, of whom there were two that year, one male and one woman. They were very much deputy principals and either of them would have made a principal in the sense that he did. The only time I knew him was at the Valedictory Dinner, when I stopped him falling over the edge of the Dytch because he'd had a bit too much to drink.

How well did he know you?

He was the sort of person that you got the impression that he did know who you were. There were 146 students living in college, so not a massive number, and I always had the impression that he did know who you were. That was in 1959. But in the second year I did actually see quite a lot of him. He gave the impression that he knew your name and knew you as well. I did actually go to a sherry morning once I remember, I was invited once in the second year, so I had no reason to actually know him but he gave the impression that he knew you.

What about the staff?

Well on reflection I think I was fairly lucky to pass now I think about it and I supposed that the staff did know me. I suppose I did quite well on teaching practice and that swung things in my favour because I was the first entertainments secretary to actually pass for several years and the sort of thing you had was my friend BJ, who I'm still friends with now, we got onto a history trip, got onto the coach just before we took the final history exam, and Mr. Shipley, Head of History, turned round and said 'Ah Mr. J and Mr. C, a last ditch effort to pass!'. He wouldn't have said that had you just been a number on a list. He wouldn't have known that. Because in my case he was absolutely accurate. It didn't occur to me at the time that I'd fail but I thought I must be fairly close to the mark. I did very little work. I set out at the beginning not to do any work or as little as possible. I'd just done Classics at A level and had to work quite hard with that and decided I'd had enough. That's why I didn't go to university basically. I don't think I'd have survived the first year really. I'm not the greatest studier in the world. I have got a degree. I went to Birkbeck College and worked hard there but at Winchester I set out to do PE and woodwork, a combination you could do but mine was the first year that they stopped that combination. So I had a go at PE and music and dropped music and did PE and history. I did a long study for history but never managed to complete one for PE and did all my PE assignments in the holidays, nothing during the term. In the second year we had a new history lecturer, Jennifer Nias, and I've corresponded with her at some point. I think she went back to Oxford or Cambridge, she was quite well known in areas of primary school education. She arrived with a new broom and I think she was probably quite young and we were caught up suddenly in having to do quite a lot of history essays which we really might have got away without doing had it been up to Mr. Shipley.

So what were you doing?

The clubs and societies were important. I was very, very busy the whole time. Very busy indeed. I played rugby, squash, swimming, hockey at various times. You have to remember that it's not actually a two year course if you add up the months. It's a really, really quick course. By the time we got to November of the first term, having started in the second or third week in September, we were out in schools and that was really a sudden death to weed a few people out who looked at it and decided they didn't want to do it. So that was the whole of the first term taken up. In the third term, the summer was taken up by the teaching practice as well, the whole of the second half or more of the term. I presume that meant they could deal with exams because there weren't that many staff in terms of the way exams are run now. Then there was a long TP in the second term of the second year and the last year finished by June, so it's a fairly short time.

But you managed to fit in other activities.

Yes, obviously in the second year I not only played sport but organised all sorts of dances. I only have shadowy memories of that because binge drinking wasn't invented this year, it did actually take place then amongst certain groups. Obviously a good half, if not more, were ex-servicemen, so many were used to it, and the rest of us younger ones were treated very much as being younger by them. So we either had to catch up and join in or go and do something else. We went away to all of the women's colleges. We had a coach and went out on Saturday nights. There was one in Salisbury, one in Chichester, a couple in Southampton, we went to Weymouth once and I'm sure there were a couple of others too. They did come to us as well because there's a picture there of a woman from Southampton at a Christmas dance, so yes, they returned. So there were all those things to keep fixing up and then there were contacts with the nurses at the hospital. I spent a lot of time on the night shift there and we had a Christmas dance, a fancy dress dance in the second term and a valedictory ball. So there were three of those to arrange as well. I gave a speech at a Christmas dinner when we made fun of the staff. I think mine was the last uncensored one. After that they decided to censor them. There's a sword of Damocles over the head of the Principal if you look at the picture. I don't know why – that was the first year there were women on the staff. There were no women lecturers at all I don't think – yes, there were in the Music Department but I don't think she figured very much in the College. I think it was a robust occasion. I didn't write the speech, merely gave it. The actual speech was written by another student, who was actually quite clever at that sort of thing. This was in my second year, so I'd already watched one. So there were women in the College. The previous year there were no women at that event. I remember the speech being given and from my point of view that was the biggest thing I had to do during the year. Arranging dances is fairly straightforward, collecting money and arranging things.

How different was it in the second year when you actually had women?

There weren't that many women. There were sixty, so it was a fairly small number. I've got pictures of the women and I was obviously doing some sick bed visiting by the look of things. The big thing in the second year as far as the council was concerned was what you did about hostels. There were no hostels locked when it was men only. Theoretically there were books you put your name in if you went away or things like that. There were books there and I'm sure I must have signed one at one time, but there wasn't a lot of signing going on. The regime was necessarily very, very flexible because most of the men had done National Service and if any rules were put on you simply got a reaction. Not only had they done National Service but they'd actually been on active service as well. If you've done that and come back you're not going to take too much notice of rules.

So the idea of it being monastic is completely false?

I think so, yes. The friend I've kept in touch with over the years, the reason we became friends in the beginning was that we were in the same hostel, he hadn't done his National Service, neither had I, but we were both in rooms with men who had and they simply locked us out of their room when they were with nurses. So the first time we must have met sitting on the stairs. It was quite impossible for us to make any remonstration at all because nobody would have taken any notice. Both had done their National Service and signed on for a third year as well and in fact one was probably in the Services for five years. So they wouldn't have taken any notice of eighteen-year olds.

What role did the Student Union or Student Council have on your life?

As unions exist now, that didn't exist because of the building work that went on. What happened the year before I don't know. Say in '57 – '59. I think the building work must have started round about early '59, so the main building was almost completely gutted and there was nowhere to go in the sense of what people call a Students Union now, which of course is where the café down the town came in. That didn't seem to make too much difference really, it still had this sense of community and I think it must have been a function of size. 146 people and then the extras on top is quite small really, like a primary school. It's pretty small.

I've read something in the Record Office that suggested that it was going to be a very difficult job for the Student Council the next year because of the women.

Yes it was. When we went back in September the second year the president was PB and he was very, very astute. I think he probably got a distinction and went on to Oxford afterwards. Actually I've met him a few times as well. He was very astute, hardworking and clear about what we had to do and from September until the elections of the first years – there were always first year elections in about October after people had been there for a month – for that first month there were all sorts of things that the Student Council were faced with. For example, if you'd gone to any meal, and I never went to breakfast or I managed it once or twice, you had to go in what was called formal dress. Certainly that was the case in the evening. I find it hard to believe it was lunchtime as well, but maybe it was. The question for the Student Council in the first month was what exactly was formal dress for females. There were no females on the Student Council at that time, although maybe people there had asked them. At the time melon seeds on strings were very popular for beads and the question was 'Is that formal or not?' and we discussed what exactly was a formal sweater. That was the first thing. Secondly it was quite clear that the woman deputy was very uncomfortable about this question of whether hostels should be locked. That was Miss Macintyre. She came from a particular background and it was fairly clear it wasn't the same as most of them had been used to. We were being spoken to by people not on the Students Council 'We're not having this/that, so don't you agree to anything like this'. So we were being pressured by other students as well. Mainly to do with hostels, rules, and nobody ever said,' That's a rule, you're supposed to do this'. That came up very, very quickly indeed, that there would be changes, even if they weren't that year. In fact I can still see the meeting now with both deputy principals and it did boil up and up as far as they were concerned and Humphreys finally said, when everything was pushed in a corner ,'I'm the deputy principal and on this matter we will decide and you'll simply do as you're told,' or words to that effect. He didn't quite put it aggressively but made it quite clear that there were going to be some limits and that would be that. Which of course is factually correct, since we were all going to leave at the end of the year. So we only had a few months to go.

Somebody said the work/socialisation balance was about sixty/forty, but I don't think that applies to you.

No, it probably doesn't. I think it did apply to other people. There were very few occasions where I was studying late at night or anything like that. Very few. I did find a couple of books in the library which I've carried in my mind ever since and that was quite good. Only a couple. Of course I think we must have done eight hours of practical work in PE a week – sports, gymnastics, all sorts of stuff – and it seemed there was a lot of that. The actual number of hours we spent in classes were actually quite small. We did a thing that was learning to write on a blackboard and giving a talk was another one. This was almost as soon as we were there. And these were practical things you were going to have to do in November. But that of course came to an end fairly rapidly. In the second year psychology lectures started to appear but they weren't psychology. I think they were called 'education', but as far as I remember we had none of those in the first year. I have to explain that I did a secondary course on the basis that there were less hours in it than the primary course. I seem to remember something like that. So I wouldn't know what the primary course was like at all.

Why did you choose to attend a Church college?

I didn't make a choice based on that. I went to boarding school when I was nine and spent three years there. On Sundays we went to Chapel twice and we were in a prep school. In the senior school I became a day boy and we must have gone to Chapel probably two or three times a week. So the fact that there was a Chapel there, that's just what there was and it's what I'd experienced. The reason I went to Winchester was that mother had gone to school there. She chose it. She said I'd like it.

How comfortable was it to be a non-attendee at Chapel services?

I was thinking about that. Nobody ever made any comment at all.

How usual was it not to go?

Thinking of the people I know, I don't know whether they went or not. I think I probably went on the first day of my first year and probably the first day of my second year and I think those are the days I actually went to breakfast as well. Maybe I went to carol services as well.

But there was no compulsion to go?

No, no comment was made on it by anybody at all ever. We did have big religious knowledge lectures I seem to remember in the hall, down at the bottom of the Dytch. But it's very vague.

How much did students help each other out in good and bad times?

I don't remember really. On an obvious level there was a matron, so that tended to be physical things. I was in West Hayes in the first year and where the library was, I think it was called the Court and both those tended to be big hostels in comparison to the others, so the staff there were relatively distant from us. But there were much smaller hostels, one called the Vatican where the priest in charge of the Chapel lived and he was a lecturer as well. There was the Principal's one and there was one run by Blackburn, a third year PE lecturer. They were much smaller and I got the impression those students knew those people much better. But my own experience of being at boarding school so young was that you became very self-reliant. There was no other way of doing it. You had to be.

If you'd had problems you'd have kept them to yourself?

Yes, that's right, that would have been my way of doing it. I think in some of the smaller ones they might have gone to the staff in charge and certainly those staff members did take quite an active part I got the impression. In my second year, the only time I ever spoke to Derek Pass, a PE lecturer who never taught me, was at 1.30am when I came in from the hospital and it was March or April and he said 'I have to remind you that the last few entertainment secretaries haven't passed'. He had to say something because I was obviously in the wrong and that was about it.

But the girls wouldn't have been allowed to come in that late?

I think very quickly a different regime was established in those hostels and of course as far as I know most of the girls were fairly young, eighteen or nineteen. So I guess a lot of men went to all male schools as well. I did and I guess more of them had that experience, so in the same way maybe a lot of girls went to girls' schools.

We had a comment from someone that the institution championed giving everybody the dignity and respect they deserved and having humble compassion for the less fortunate. Would you agree with that?

I came out of the public school system fairly alienated from the whole thing, which was another reason for not going to university. I wanted to do National Service because that would get me out of it and I didn't have to do anything for two years and maybe something would turn up. There was, particularly in the second year, a lot of talk about things like social equality and things like that. There were students who were more politically minded and have shown that since, but that didn't actually come into college life a lot.

But I remember those discussions going on and being talked about. I was aware of that because I'd had a privileged background. Others there were very quick to tell me that I had and how different their background had been. There were quite a few coal miners' sons. The person who put me right had been a drill sergeant in the guards and he'd obviously spent a long time with officers who'd had a similar background to me and he told me I was arrogant.

How true was that?

I would think it was. In my second TP I taught in a secondary modern in Andover and the gym was a shared hall with wall bars on the side. The school I went to had three gymnasiums and a lot of the people who did PE, if they hadn't been in the services, when they got to college the gymnasium was an absolute revelation. The facilities there were absolutely amazing. Whereas to me they were tiny really. So looking back on it we were aware I think that there were a lot more of us than there had been before and on that basis we were aware that there was a lot more of us because education was expanding. Schools were expanding. I did a final TP at Romsey secondary modern, but it was a comprehensive in all but name, because looking at things later on I discovered that whether you got through the Eleven-plus or not in a lot of areas depended on how many grammar schools there were. If there weren't any grammar school places then only two per cent passed. If in Wales, where they said they were going to have grammar schools all over the place, thirty per cent passed. In Romsey there was nowhere for anybody to go so somebody farsighted had already turned the secondary modern into a comprehensive and I work in a comprehensive now and I could recognise this one as being pretty much identical to the one I taught in then. So it was way ahead of its time.

How did the sense of camaraderie change when it became coeducational?

Well I think that second year that I was there was very much a settling down period. Before that year, to all intents and purposes it hadn't really changed but it was obviously going to. I suppose it was odd, this heavy number of people coming out of the services at the time, not only National Service people but all the Services threw out large numbers of people because it was post-Suez. When they closed the National Service they didn't need all those people because the numbers weren't there, so there were all these older people. If we look in here (photograph album) he was a submariner, so must have been in the Navy for at least three years, he was out of the RN too, so was a full-time professional and I think he'd been in the Navy as well. So apart from National Service people like these three, you'd got these older people and they had a life outside the College in the main. That first year things ostensibly didn't change and I dare say the new female lecturers said 'Well it will be different from next year', because I think there was a feeling that this wasn't going to be different this year.

How did you feel about it becoming coeducational?

I certainly wasn't shocked or anything and I think it was a change that was going on generally outside colleges like that because I did two years. There were a few two year people the following year, but only a few. If you're going to expand it to three years obviously the course is going to change and I think that caused quite a lot of problems as well in terms of what exactly they were going to do. Some people would have said 'They're going to have to go out on long TPs', but organising those is a massive task and very expensive in terms of supervision, with all these lecturers driving around wasting their time going from place to place. So things were going to change and this was part of it.

Why did you take part in the three-legged race?

Because it was there I suppose. I've thought about that and I had only the vaguest notion it was going on. My wife says I'm late for everything anyway and I was late for that. I've got a picture to prove I was there but I don't remember talking about it much beforehand. I did write a letter about it, that the actual weather at the time, which I think might have had something to do with it, was that it was too snowy to do sport. If you look at who took part they were mainly people in my year. It was also a time of the final TP for the second year, so they weren't in college in that sense because you were bussed out early in the morning or went out altogether. So if I had four hours of lectures at the time I think I was probably lucky because the staff couldn't do both – giving lectures and supervising. So practically speaking there was every element there. But I'm prepared to believe there were people in that group who'd thought about it and said 'Right, we must make a statement here'. But it might have been self-publicity in a way. It might have been a rite of passage as well.

Some people have used the words 'family' and 'home' to describe the community. Does that correspond to your experience?

It was more or less exactly like a public school. There was very little to choose, the only difference being that you couldn't be bullied by the staff. That was quite a big difference. There weren't endless rules like there were at school – like, 'You can walk along here but not along there', 'you can't put your hands in your pockets if you're under a certain age', etc. There was none of that and it was a very, very pleasant atmosphere the whole time I was there. Very pleasant indeed. And in fact I found adjustment after it quite difficult really in the sense that everything was there. It was very easy as far as I could see to do this, that and the other and see or not see people. That's not the case in other circumstances. You have to be much more proactive in the real world. You couldn't describe any of this as the real world. Not really.

How remote was the College from Winchester?

I would think we must have been seen because everybody wore scarves. Everybody. And they were fairly bright orange striped things. So we must have been seen. We had some dealings with Winchester College in that we used some of their facilities. I played squash there but you didn't really see anybody around. The football team actually played them at football every year and I remember from my friend they were absolutely spellbound by the whole thing because it was straight out of a book really. The seventeen-to-eighteen-year-olds would be calling for a fag, they'd call them out to run their bath and so on and they found that astonishing.

We must have been seen in some of the pubs and quite a lot of us used to go walking round The Close on Sundays, so we appreciated that bit of Winchester.

Did you feel inferior?

No.

When you were out and about, were you made welcome?

Yes, we were never excluded from anywhere I don't think.

Were the community involved in College Rag Week?

No, the previous year to me I think they painted footsteps down King Alfred's statute across to the gents and back up, but I think that's a bit of a myth. It appears that people in different years think they did it. I don't know. We must have been apparent there. There wasn't a Rag Week at that time but we did take part in this bonfire and I have a picture of the guy. That was quite a big carnival.

The three-legged race itself was a bit of a rag?

Yes, it was. Everybody went past tooting. It was in the local paper.

The Guy Fawkes parade was a big event and I think that was the first one for some time or the first year we decided to build a guy and take part in it. It was very much a carnival, a town carnival. That would have been quite a thing to take part in. It was a very, very big procession as I remember it, which is why we ended up with this – this is the trailer and there was a tractor there, which meant people had contacts with people who had these things, and that chap there was quite important in building it. He was a third year woodwork student who had been in the Guards, the drill sergeant who told me off. These two were the driving force and had done their National Service. I think he'd been a military policeman and he became an inspector in Somerset but he's dead now. He died quite young. They decided we'd build this but it would be very, very big and impressive and they built it together. And I think it must have been half term or something like that. All these people took part in the procession. I was inside shouting through a megaphone for a lot of the time, and this came out the chest I think. So I don't remember seeing very much.

Do you remember any countryside around Winchester?

Yes, St Catherine's Hill. Largely in the summer time I seem to remember either people sleeping up there or going up there or something like that. Also Farley Mount we spent a lot of time running up towards in that second term when we had so few lectures. By the river, walking by the river down in The Close. Even going to the games pitches down at Bar End. We all walked or rode bikes down there.

You've mentioned the ladies' colleges. What about cafes and pubs?

The ones near West Hayes. One of them is still there, I think it was probably the County, on the corner of the road. That provided pork pies for morning breakfast and also my friend was a keen backer of horses and someone took bets there. The Southgate, the hotel, because it was the manager there who challenged me to work in the kitchens. He reckoned we were an idle lot who didn't do anything much and I actually worked in the kitchens as the chef's washer up at one point. Then there was a pub right down near the College itself on a corner. I can't remember the name. And another one on a corner further on coming out of Winchester, another corner, but the same road as the Southgate. Those are the ones I remember.

How important was the sense of history to you?

If you'd never experienced it you would be, and people probably are, amazed when you see that sort of setting for the first time. But as we experienced it, it did have an effect on us I think, that you carried with you. Just a subtle sort of effect really, because it's quite impressive really. That's why tourists go and visit it. Then there's gates they walk through. That three-legged walk started in a gate. The Round Table, I never went there but it's there. And the statue of King Alfred. You accept it because it's part of it. It's only if you took it away and it's not there and then you see it in a different setting that you think, 'This is wonderful'.

You talked about the different socio-economic differences when you went to TP.

Yes, because we were secondary students we had to do a primary first of all and we went to the primary school in

New Alresford and we could walk out of that school, and there were six of us there, and we were all P.E. students, so we practically flooded the whole school with students and we weren't allowed to go in the staff room because there were just too many of us. They had the most fantastic school dinners as well. It was what you would imagine a rural primary school to be at that time and we could walk down the bottom and look at the trout in the stream. So that was pretty idyllic. The secondary modern in Andover was pretty depressing, both for students and staff really and I spent a lot of the time there in the swimming pool. There was a pool down the road and as I was supposed to do P.E. I managed to fill my TP timetable with largely teaching swimming. I remember my tutor, who was an English lecturer who wrote books – not Ryman, the other one – and I had him on two TPs and managed to convince him that it was very demanding being in the sunshine all day in the pool and he was a bit sceptical at the time but I convinced him that it was easy teaching inside a classroom where you have all the books but being in a pool anything could happen couldn't it. He seemed to go away happy.

How important was King Alfred's to you?

When I was at public school I had an interview at Southampton and Nottingham and was offered places in both and the one I might have taken was Nottingham. My housemaster wrote to my parents because they didn't know what King Alfred's was. When he had to write a reference he didn't know what King Alfred's was or where it was. They had no notion at all about training colleges. They were all Oxbridge graduates and then done a version of the PGCE. He wrote in the letter 'It's more normal to do the degree first and the teacher training afterwards'. Over the years I've never once regretted doing it the other way round. Never.

Someone said they wouldn't change their experience at all.

No, I wouldn't. And of course PB did exactly the same thing. I think he probably had a place at Oxford already, a scholarship, but he deferred it and did two years and then went on. I've never ever regretted that.

What did you gain from the institution?

I think it introduced me to a much wider social set of people than I'd experienced at school. I had led this time at school, which was six days a week, so it was pretty constant all the time, but I also had lots of contacts in Romford Market. I knew people there and done little jobs in the market when I was younger. But that was totally different to the people I met at school and when I was at school I gravitated towards people who were eventually thrown out of school for one reason or another. I was amazed after forty years that many of these people are still teaching and you might say they're doing it for their pension or whatever, but they're not. They had an opportunity to go there. It was totally beyond their wildest expectations. They were full of enthusiasm and energy and in a light way they were going to make a difference and I think that's probably what they did. If you think about what happened in schools during the sixties and seventies they did.

What standards do you carry with you?

When I left the school I went to work in a boarding school. There was a fairly major problem in actually existing on the salary at the time. I think it was about £420 per year or something, maybe even less. My friend Bill did a third year, so started on more money than I did, but he also worked in prison in the evening. The chap I had a room with in the first year probably worked in a borstal as well. In order to survive they had second jobs. I went to a boarding school, which meant I lived in and had things paid for. I just paid a small amount and I had somewhere to live immediately. And after forty years another student said to me, 'Oh you sold out'. I've met him since and he was a head when I was and he would be a person who had a political agenda at that time and age. But in fact those two years for me at the boarding school were simply an extension of the two years at King Alfred's. So I really did four years, but got paid for it. But following that I then made efforts to get out of teaching, but not very successfully. All the way through that same impression of making a difference to those people who might not have thought they were going to get that opportunity – that's what I took away. When I was head of a primary school I had a large unit for gypsies within the school because nobody else would take them and we went on to have about seventeen gypsies within a primary school and it came from that chap saying to me, 'You've had every advantage and have to be a bit more humble and think that these are different people with different views'.

Anything else you'd like to say?

No, it's been interesting trying to recall things because memory is a funny thing. I've been teaching psychology since 1989, which I avoided like the plague having done it in my degree at Birkbeck. You think, 'Was it really like that?' and little things connect together. I think you have to take any reminiscences with a very large dose of salt really, but I think the main thing was that it was definitely a time in which things changed quite drastically and there were people who intended them to change as well in all different spheres as well.

And King Alfred's gave them the opportunity?

Yes, I think so. There was only one person you could blame if you didn't get anything out of it and that was yourself. I don't remember many people leaving during the course.

End of interview

Bibliography

Aiston, Sarah, '"A Woman's Place …": Male Representations of University Women in the Student Press of the University of Liverpool, 1944-1979', *Women's History Review*, 15.1 (2006): 3-34.

Aldrich, Richard, 'The Three Duties of the Historian of Education', *History of Education Journal* 32.2 (2003): 133-43.

Aldrich, Richard, *The Institute of Education 1902-2002: A Centenary History* (London: London University, 2002).

Anderson, Eric, *Inclusive Masculinity: The Changing Nature of Masculinities* (London: Routledge, 2011).

Anderson, Robert. *British Universities, Past and Present* (London: Continuum, 2006).

Arthur, James, 'Changing Patterns of Church College Identity and Mission', *International Journal of Research and Method in Education* 24.2 (2001): 137-143.

Arthur, James, *Faith and Secularisation in Religious Colleges and Universities* (London: Routledge, 2006).

Bell, Les, 'Chronicles of Wasted Time? Initial Teacher Education in England: 1960-1999', *Australian Journal of Education* 43.2 (1999): 186-204.

Benne, Robert, *Quality with Soul: How Six Premier Colleges and Universities Keep Faith with Their Religious Traditions* (Grand Rapids: William B. Erdmans Publishing, 2001).

Black, P. J., *National Curriculum Task Group on Assessment and Testing*, known as *The Black*

Report, (London: Dept. of Education and Science and Welsh Office, 1988).

Bone, Jennifer. *Our Calling to Fulfil: Westminster College and the Changing Face of Teacher Education 1951-2001* (Bristol: Tockington Press, 2003).

Bornat, Joanna, and Hanna Diamond, 'Women's History and Oral History Developments and Debates', *Women's History Review* 16. 1 (2007): 19-39.

Bowen, Marjorie, *Making Our Boys Effeminate*, National Association of Schoolmasters, Warwick Modern Records Centre, MSS.38C/4/2/2.

Brown, Callum G., Arthur J. McIvor and Neil Rafeek, *The University of Strathclyde 1945-1975: An Oral History of the University of Strathclyde* (Edinburgh: Edinburgh University Press, 2004).

Brown, Hilary, 'Whose Story Counts?: Constructing an Oral History of the Open University at 40', *Oral History Autumn* (2011): 94-106.

Burchall, James T., *The Dying of the Light* (Grand Rapids: William B. Erdmans Publishing, 1998).

Cathedrals Group, 'Welcome to The Cathedrals Group', *The Cathedral Group*: cathedralsgroup.org.uk.

Church of England, *An Excellent Enterprise: The Church of England and its Colleges of Higher Education* (London: Church House Bookshop, 1994).

Connell, Raewyn, *Masculinities* (Cambridge: Polity, 1995).

Cox, Andrew, Tim Herrick and Patrick Keating, 'Accommodations: Staff Identity and University Space', *Teaching in Higher Education* 17.6 (2012): 697-709.

Cunningham, Peter, and Philip Gardner, *Becoming Teachers: Texts and Testimonies 1907-1950* (London: Woburn Press, 2004).

Dale, Edmund H., *Relentless Struggle: An Autobiography* (Victoria: Trafford Publishing: 1999).

Dale, Reginald R., *Mixed or Single-Sex School?* (London: Routledge, and Kegan Paul, 1974).

Davie, Grace, *Religion in Britain since 1945: Believing without Belonging* (Oxford: Blackwell, 1994).

Davies, Clive Jones, 'The Anglican Colleges of Higher Education', in *Faith for the Future*, ed. Graham Leonard (London: National Society Church House Publishing, 1986), 87-93.

Dearing, Ronald, *The Way Ahead: Church Schools in the New Millennium* (London: Church House Publishing, 2001).

Deboick, Sophia, 'Newman Suggests a University's "Soul" Lies in the Mark it Leaves on its Students', *The Guardian* (20 October 2010): www.guardian.co.uk.

Dent, Harold C., *The Training of Teachers in England and Wales 1800-1975* (London: Hodder and Stoughton, 1977).

Dickinson, John, 'The Making of the University of Winchester', an unpublished typescript (University of Winchester Records).

Doherty, Geoffrey D. C., *A Case Study of the amalgamation of Crewe and Alsager Colleges of Education* (Crewe: Crewe and Alsager College of Higher Education, 1981).

Domanska, Ewa, 'Frank Ankersmit: From Narrative to Experience', *Rethinking History* 13.2 (2009): 175-195.

Dyhouse, Carol, *Students: A Gendered History* (London: Routledge, 2006).

Elias, Norbert, Forward in *The Sociology of Community: A Selection of Readings*, ed. Colin Bell and Howard Newby (Abingdon: Frank Cass and Company Ltd, 1974) ix-xlii.

Encyclopaedia Britannica, 'Ferdinand Tönnies,' *Encyclopaedia Britannica*: www.britannica.com.

Freathy, Rob, 'The Triumph of Religious Education for Citizenship in English Schools, 1935-1949', *History of Education* 37.2 (2008): 295-316.

Freathy, Rob, and Stephen G Parker, 'Secularists, Humanists and Religious Education: Religious Crisis and Curriculum Change In England, 1963-1975, *History of Education* 42.2 (2013): 222-256.

Gandy, Frances, 'The University and Life Experience Project: Phase Two', in *The Year: The Annual Review of Girton College* (2011-2012): 32-33.

Gardner, Philip, 'Oral History in Education: Teacher's Memory and Teachers' History', *History of Education Journal* 32.2 (2003): 175-188.

Garnett, Jane, Matthew Grimley, Alana Harris, William Whyte and Sarah Williams, *Redefining Christian Britain: Post 1945 Perspectives* (London: SCM Press, 2006).

Gates, Brian Edward, 'Diversifying the Colleges' in *150 Years: The Church Colleges in Higher Education*, ed. Trevor Brighton (Chichester: West Sussex Institute of Higher Education, 1989) 50-57.

Gay, John, Brian Kay, George Perry, Diana Lazenby, *The Future of the Anglican Colleges, Final Report of the Church Colleges Research Project* (Abingdon: Culham Educational Foundation, 1986).

Gillard, Derek, *Education in England: A Brief History* (Edinburgh: www.educationengland.org.uk, 2011).

Gilligan, Carol, *In a Different Voice: Psychological Theory and Women's Development* (Cambridge: Harvard University Press, 1982).

Glaser, Barney, and Anselm Strauss, *The Discovery of Grounded Theory: Strategies for Qualitative Research* (Chicago: Aldine Publishing, 1967).

Gluck, Sherna, and Daphne Patai, *The Feminist Practice of Oral History* (London: Routledge, 1991).

Grimley, Matthew, 'Moberly, Sir Walter Hamilton (1881-1974)', *Oxford Dictionary of National Biography*, (Oxford: www.oxforddnb.com, 2007).

Hampshire Record Office, 'University of Winchester', HRO47M91W, Hampshire Record Office.

Hansard HC Deb 888 (11 March 1975): 468-80.

Hawkins, Sue, '"Whose Story is it Anyway?": The Challenges of Conducting Institutional Histories', *Journal of Conservation and Museum Studies*, 10.1 (2012): www.jcms-journal.com.

HESA, *Statistics*, Higher Education Statistics Agency, HESA: www.hesa.ac.uk, 2011.

Hicks, Leslie, Diane Simpson, Ian Mathews, Karen Crawford, Harriet Koorts with Kevin Cooper, 'Connected Communities', Arts and Humanities Research Council (2011): www.ahrc.ac.uk.

Hopkins, Laurence, 'The Path of Least Resistance: A Voice-Relational Analysis of Disabled Students' Experiences of Discrimination in English Universities', *International Journal of Inclusive Education* 15.7 (2011): 711-727.

Hull, John, *Studies in Religious Education* (Lewes: Falmer Press, 1984).

Hunter, Lisa, Toni Rossi, Richard Tinning, Erin Flanagan and Doune Mcdonald, 'Professional Learning Places and Spaces: The Staffroom as a Site of Beginning Teacher Induction and Transition', *Asia-Pacific Journal of Teacher Education* 39.1 (2011): 33-46.

Jacobs, Andrea, and Camilla Leach, '"No Women, Please": Co-education and Expansion, Crisis and Change at King Alfred's College Winchester in the Mid-Twentieth Century', in *Persistence and Disappearance: Educational Organizations in their Historical Contexts*, ed. Michael Göhlich, Caroline Hopf and Daniel Tröhler (Wiesbaden: VS Press Fur Sozialwissenschaften, 2008) 41-53.

Jacobs, Andrea, Camilla Leach and Stephanie Spencer, 'Learning Lives and Alumni Voices', *Oxford Review of Education* 36.2 (2010): 219-232.

Jacobsen, Rhonda H., and Douglas G. Jacobsen, *No longer Invisible: Religion in University Education* (Oxford: www.oxfordscholarship.com, 2012).

James, Tom, and Martin Doughty, *King Alfred's College Winchester: A Pictorial Record* (Stroud: Alan Sutton Publishing, 1991).

Jessop, Tansy, Laura Gubby and Angela Smith, 'Space Frontiers for New Pedagogies: A Tale Of Constraints and Possibilities', *Studies in Higher Education* 37.2 (2012): 189-202.

Kelsall, Roger K., Anne Poole and Annette Kuhn, *Graduates: The Sociology of an Elite* (London: Methuen, 1972).

Kotter, John, 'Leading Change: Why Transformation Efforts Fail', *Harvard Business Review* (1995): 59-67.

Kotter, John, *What Leaders Really Do* (Cambridge: Harvard Business Press, 1999).

Lawton, Dennis, *Education and Politics in the 1990s: Conflict or Consensus?* (London: Falmer, 1992).

Lofthouse, Mark, *Faith, Class and Politics: The Role of the Churches in Teacher Training, 1914-1945* (Oxford: University of Oxford Department of Education, 2009).

Lowe, Roy, 'The Changing Role of the Academic Journal: The Coverage of Higher Education in *History of Education* as a Case Study, 1972-2011', *History of Education Journal* 41.1 (2012): 103-115.

Marjon, 'About Us', *Marjon University*, Marjon University of Plymouth: www.marjon.ac.uk, 2012.

Marsden, George, *The Soul of the American University: From Protestant Establishment to Established Non-Belief* (New York: Oxford University Press, 1994).

Massey, Doreen, 'Places and their Pasts', *History Workshop Journal* 39 (1995): 182-192.

Massey, Doreen, *For Space* (London: Sage, 2005).

Massey, Doreen, *Space, Place and Gender* (Oxford: Polity, 1994).

Mathers, Helen, *Steel City Scholars: The Centenary History of the University of Sheffield* (London: James and James, 2005).

Matterson, Alan, *Polytechnics and Colleges* (London: Longman, 1981).

Mauthner, Natasha, and Andrea Doucet, 'Reflections on a Voice Centred Relational Method', in *Feminist Dilemmas in Qualitative Research: Public Knowledge and Private Lives*, ed. Jane Ribbens and Rosalind Edwards (London: Sage, 1998) 119-146.

McCleod, Hugh, *The Religious Crisis of the 1960s* (Oxford: Oxford University Press, 2007).

McCulloch, Gary, 'Historical Insider Research in Education', in *Researching Education from the Inside: Investigations from Within*, ed. Pat Sikes and Anthony Potts (London: Routledge, 2008) 51-63.

McDowell, Linda, 'Acts of Memory and Millennial Hopes And Anxieties: The Awkward Relationship Between the Economic and the Cultural', *Social and Cultural Geography* 1.1 (2000): 15-24.

McDowell, Linda, ed., *Undoing Place? A Geographical Reader* (London: Arnold, 1997).

McGregor, Gordon P., *A Church College for the 21st Century: 150 Years of Ripon and York St John* (York: University College of Ripon and York St John, 1991).

McNair, Arnold, *Teachers and Youth Leaders: Report of the Committee Appointed by the President of the Board of Education to Consider the Supply, Recruitment and Training of Teachers and Youth Leaders.* Known as *The McNair Report* (London: HMSO, 1944).

Mind Tools, 'Kotter's 8-Step Change Model', www.mindtools.com

Minister, Kristina, 'A Feminist Frame for the Oral History Interview', in *Women's Words, the Feminist Practice of Oral History*, ed. Sherna Gluick and Daphne Patai (London: Routledge, 1991) 27-41.

Moller, Michael, 'Exploiting Patterns: A Critique of Hegemonic Masculinity', *Journal of Gender Studies* 16.3 (November 2007): 263-276.

Newman, Melanie, 'Christian Colleges: Our Higher Purpose', *Times Higher Education Supplement* (30 November 2007), www.timeshighereducation.co.uk.

Nias, Jennifer, 'Primary Teaching as a Culture of Care' in *School Culture*, ed. John Prosser (London: Sage, 1999) 66-81.

Nias, Jennifer, 'Value-persistence and Utility in Colleges of Education', *Education for Teaching* (1972): 29-34.

Niblett, W. R., *The Church's Colleges of Higher Education* (London: Central Board of Finance of the Church of England, 1976).

Noddings, Nel, *Caring: A Feminine Approach to Ethics and Moral Education* (California: University of California Press, 1984).

Noddings, Nel, *Educating Moral People: A Caring Alternative to Character Education* (New York: Teachers College Press, 2002).

Nora, Pierre, 'Between Memory and History: Les Lieux de Memoire', *Representations* 26 (Special Issue: Memory and Counter-Memory, Spring 1989): 7-24.

Parker, Stephen G., and Rob J. K. Freathy, 'Ethnic Diversity, Christian Hegemony and the Emergence of Multi-Faith Religious Education in the 1970s', *History of Education* 41.3 (2012): 381-382,

Pickford, Giles, 'Town Gown Relations', *Journal of Tertiary Educational Administration* 11. 1 (1989): 201-210.

Pigott, Robert, 'Is Christianity Shrinking or Just Changing?', BBC News (11 December 2012): www.bbc.co.uk/news.

Plowden, Bridget. *Children and their Primary Schools.* Known as *The Plowden Report* (London: HMSO, 1967).

Power, Sally, Geoff Whitty and Tony Edwards, 'Success Sustained? A Follow-up Study of the "Destined for Success?" Cohort', *Research Papers in Education* 21.3 (2006): 235-253.

Putnam, Robert D., *Bowling Alone: The Collapse and Revival of American Community* (New York: Touchstone, 2000).

Quality Assurance Agency (QAA), *Institutional Report on the University of Winchester* (www.qaa.ac.uk).

Rheinharz, Shulamit, *Feminist Methods in Social Research* (New York: Oxford University Press, 1992).

Robbins, Lionel, *The Report of the Committee on Higher Education*, known as *The Robbins Report* (London: HMSO, 1963).

Roberts, Helen, *Doing Feminist Research* (London: Routledge and Kegan Paul, 1982).

Rogers, Bridget, *Council for National Academic Awards 1964-1993* (CNAA: archiveshub.ac.uk, 1993).

Roper, Michael, and John Tosh, 'Mummy, Matron and the Maids: Feminine Presence and Absence in Male Institutions 1934-63', in *Manful Assertions*, ed. Michael Roper and John Tosh (London: Routledge, 1991) 168-190.

Rose, Martial, *King Alfred's College, Winchester, 1980-1990: A Decade of Change* (Salisbury: Salisbury Printing: 1990).

Rose, Martial, *A History of King Alfred's College, Winchester 1840-1980* (London: Phillimore and Co., 1981).

Scott, Joan, 'Gender as a Useful Category of Historical Analysis', *American Historical Review* 91.5 (1986): 1053-1075.

Siegal, Wes, Allan H. Church, Miriam Javitch, Janine Waclawski, Steffani Burd, Michael Bazigos, Ta-Fu Yang, Kate Anderson-Rudolph and W. Warner Burke, 'Understanding the Management of Change: An Overview of Managers' Perspectives and Assumptions in the 1990s', *Journal of Organisational Change Management* 9.6 (1996): 54-80.

Silver, Harold, '"Things Change but Names Remain the Same": Higher Education Historiography 1975-2000', *History of Education Journal* 35.1 (2006): 121-140.

Silver, Harold, 'Higher Education and Social Change: Purpose in Pursuit', *History of Education Journal* 36.4-5 (2007): 535-550.

Silver, Harold, *A Higher Education: The Council for National Academic Awards and British Higher Education 1964-1989* (London: Falmer, 1990).

Silver, Harold, *Tradition and Higher Education* (Winchester: Winchester University Press, 2007).

SI-UK Education Council, 'University of Winchester', *University Profile* (SI-UK: www.studyin-uk.com, 2012).

Spencer, Stephanie, 'A Uniform Identity: Schoolgirl Snapshots and the Spoken Visual', *History of Education* 36.2 (2007): 227-246.

Spencer, Stephanie, *Gender Work and Education in Britain in the 1950s* (Basingstoke: Palgrave Macmillan, 2005).

Summerfield, Penny, *Reconstructing Women's Wartime Lives: Discourse and Subjectivity in Oral Histories of the Second World War* (Manchester: Manchester University Press, 1998).

Thompson, Paul, Introduction in *Oral History, Health and Welfare* ed. Joanna Bornat, Robert Perks, Paul Thompson and Jan Walmsley (London: Routledge, 2002).

Tippett, Brian, 'Diversifying the Colleges' in *150 Years: The Church Colleges in Higher Education*, ed. Trevor Brighton (Bognor Regis: West Sussex Institute of Higher Education, 1989).

Tobin, Lucy, 'Rise of the Stay-at-Home Students', *The Guardian* (12 August 2011): www.theguardian.com.

Tönnies, Ferdinand, *Community and Association (Gemeinschaft und Gesellschaft)* (London: Routledge and Kegan Paul, 1955).

Vogt, Francesca, 'A Caring Teacher: Explorations into Primary School Teachers' Professional Identity and Ethic of Care', *Gender and Education* 14.3 (2002): 251-264.

Waddell, Diane, and Amrik Sohal, 'Resistance: A Constructive Tool for Change Management' *Management Decision* 36.8 (1998): 543-548.

Warnock, Mary, *Meeting Special Educational Needs* (London: HMSO, 1978).

Warwick Modern Records, *National Association of Schoolmasters, 1914-1970s.* Accession Number: MSS 38 (Warwick Modern Records Centre: warwick.ac.uk, 1974-92).

Weaver; T. R., *Study Group on the Government and Colleges of Education* (London: HMSO, 1966).

Wikipedia, 'Community', *Wikipedia:* en.wikipedia.org.

Wooldridge, Ewart, and Eddie Newcombe, *Distinctiveness and Identity in a Challenging HE Environment: A*

Unique Opportunity for Cathedrals Group Institutions (Chester: The Cathedrals Group, 2011).

Woolf, Virginia, *A Room of One's Own.* 1928. (London: Penguin, 1945).

Yukl, Gary, *Leadership in Organisations* (Boston: Pearson, 2010).

INDEX

ACTL (Association of College Teachers and Lecturers) 213, 224 n. 47
Anglican Church, The 27, 82, 83, 97, 100, 110, 112 n. 40, 233
Armstrong, Ernest (Under Secretary of State for Education and Science) 202
Association of Assistant Mistresses 164, 189 n. 27
Association of Schoolmasters 164, 189 n. 27
Athiny Training College (Kingston upon Hull) 202

Bar End 276
Basingstoke 'Outpost' 34
Battery, The 143
Baylor University, Texas 82, 111 n. 20
Birmingham Agreed Syllabus for Religious Instruction 112, 113 n. 58
Bishop Grosseteste University (Lincoln) 82
Bishop of Winchester 106, 113 n. 77, 244 n. 24
Bishop Otter College (now University of Chichester) 27, 168, 198, 260, 266
Bishop's Palace, The 139
Blackburn, Frank 271
Black Papers, The 215
Black Swan, The 13
Board of Education 81, 91
Browne Report (2010), The 19 n. 4
Burma Road, Winchester 124, 126, 149 n. 17

Cadena Cafe, The 13
Canterbury Christ Church University 82, 198
Carfax Hotel, The 117, 121
Carmarthen College 28, See also Trinity St David, University of Wales
Carter, Professor Joy (Vice Chancellor) 196, 201
Cathedrals Group, The 80, 82, 108, 109 n. 2, 233
Chair of Governors 98, 113 n. 77

Chester College (now University of Chester) 27, 180
Christchurch Road (student residences) 122, 123
Christian Union 16, 51, 62, 85, 93, 95, 96, 101, 105
Christmas Carol Service 58
Clarke, Kenneth 202
Congregationalists, The 80
Council for National Academic Awards (CNAA) 35, 37, 41 n. 13, 42 n. 19, 70, 71, 191, 192-193, 205-214, 220, 221, 228
Council of Church Colleges and Universities (CCUC) 79-80
County Arms , The 143, 261, 276
Cranmer, John (Principal) 36
Crewe and Alsager College of Education 42 n. 17
Crombie Code 201-202, 203
Crombie Hall, Aberdeen 169
Crosland, Antony 33
Culham College, Abingdon 28

Dale, Edmund 111 n. 29
Dearing Report 2001,The (*The Way Ahead: Church Schools in the New Millennium*) 82, 108, 110 n. 17,
Degree awarding powers 38, 39, 192, 204
Dickinson, John (Principal) 36, 37, 43 n. 30, 201
Dickinson, W.P. (Principal) 28, 29, 30, 31, 51, 55, 87, 112 n. 38, 234, 259
Dining Hall 29, 58, 61 fig, 130
Drey, C. N. C, (Tim) (Vice Principal) 36, 43 n. 27

Education Act 1944, The 86, 90, 111 n. 34, 164
Education Act 1962, The 41 n. 8
Education Reform Act 1988, The 36, 215
Education Act 1996, The 43 n. 31
Education Act (Student Loans) 1996, The 43 n. 31.
Exchange, The 143

Farley Mount 141, 260, 276
Freshers' Week 66, 136
Friends Reunited 245

Gemeinschaft and Gesellschaft 46-47, 55, 62, 68, 71, 73, 74 n. 6, 89, 98,107, 108, 120, 121, 122, 129, 133, 156, 159, 160, 162, 175, 178, 195, 199, 206, 221, 230-232, 240
Gloucestershire University, formerly Cheltenham and Gloucester College 34, 38
Girton College, Cambridge 21 n. 14, 22 n. 23
Green Jackets Barracks 117
Green Man, The 117, 143, 261

Grounded Theory Methodology 18, 25 n. 43
Guy Fawkes Parade 275

Hampshire County Youth Orchestra 16
Hampshire Record Office 7, 23 n. 26
Herbert Jarman Building 34, 124
Holm Lodge 32
Homerton College, Cambridge 181, 190 n. 68
Humphrey, Hugh (Vice Principal) 269

Institute of Education, University of London, 21 n. 13

John Stripe Theatre 33
Joint Four, The 164, 189 n. 27

Kay-Shuttleworth, Sir James 81, 109 n. 12
Ken's cafe 137, 143-146, 147
Kettle, Kenneth 124
King Alfred's Day 29, 30
King Alfred's Statue 53-54, 118, 123, 276

Ladies' Day (Dramatic performance) 62
Lancaster University 104
Learning Cafe 130
Lee, Sir Desmond 31
Leeds Trinity University 82
Leeson, Reverend Spencer 29
Light, Professor Paul (Vice Chancellor) 201
Liverpool Hope University 198
Liverpool University, 155, 187 n. 6

Macintyre Hall 64
Macintyre, Robina (Vice Principal) 32, 157, 180-183, 181 fig, 184, 190 n. 69, 234, 269
Main Building 29, 121, 123, 170, 263, 268
Maria Assumpta Roman Catholic Training College 181, 190 n. 63, 243 n. 20
Martial Rose Library 124
Mary Ward College 202
MaxQData 247
McCleod, Hugh 91
McNair Report 1944, The 23 n. 23, 30, 40 n. 5, 55, 80
Medecroft 133-135
Moberly, Sir Walter 85
Montessori Schools 181, 235, 243 n. 20
Mrs Meyrick's Night Clubs 182
Muslim prayer room 234

NATFE (National Association of Teachers in Further Education) 213, 224 n. 47
National Association of Schoolmasters 164
National Service 13, 28. 52, 55, 86, 154, 161-162, 164, 267-268, 271, 273, 275

NUS (National Union of Students) 127
NUT/NUWT (National Union of Teachers/Women Teachers) 128
Newman, John Henry (Cardinal) 2, 19 n. 5
Newman University, Birmingham 82
Nias Jennifer 32, 156, 157, 158-160, 180, 181, 183, 184, 236, 265

Oral history 2, 3, 4, 5, 8-12, 27, 51, 83, 120, 124, 131, 134, 139, 140, 146, 185, 191, 193, 194, 197, 200, 219, 222, 228, 231, 233, 236
Oxbridge 28, 53, 54, 57, 76 n,24, 119, 129, 148-149 n. 7, 160, 178, 263, 277

Participant Elicitation through Peer Comments 10, 247, 258
Pass, Derek 271
PE 'Lads' 129, 173, 175
Pemberton, Pat 32
Playing for Time Theatre Company 239
Plowden Report Children and their Primary Schools 1967 , The 156, 181, 235

Quality Assurance Agency (QAA) 38, 41 n. 9

Rag Week 14, 101, 136, 275
Reading University 35
Regional Advisory Council (RAC) 35
Report of the Working Party on the Communications of the Christian Faith 113 n. 59
Research Degree Awarding Powers (RDAP) 39, 192, 204
Rising Sun, The 117
Robbins Report (1963), The 33, 41 n. 13, 228
Roman Catholic Church, The 80, 81
Rose Martial (Principal) 33, 36, 38, 191, 194-195, 196, 200-201, 205, 213, 223
Round Table, The 276

St Alphege (building) 123
St Catherine's Hill 141, 142, 260, 276
St Cross 142, 260
St Edburga (building) 123
St Giles Hill 138, 139, 141, 142, 150 n. 44, 237
St Grimbald (building) 123
St John's College (Battersea) 27. See also St Mark and St John University
St Mark and St John University, Plymouth 82
St Mary's University (Twickenham) 82
Salisbury, Sarum St Michael College 27, 34, 168, 260, 266
Senior Common Room (SCR) 36, 60, 72, 103,

129, 130, 131, 132, 133, 147, 176, 210, 215, 240
Sheffield University 21 n. 13, 133
Shoei College, Tokyo 42 n. 24
Smart, Professor Ninian 91, 104, 112 n. 58
Southampton Institute (now Southampton Solent University) 203
Southampton University 34, 35, 37, 38, 39, 192, 193, 210
Southgate Hotel, The 276
Spoken Visual Methodology 13, 118, 131, 238,
SPSS (Statistical Package for the Social Sciences) 229, 247
Strathclyde University 4,
Stripe Lecture Hall 124
Stripe, John (Principal) 31, 32, 41 n. 21, 55, 122, 194, 196
Student Services Centre 129
Student Union 54, 119, 124, 125, 127, 128 fig , 129, 143, 147, 170, 182, 268
Sunday Express, The 182
Surplice, Alwyn 139
Sussex University 21 n. 14, 170

Thatcher, Margaret 215
Three-Legged Race 102 fig, 153, 165, 170, 274-274, 276
Times Higher Educational Supplement 70, 82, 198
Tom Atkinson Building 34,124
Town and gown 118, 121,135, 146, 150 n. 41, 151 n. 66, 238, 239
Trinity St David, University of Wales 82
Trotter, Dame Janet 38, 183-184

University College Winchester 27, 38, 198, 248
University of Notre Dame, Indiana 82
University Teachers' Group 85

Valedictory Dinner 58, 59 fig, 264
Voice Relational Methodology (VRM) 3, 5, 11- 12, 13, 118, 136, 144, 194, 207, 224 n. 32, 229-230, 238

Warnock, Lady Mary 42 n. 21
Water Meadows 118, 119, 136, 138, 141, 142, 147, 260
Weaver Report (1966), The 33, 41 n14
Wesleyan Methodists, The 81
Wessex Hotel, The 117
West Downs 118, 124, 137
West Hayes 29, 45, 51, 270, 276
West Hill 118
Westminster College (now part of Oxford Brookes University) 21 n13, 212, 220
White, R.C. (Principal) 28
William of Wykeham 123

Winchester Cathedral 14, 82, 87, 93, 100, 118, 119, 120, 136, 138, 139, 140, 142, 144, 147, 237 fig, 260, 275, 276
Winchester City Trust 239
Winchester College 29, 31, 40 n. 3, 123, 149 n. 15, 151 n. 59,260, 274
Winchester Experience 137, 175, 191
Winchester Prison 53, 239
Winton Club, The 53, 245, 249
Wintonian, The 109 n. 1, 165, 166, 188 n. 21, 234
Wykeham Arms, The 142, 151 n. 59

York St John University 82, 87, 112 n. 41
York University 21 n. 14

Lightning Source UK Ltd.
Milton Keynes UK
UKOW06f1551160315

247959UK00001B/2/P

9 781906 113155